EAST GERMANY
—— IN ——
COMPARATIVE
PERSPECTIVE

Edited by
DAVID CHILDS,
THOMAS A. BAYLIS,
MARILYN RUESCHEMEYER

ROUTLEDGE
London & New York

First published 1989
by Routledge
11 New Fetter Lane, London EC4P 4EE
29 West 35th Street, New York, NY 10001

Printed in Great Britain by
Billing & Sons Ltd, Worcester

British Library Cataloguing in Publication Data
East Germany in comparative perspective.
 1. East Germany. Social conditions
 I. Childs, David   II. Baylis, Thomas A.
 III. Rueschemeyer, Marilyn
 943.1087'8

Library of Congress Cataloging in Publication Data
East Germany in comparative perspective / edited by David Childs,
 Thomas A. Baylis, Marilyn Rueschemeyer.
   p.   cm.
 Includes index.
 ISBN 0–415–00496–9
 1. Germany (East)—Politics and government. 2. Germany (East)–
 –Social conditions. 3. Germany (East)—Economic conditions.
 I. Childs, David, 1933–   . II. Baylis, Thomas A.
 III. Rueschemeyer, Marilyn, 1938–
 DD283.E27   1989
 943.1—dc19
                                                         88–31913
                                                              CIP
 ISBN 0–415–00496–9

£35

£10

EAST GERMANY IN COMPARATIVE PERSPECTIVE

The German Democratic Republic has recently assumed increasing importance within the Eastern bloc, both economically and strategically, largely as a result of its favourable trading position with the West.

This book, written by leading American and British specialists in the field, seeks to illuminate the current position of the GDR in key political, economic and social areas. It looks at the political leadership and changes in the ruling party, the informal 'comrades' or social court system, the position of women in politics and society, church–state relations, the economics of consumer shortages, the role of the industrial enterprise in the planning system, foreign economic policies and relations with revolutionary movements in the Third World. It discusses recent developments in the context of the Soviet–East European bloc, in which the apparent uniformity of the past is giving way to the likely-shape and distinctiveness of the East German course in the Gorbachev era and beyond.

The Editors: David Childs is Reader in Politics and Director of the Institute of German, Austrian and Swiss Affairs at the University of Nottingham; Thomas A. Baylis is Associate Professor of Political Science at the University of Texas, San Antonio and Marilyn Rueschemeyer is Associate Professor of Sociology at the Rhode Island School of Design and Adjunct Associate Professor at Brown University.

Contents

Tables

Figures

Contributors

Thomas A. Baylis is Associate Professor of Political Science at the University of Texas at San Antonio, and author of *The Technical Intelligentsia and the East German Elite* (1974) and *Governing by Committee: Collegial Leadership in Advanced Societies* (1989).

Phillip J. Bryson is Professor of Economics at the University of Arizona, and has written *Scarcity and Control in Socialism* (1976) and *Consumers under Socialist Planning* (1984), as well as numerous articles on the economics of socialism.

David Childs is Professor and Director of the Institute of German, Austrian, and Swiss Affairs at the University of Nottingham. He is the author of numerous books and articles on East German, West German, and British politics, including *The German Democratic Republic: Moscow's German Ally* (1983, 2nd edn 1988), editor of *Honecker's Germany* (1986), and *East Germany to the 1990s: Can it resist Glasnost? (1987).*

Irwin L. Collier is Assistant Professor of Economics at the University of Houston. He is the editor of an issue of *Comparative Economic Studies* (June 1987) devoted to the East German economy and the author of a monograph and several articles also dealing with the subject. His article in this volume is part of a larger project supported by the National Council for Soviet and Eastern European Research.

Ronald A. Francisco is Associate Professor of Political Science and Soviet and East European Studies at the University of Kansas. He is co-editor of *Berlin Between Two Worlds* (1986). His previous articles and books have dealt with the international relations and economic concerns of the GDR and the Soviet bloc.

Robert F. Goeckel is Assistant Professor of Political Science at the State University of New York at Geneseo. His primary area of research interest is church–state relations in Eastern Europe, and he has published a number of articles on that subject in books and such journals as *World Politics* and *Studies in Comparative Communism*.

Henry Krisch is Professor of Political Science at the University of Connecticut. He is author of *German Politics under Soviet Occupation* (1974) and *The German Democratic Republic: The*

Search for Identity (1985) as well as articles on Soviet and GDR politics. His current research focuses on the political and ideological response to social change.

Manouchehr Mokhtari is a graduate student in Economics at the University of Houston.

Marilyn Rueschemeyer is Associate Professor of Sociology at the Rhode Island School of Design and Adjunct Associate Professor at Brown University. She has written *Professional Work and Marriage: An East–West Comparison* (1981), co-authored *Soviet Emigré Artists: Life and Work in the Soviet Union and the United States* (1985), and co-edited *The Quality of Life in the German Democratic Republic* (forthcoming).

Brigitte H. Schulz is Assistant Professor of Political Science at Seattle University. She is co-editor of *The Soviet Bloc and the Third World* (1988).

Szonja Szelenyi is Assistant Professor of Sociology at Stanford University.

Nancy Travis Wolfe is Associate Professor in the College of Criminal Justice, University of South Carolina. She has written numerous articles in the field of criminal justice and has conducted research on lay courts in both Germanys under awards from the Fulbright programme and the International Research and Exchanges Board.

Preface

For many years the study of the German Democratic Republic in the United States, Great Britain, and the Federal Republic of Germany proceeded in relative isolation from the scholarship on the Soviet Union and the other countries of Eastern Europe. One of the purposes of the conference on 'The GDR in the Socialist World' (organized by the GDR Studies Association of the United States and held at the Wingspread Conference Center in Racine, Wisconsin in September 1986) was to examine the politics, economy, and society of the GDR in the context of its membership in the bloc of states led by the Soviet Union. We wanted both to compare the institutions, policies, and practices of the GDR with those of its neighbours and to examine the role played by the GDR in bloc-wide policy. While the senior authors of each of the papers given at the conference are members of the Association and have devoted special professional attention to the study of the GDR, each sought to place the East German experience in a broader setting. Scholars whose specialization lies in other parts of the Soviet bloc then provided commentaries from the perspective of their own areas of concentration, and the papers were then revised for this volume taking these and other comments into account. In view of the current rapid pace of changes in the USSR and Eastern Europe, it is important to note that these revisions were completed by December 1987.

We would like to thank, first, the four 'outside' scholars whose stimulating and often provocative comments on the original papers proved so helpful in their revision. They are Daniel Chirot, Gregory Grossman, Sarah Meiklejohn Terry, and Ivan Volgyes. Three papers not revised for inclusion here – at the discretion of their authors – also contributed significantly to our discussion: they were presented by Joan DeBardeleben, Dale Herspring, and John E. Parsons. Manfred Ackermann of the Federal Ministry for Inner German Relations, E. Wayne Merry of the U.S. Department of State, and Ian Wallace of Loughborough University all made stimulating informal presentations. The four panels given at the conference were organized by Thomas Baylis, Erwin Collier, Marilyn Rueschemeyer, and

Angela Stent, and were chaired by C. Bradley Scharf, John Garland, Angela Stent, and Melvin Croan.

We would like to express our special gratitude to the Ford Foundation and to the Johnson Foundation for their generous support for the Conference and for the preparation of this book, and to Rita Goodman and the staff at Wingspread for their efficiency and hospitality. Finally, we would like to thank the principal organizer of the conference, Michael J. Sodaro, the former President and current Secretary-Treasurer of the GDR Studies Association, and to pay tribute to the late Charles R. Foster, who deserved much of the credit for the establishment of the Association and the organization of its first Wingspread Conference in 1983.

David Childs
Thomas A. Baylis
Marilyn Rueschemeyer

Abbreviations

ANC	African National Congress
CAD/CAM	Computer-Assisted-Design/Computer-Assisted Manufacturing
CC	Central Committee
CDU	Christlich-Demokratische Union (Christian Democratic Party)
CMEA	Council for Mutual Economic Assistance
CPE	Centrally planned economy
CPSU	Communist Party of the Soviet Union
DDR	Deutsche Demokratische Republik (German Democratic Republic)
DFD	Demokratische Frauenbund Deutschlands (Democratic Women's League of Germany)
DIW	Deutsches Institut für Wirtschaftsforschung
DM	Deutsche Mark
EPP	Effective Purchasing Power
FDGB	Freie Deutsche Gewerkschaftsbund (Free German Trade Union League)
FDJ	Freie Deutsche Jugend (Free German Youth)
FRG	Federal Republic of Germany
GATT	General Agreement on Tariffs and Trade
GDR	German Democratic Republic
GNP	Gross National Product
GO	Grundorganisation = Basic Organization
HSWP	Hungarian Socialist Workers' Party
IBRD	International Bank for Reconstruction and Development (World Bank)
ICP	International Comparison Project
IIB	International Investment Bank (CMEA)
IMF	International Monetary Fund
INF	Intermediate-range Nuclear Forces
LDPD	Liberaldemokratische Partei Deutschlands = Liberal Democratic Party
LWF	Lutheran World Federation
MPLA	Popular Movement for the Liberation of Angola
NDPD	National Democratic Party of Germany
NEP	New Economic Policy
PI	Planning Improvement

PPO	Primary Party Organization
PPP	Purchasing Power Parity
R & D	Research and Development
RFE	Radio Free Europe
RSFSR	Russian Soviet Federated Socialist Republic
SED	Sozialistsische Einheitspartei Deutschlands (Socialist Unity Party)
SPD	Sozialdemokratische Partei Deutschlands = Social Democratic Party
SSD	Staatssicherheitsdienst = State Security Police
UNCTAD	United Nations Conference for Trade and Development
UNITA	National Union for the Total Independence of Angola
USSR	Union of Soviet Socialist Republics
ZK	Zentralkomittee

Note: Abbreviations for the legal documents cited and terms used in Nancy Wolfe's article are listed at the end of that article.

The SED Faces the Challenges of Ostpolitik and Glasnost

David Childs

THE GDR BETWEEN BONN AND MOSCOW

Abgrenzung

There are few states of any standing with which the GDR does not enjoy full diplomatic relations: Chile, Israel, South Africa and South Korea are among them, as is the Federal Republic of Germany (FRG). However, unlike the other four states mentioned, the GDR has conducted formal relations with Bonn since the Basic Treaty establishing such relations came into force in June 1973. Under the Treaty, the two states affirmed the inviolability of the frontier between them 'now and in the future' and total respect for each other's territorial integrity. Article 6 committed them to respecting each other's independence and separateness (*Unabhängigkeit und Selbständigkeit*) in their internal and external affairs. They also agreed to exchange permanent representatives. Yet, despite this agreement, the Federal Republic does not classify these relations as normal diplomatic relations between foreign states. It does not regard the GDR as a foreign state nor does it regard its citizens as foreigners. It is merely a German state which is part of the same German nation as itself. The theory is 'two states, one nation'.

On the day the Treaty was signed, the Federal Government, through its representative Egon Bahr, informed the GDR in a letter that the Treaty, 'does not contradict the political aim of the Federal Republic of Germany to work towards a state of peace in Europe in which the German people will be able to achieve once again, in free self-determination, its unity'. When the representatives of the two states took up their work in 1974, the West German was dealt with as a foreign diplomat who conducts his relations through the GDR Foreign Ministry, whereas the GDR's man in Bonn was told by the Federal Republic that he was to work through the Chancellor's office. The Federal Republic continued to regard GDR Germans simply as Germans and, a great advantage to the GDR, continued with the previous trade relations. The ruling SED's response was a policy of *Abgrenzung*, or delimitation, between the GDR and the Federal Republic. It sought to wipe from the consciousness of the 17 million people it ruled, the common ties between themselves and the 60.7 million Germans of the Federal Republic. This policy, already annunciated by Hermann Axen in September 1970, denied any common German history or culture. According to this theory, expounded by Erich Honecker in May 1973, there had always been two cultures in Germany, the culture of the ruling exploiter class and the culture of the progressive working class. Since 1945 these two had developed further still in different directions: West German culture had become decadent and the progressive working class culture had evolved into the socialist national culture of the GDR. In practical terms, the policy of *Abgrenzung* meant that many public bodies in the GDR were required to change their names to remove the word 'German' from them. The East German radio, for instance, changed its name from the *Deutschlandsender* to the 'Voice of the GDR' (*Stimme der DDR*). This was just one of very many changes. Remarkably, some retained their old names – perhaps the strangest case being the railway which continued to be called the *Deutsche Reichbahn* as it had been before May 1945. The political parties retained their old names as well. Thus the SED is still the Socialist Unity Party of Germany, the LDPD is still the Liberal Democratic Party of Germany and the NDPD remains the National Democratic Party of Germany. Another visible sign of change was that from January 1974 all GDR vehicles leaving the Democratic Republic had to carry the international registration letters 'DDR' and not, as previously, 'D' for Germany. The banknotes were also changed to give the necessary emphasis on the GDR. Embarrassingly, the 'national hymn' of the GDR was no longer sung because verse one contains the line, 'let us serve you well, Germany, united fatherland'. The constitution was also revised in 1974, removing the references in the 1968 constitution to Germany and stressing the eternal ties with the Soviet Union. Unlike 1968 there was no referendum to attempt to popularize and then legitimize the changes.

The *Abgrenzung* measures were the SED's nervous response to the closer relations with West Germany in the wake of the Basic Treaty. The SED was in a difficult position, and Moscow required it to be more ready to compromise with West Germany because the Soviet Union itself wanted better relations with Bonn. Many in the SED leadership feared this development as a policy which they considered to be detrimental to the GDR's vital interests. Walter Ulbricht, who headed this group, was forced to stand down in 1971 and make way for the more flexible Honecker. The SED realized it needed Bonn to help it get more recognition on the international stage and to assist it economically. Both these factors, recognition and an improving economy, were vital to stability. Yet the closer ties leading inevitably to more human contacts could slow the development of Marxist–Leninist consciousness in the GDR and threaten the SED's way of doing things and could, perhaps, even threaten the system ultimately.

Trade with Bonn

In most respects the Moscow-decreed policy towards West Germany brought with it great benefits for the SED's GDR. International recognition came swiftly once Bonn and the Western powers had signalled that they had abandoned their veto. In December 1972 alone, twenty states took up diplomatic relations with the GDR – including the Western neutrals Switzerland, Sweden and Austria, the first NATO state Belgium, and pro-western Iran. In January 1973 thirteen other states, including other NATO members, followed. Britain and France agreed relations in February. (The USA waited until September 1974.) In September 1973 the GDR and the FRG were admitted to the UNO as members 133 and 134 respectively. Economic aid and trade helped the economy as did the millions of visitors from the West.

The units of account in Table 1.1 approximate to one DM per unit. For the Federal Republic, trade with the GDR is not of great significance in terms of its total economy, as it represents only 1.5 per cent of its external trade in 1985. Certain *Länder* where unemployment is above average – the Saar and North-

Table 1.1. Development of trade between the GDR and FRG 1960–1986 (in millions of units of account)

	deliveries to GDR	deliveries from GDR
1960	1,030	1,007
1970	2,484	2,064
1975	4,028	3,391
1980	5,875	5,855
1981	6,129	6,350
1982	7,080	6,988
1983	7,681	7,562
1984	7,251	8,241
1985	8,586	8,158
1986	7,837	7,344

Source: Beilage *Informationen* (Bundesminister für innerdeutsche Beziehungen) No. 1, 1988, p. 17

rhine-Westphalia for instance – would like to export more coal and steel to the GDR. There is a consensus in West Germany among all parties that trade with the GDR should be encouraged for political reasons, as a means of keeping Germany together by creating a vested interest on the part of the GDR in better relations with Bonn. For the Democratic Republic, trade with the FRG is of far greater significance. In 1985 it represented 8.3 per cent of its total external trade. Only the Soviet Union, with over 38 per cent of the GDR's external trade in 1985, is more important. The trade with West Germany is far more important to the GDR than the percentage would indicate. It is responsible for a considerable part of the GDR's hard-currency earnings. It is trade conducted under favourable terms because it is not treated by West Germany as foreign trade. It therefore avoids the tariff barriers of the European Community. In addition, the agreements regulating this trade do not oblige the partners (in practice the GDR) to balance their trade in any one year due to the existence of the so-called 'swing'. This represents in effect an interest-free credit. West Germany has also been a source of direct credits in the 1980s. In 1983 a credit of 1 billion DM was made available and in 1984 a further credit of 950 million DM. The Federal Republic has also helped towards improving the physical communications between West Germany and Berlin, used by East German as well as by West German traffic. In 1980 the Federal Republic agreed to pay (for the period up to 1989) 50 million DM for West German and West Berlin use of the transit routes between West Germany and West Berlin. Much revenue from private sources flows into the GDR from the West. The churches help to maintain their sister organizations in the GDR and West Germans appear to give generously to their relatives in the East. How else can we explain the many hard-currency-only Intershops throughout the GDR?

'Human Contacts'

It would be wrong to presume that it was only after the beginning of Brandt's *Ostpolitik* was introduced that West Germans started to visit the GDR. There were many visitors before the improvement in relations in the 1970s. In the main, these visitors were individuals who had relatives in the GDR or who were there on business. Many who had left the GDR without official permission could not return there for fear of arrest. For those without compelling reasons to go there the GDR was not an attractive place. West Germans who wanted to visit the GDR and who did not have relatives there were sometimes regarded with some suspicion in the Federal Republic itself. After the Basic Treaty was signed, the West German authorities encouraged people to visit the other German state and there were few restrictions on who could, and who could not, go to this Warsaw Pact state. The GDR was persuaded to ease matters by passing legislation releasing those who had fled from the GDR from their citizenship and from fear of prosecution (in most cases) if they visited their old homeland. The Berlin Agreement, signed in 1971 by the USA, the Soviet Union, France, and Britain, laid the basis for regular visits by West Berliners to East Berlin and the GDR. Various other agreements led to the improvement of physical communications between the two states, as well as the postal and telecommunication services.

In an effort to restrict the number of visitors from the West, the GDR put up the minimum daily currency exchange rate of Deutschmarks into GDR-marks per visitor per day in November 1973 and in October 1980. In addition to the visits shown in Table 1.2, millions more visits have been made by West Berliners over the period since 1971. In both cases the visits

Table 1.2. Visits by citizens of the FRG to the GDR (stays of one or more days)

1967	1,423,378	1976	3,120,962
1968	1,261,441	1977	2,987,754
1969	1,107,077	1978	3,177,273
1970	1,254,084	1979	2,923,212
1971	1,267,355	1980	2,746,273
1972	1,540,381	1981	2,088,213
1973	2,278,989	1982	2,218,486
1974	1,919,141	1983	2,219,868
1975	3,123,941		

were hit by the increase in the minimum currency exchange rate.

What of visitors in the other direction? Since the end of 1964 the GDR had been allowing its pensioners to visit relatives in the West. They were sent forth with virtually no money and were forced to rely very largely on their relatives and some small official West German help. Few others, except for those on official business, were allowed to journey to the West. The pensioner traffic developed as follows:

1965	1,218,825
1970	1,048,070
1975	1,330,389
1980	1,554,764
1985	1,609,000
1987	3,800,000

As a result of the *Ostpolitik* a new category of visitor from the GDR could be received in the West. These were travellers on 'urgent family business' – such as the marriage, serious illness, or death of a close relative. In 1973, the first full year of this scheme, 41,498 East Germans were allowed to make the trip. The figure then fluctuated around the 40,000 mark until 1977. Over the last 10 years it has developed as follows:

1978	48,659
1979	41,474
1980	40,455
1981	36,667
1982	45,709

1983	64,025
1984	61,133
1985	66,000
1986	573,000
1987	1,200,000

These visitors from the GDR arrive in West Germany with virtually no money as they are only allowed to change 15 GDR-marks per annum into West German currency. (Before 30 June 1987 the amount was 70 marks per annum.) The Federal Republic now helps such visitors with a gift of 100 marks per year, and visitors from the GDR are also entitled to free medical care during their stay in West Germany.

One other form of human contact which has greatly developed since the early 1970s is the East–West telephone conversation. Before the Basic Treaty was negotiated this form of communication was very restricted, due to neglect of existing equipment and failure to modernize the telephone service between the two German states. This was, of course, due to political factors. In 1975 there were only 9.7 million calls from West Germany to the GDR, which was itself an improvement on earlier years. Telephone traffic then developed quite rapidly as new lines were installed and the political situation improved. By 1980 there were over 23 million calls from the Federal Republic to East Germany. In 1985 a record number of 26.4 million calls were made and in 1986 there were 30.3 million. It is estimated that for 1987 the number was 32 million. There are no figures available for calls made in the East–West direction. As one might expect, given the increase in telephone traffic, the number of letters sent between the two parts of Germany has fallen in recent years. The number of letters sent from West to East fell from 80 million in 1975 to 75 million in 1980 and 61 million in 1985. It rose to 63 million in 1986. In the other direction 140 million were dispatched in 1975, falling to 70 million in 1980 but rising again to 108 million in 1985. In 1986, 105 million letters were sent from the GDR to the Federal Republic. No explanation has been offered for the apparent greater enthusiasm of East Germans to write letters, bearing in mind the great difference in the size of the populations. Perhaps the greater difficulty in phoning was a factor. The greater number of letters from the GDR to West Germany is even more surprising when one considers that many East Germans

7

are not supposed to have any contact with citizens of Western states. The total number of letters sent through the GDR post in all directions has remained fairly constant: it was 1,249 million in 1955; 1,376 million in 1970; 1,256 million in 1980; and 1,271 million in 1986.

Strauss in the GDR

The SED has had to cope with distinguished political visitors from West Germany as well as with millions of ordinary tourists. The first of these were Herbert Wehner, chairman of the parliamentary group of the Social Democratic Party (SPD) and Wolfgang Mischnick, chairman of the Free Democratic (FDP) parliamentary group. They met Honecker at the end of May 1973. Interestingly enough, both were born in Dresden in what became part of the GDR. It was an astonishing visit because both were technically, according to SED ideology, 'class enemies'. Wehner, a Communist in the Weimar Republic, had been denounced on many occasions in *Neues Deutschland*. Later, pictures of Honecker with other 'class enemies' were to appear in the East German media. In 1975 he met Chancellor Helmut Schmidt in Helsinki at the Conference on Security and Co-operation in Europe. The two leaders met again in Belgrade in 1980 at the funeral of President Tito. On the same occasion Honecker met Willy Brandt, SPD chairman, and Federal President Karl Carstens. Schmidt and Honecker met again in 1981 when the Chancellor visited the GDR. Other funerals provided useful opportunities for Honecker to have conversations with West German leaders. He met President Carstens at Brezhnev's in 1982, Chancellor Kohl at Andropov's in 1984 and again at Chernenko's in 1985. Meanwhile the visit of the Bavarian leader Franz Josef Strauss to the GDR in July 1983 was something of a minor sensation. For decades Strauss had been a popular target for *Neues Deutschland* and East German cartoonists. Despite the ups and downs of USA–USSR relations, and even GDR–FRG relations, top politicians were increasingly on the move in both directions. In the 1980s West German politicians seemed to be compelled to make a ritual visit to the GDR. In January 1985 Johannes Rau, Prime Minister of Northrhine-Westphalia and SPD Chancellor candidate in the 1987 elections spent four days in the GDR during which he met Honecker. In November of the same year his colleague from the Saar, Oskar Lafontaine, made the same trip. Both have been among the many West German political visitors since then. In the meantime, most of the senior members of the Politburo of the SED had been to Bonn. What do all these trips add up to? In the case of the GDR, trade has been an important consideration, less so in the West German case. More important in both cases has been the need to prove to their respective peoples that they care about *détente* in Germany. For the GDR leaders their encounters with West Germans are an important part of their bid to win recognition from their own people but, for this, they have to pay a price. It becomes increasingly difficult to present the West German leaders as 'class enemies', 'imperialists', and 'warmongers'. Thus, it follows that, if they are not such wicked creatures, then their 'NATO state' cannot be the danger it has been presented as being, and that many restrictions on individual rights in the GDR are totally unnecessary. These contacts are, then, on the one hand, a means of stabilizing the regime, but, on the other, they make the old-style Marxist–Leninist state more difficult to uphold.

The old-style Marxist–Leninist state, which probably reached its true zenith under Ulbricht – despite some of Honecker's early moves to go further down this road – has been under severe pressures from other sources since 1971. These have been: western television; Eurocommunism; Solidarity in Poland; the peace movement in West Germany; and, more recently, Gorbachev's version of reform Communism in the Soviet Union.

When the Berlin Wall went up in 1961 only about 17 per cent of East German homes had television and in those days it was fairly easy for the authorities to make it difficult for individuals to watch western television. Thus, few would have been stirred by western television material on the tense situation in Berlin and escapes across the early, primitive wall. When Willy Brandt became deputy Chancellor and Foreign Minister in the 'grand coalition' of the Federal Republic in 1966, about half of East German homes had television. Over 50 per cent could have seen the invasion of Czechoslovakia in 1968 and 70 per cent the dramatic change in government in Bonn in 1969. The age of the new *Ostpolitik* and the age of Honecker has also been the age of almost total availability of western television in the great majority of GDR homes. It is impossible to measure the effect of this exactly but it has been of major political significance. East German leaders have complained about the effects of Western television, refugees have commented on it, and the attempts of the GDR's own television to be more engaging (compared to the lack of such attempts by the press) confirm its influence.

The SED and 'Euro-Communism'

The Warsaw Pact invasion of Czechoslovakia in 1968 was one of a number of factors which forced western Communist parties to re-examine their ideologies. Other factors were: the overthrow of the right-wing dictatorships in Portugal and Greece; the peaceful transition to democracy in Spain; the revival of democratic socialism in Western Europe; and the decline of the Communist vote. Another factor was the increasing contrast between (relative) working class affluence in the West and (relative) poverty in the East. One other factor was the imprisonment of those who sought civil rights in the 'socialist camp'. The result of this re-examination came to be known as 'Euro-Communism'. This tendency could be summed up as the acceptance of 'bourgeois democracy', the abandonment of the 'dictatorship of the proletariat', the acceptance of free trade unionism (free of state and party control), and intellectual and religious freedom. Finally, there was acceptance of the fact that a Communist-led government could be turned out by the voters at free elections. The GDR threw up a number of intellectuals who sought democratic reforms along these lines whilst still claiming to be Marxists. Among the better known of them were Robert Havemann, Stefan Heym, and Rudolf Bahro. All were long-standing SED members. Havemann was a well-known scientist and Heym a well-known writer. In their different ways they attracted much attention but they did not attempt to build up reform groups within or outside the party. All were persecuted by the regime which gave them more publicity through the Western media. After he was released from prison and went to the West, Bahro gave up Marxist socialism and seemed to lose his influence. Placed under house arrest and fined for publishing in the West, Havemann died of cancer in 1982. In old age, Heym appears to be tolerated as a licensed rebel. In December 1977 *Der Spiegel* published what it claimed was a manifesto written by SED reformists but no reformist group ever surfaced. One reason why reform groups have failed in the GDR is that the authorities could always expel the ringleaders to the West. To date, the best-known example of this was the refusal to allow Wolf Biermann, the singer and writer, to return to the GDR after a concert tour of West Germany in 1976.

In April 1983 the SED felt confident enough to host an international Karl Marx conference to commemorate the 100th anniversary of his death. Most of the world's Communist parties attended with the 'Euro' parties having their views published in *Neues Deutschland*. In the later 1970s in the GDR there was considerable interest in the ideas of Euro-Communism and, among other things, Rosa Luxemburg's criticism of Leninism. Today little is heard of Euro-Communism, either in the West or in the GDR. This is probably because western Communist parties have failed to become credible alternatives to the Socialists in the societies based on market economies.

The mass, free trade-union movement in Poland known as Solidarity climaxed in 1980–81. After remarkably winning its fight for legal recognition, the movement was declared illegal and martial law was declared in December 1981. Since then it has carried on a shadowy existence. It can rightly be asked why the movement did not lead to similar developments in neighbouring Czechoslovakia and the GDR. Five broad reasons can be given for this failure. First, in neither Czechoslovakia nor the GDR was the economic situation as bad as in Poland. Second, in neither state was the Catholic Church anything like as powerful as elsewhere, (i.e. a church independent of the state, wealthy, with excellent internal and external communications, with disciplined cadre, and a highly conscious following). Third, there were the national and ethnic differences, especially between the GDR and Poland. Fourth, in both the GDR and Czechoslovakia the grip of the secret police was just that much stronger in societies which were, in any case, more centralized. Finally, both the GDR and Czechoslovakia had lost very many potential opposition cadre who had left, or been forced to leave, their respective states. In the GDR, Solidarity did call forth admiration in certain circles, some were ashamed that no such movement was formed in the GDR, but it also called forth some disgust and anger. Many in the GDR, and no doubt Czechoslovakia, felt they could not win against the opposition of the Soviet Union and that they should try to make the best of their defective economic system. Strikes and production loss would only mean that the GDR and Czechoslovakia would have to help Poland, thus leaving less for themselves. Solidarity in Poland was a luxury they could not afford.

The Peace Movement in the GDR

In many respects, both the peace movement in West Germany and the Green movement have represented a bigger threat to the SED's old way of doing things. The Helsinki conference of 1975 on European Security and Co-operation gave a boost to such tendencies on both sides of the East–West divide. In July 1976 thirty-three East Germans from Riesa, a small industrial town near Leipzig, made public their petition asking for support to leave the GDR. Arrests followed, with those arrested eventually being released to go to West Germany. The numbers applying to leave steadily built up. On 17 February 1977 Honecker admitted in an interview with the *Saarbrücker Zeitung* that 10,000 GDR citizens had applied to leave. This was a big admission, even though the figure was probably considerably higher. The figure has continued to grow, with Western reports in 1988 claiming 100,000.

The ecology/peace movement in the Federal Republic grew up in the 1970s, in part as a reaction to decisions to build nuclear power stations (Brekdorf, 1976) and some radical disappointment with the SPD in office. By 1978 the Green movement was gaining sizeable votes in local and regional elections. The sharpening of the international atmosphere due to the Soviet invasion of Afghanistan (1979), the election of Ronald Reagan to the US Presidency (1981), the proclamation of martial law in Poland (December 1981), and the stationing of Cruise and Pershing missiles in West Germany (December 1983), greatly helped the Green movement along. In the 1983 federal elections the Greens gained 5.6 per cent of the vote and thus gained entry into parliament with twenty-seven seats. Opinion in the GDR was influenced by all the above developments and by what looked like a tightening up in all directions. In December 1971 Honecker had promised greater intellectual freedom in what became known as the 'no taboos' speech. This policy did not last long, as the cases of Bahro, Biermann, Havemann, Heym and two other writers, Reine Kunze and

Hans Schädlich, showed. The state introduced compulsory military training in schools for 15- and 16-year-olds in September 1978, despite opposition from the churches. In June 1979 the penal code was tightened up with increased penalties for 'agitation against the state, establishing illegal contacts, public vilification'. The law covering 'illegal contacts' was extended to writers publishing critical material in the West. At another level, GDR citizens were no longer permitted to buy goods in the *Intershops* with hard currency but were supposed to exchange such currency at banks for coupons and then use the coupons to make purchases. This measure was meant to reduce the use of hard currency as a second currency in the GDR and put a brake on the tendency of tradesmen to ask for hard currency for private work done. Calls for alternatives to military service were dismissed by the authorities. Increasingly the churches were drawn into the activities of the growing unofficial peace and civil rights' groups.

The SED hoped that the celebrations of the 500th anniversary of the birth of Martin Luther (at Eisleben in what is now the GDR) would give it an opportunity to get closer to the Protestant churches. This was only partly successful, as church and state had separate committees to celebrate the events – although there was co-operation between them. Such symbolic anniversaries could not change the opinions of many people about life under the GDR's style of Communism. In 1984 there was a wave of embassy occupations by people who desperately wished to leave the GDR. Would-be refugees entered the US Embassy in East Berlin, the West German representation building, and the West German embassy in Prague. Their efforts were successful after some secret diplomacy. The churches did not, of course, want people to leave and at the evangelical church synod at Görlitz in March 1984 it urged the SED to create the necessary conditions which would encourage people to stay. A similar call was heard at another synod in the same town in 1987, when the nuclear deterrent and the value of military service were also questioned. The much less important (in terms of its following) Catholic church has also voiced criticism of various aspects of SED practice. In July 1987, at the first meeting of the GDR's Catholics at Dresden, 80,000 Catholics heard Cardinal Joachim Meisner, chairman of the Berlin bishops' conference, call for more career opportunities for Christians.

Honecker in Bonn

There was a sign of relief all round when Honecker finally set off for Bonn in September 1987. The trip was originally planned for September 1984 but had kept being put off, it was presumed, because of Soviet objections. The visit was, therefore, a sign of the improved relations between Moscow and Bonn, as well as those between Moscow and Washington. Because the visit had been so long in getting under way, the people in both German states were less expectant than they would have been had it taken place as planned. However, it was felt that things could only get better as a result. Honecker knew he had to help to create a better climate by concessions to Western ideas on human rights. On 17 July 1987 the GDR Council of State issued decrees announcing a general amnesty and the abolition of the death penalty. As far as is known no executions had taken place since 1980, when Winfried Baumann, an admiral who was convicted of spying for West Germany, was executed. The GDR was thus the first country in the Soviet bloc to abolish the death penalty. According to GDR statements 24,621 convicted prisoners were released under the amnesty and a further 1,753 people were released from pre-trial detention. Among those released were more than eighty prisoners of conscience most of whom had been imprisoned either for trying to leave the GDR without permission or for applying to leave. Because of the secrecy involved, it is likely that the number of such prisoners released was considerably higher than the eighty known. In addition to these moves, it appears that frontier guards had been given new instructions limiting the use of firearms.

Honecker's visit went well and there were cautious hopes of more freedom in the GDR. As the figures given above indicate, there was certainly more travel between the GDR and West Germany. However, within weeks of Honecker's return, the security police (SSD) raided an ecological library in the Church of Zion in East Berlin and arrested seven people; they also confiscated equipment and documents. It was alleged that they had been caught 'red-handed' producing written material hostile to the state. The group had been involved in producing the magazines *Grenzfall* and *Umweltblätter* (environment pages). Those concerned were released after a few days. On 10 December 1987 a number of people were arrested because they intended presenting a declaration to the GDR United Nations' Association calling for 'an open and truthful democratic society'. They were subsequently released with the advice that they could go to West Germany or face possible action against them.

The next big security round-up came on 17 January 1988 when a number of people were arrested for attempting to join an official demonstration to commemorate the murder in 1919 of Rosa Luxemburg and Karl Liebkneckt, two founders of the German Communist Party. Those arrested had hoped to carry banners bearing Luxemburg's words taken from her pamphlet, *The Russian Revolution*, in which she criticized the Bolsheviks, 'Freedom is always the freedom of those who think differently'. Among those arrested were Vera Wollenberger, a former member of the SED who had been expelled in 1982 after protesting against the increasing militarization of GDR society. Since her expulsion she had helped to form an unofficial church-affiliated group *Kirche von Untern* (Church from Below). Among the others arrested were some who had been taken into custody during the raid on the ecology library. They, and Wollenberger, were sentenced to 6 months' imprisonment for 'riotous assembly'. Another former SED member arrested was Stephan Krawczyk, a song-writer and singer who had been banned from performing in public, and his wife Freya Klier. Before her arrest she had urged artists in West Germany not to perform in the GDR as long as her husband was in prison. He was charged with, among other things, treasonable contacts with secret-service-controlled circles in West Berlin. She was charged with treasonable activity. Over 100 had been arrested.

The arrests caused widespread protests in both parts of Germany. In churches in many parts of the GDR there were protest meetings and vigils. The arrests unwittingly achieved the almost impossible – all parties in the West German parliament united in condemning them. It appears that all those arrested were later released, many on the understanding that they would leave the GDR. Thus, once again, the SED was attempting to rid itself of civil rights leaders and key activists.

Speculation followed when further arrests took place on 5 March 1988. Some Western reports talked of over 200 arrests. It seemed likely that there was a rift in the GDR SED leadership, with the security apparatus worrying about the growing domestic civil rights movement and the possible example of the new protest movements in the Soviet Union. Certainly the SED leaders had not been enthusiastic about Gorbachev's reform ideas.

The SED and Gorbachev

The SED leaders had hoped they would meet the challenge of *Ostpolitik* with some mild cultural liberalism, permitting more contacts between GDR citizens and their relatives in the West and, above all, with higher living standards and welfare benefits. At the same time there would be ideological *Abgrenzung*, vigilance by the SED and firm adherence to Democratic Centralism. None of these policies were entirely successful but they were by no means total failures either. *Abgrenzung* failed in practice, and living standards did not rise enough to make people think they were being adequately compensated for the rather rigid regimentation they had to put up with and the sacrifices they were asked to make. Since 1985 the SED faced another challenge, that of Gorbachev's *glasnost* (openness) and *perestroika* (restructuring).

Gorbachev, who became the Soviet Party leader in 1985, had become convinced that great changes in the Soviet Union would be necessary if it wanted to survive as a modern nation. In brief, he decided it was necessary to make the Soviet economy much more efficient and society more democratic. He expected the Soviet media to freely discuss problems, expose corruption and educate public opinion. By the time he turned up to the eleventh congress of the SED in April 1986 his revolutionary aims had caused much discussion world-wide. He must have been quite shocked at the self-satisfied way in which the SED congress was conducted. There was not even the usual lip-service to self-criticism. The SED attempted to tempt him with their plans for developing the key technologies and how these could help the Soviet economy. Honecker also tried to sell Gorbachev the idea that the GDR could play a useful role in his efforts at peace and disarmament.

Since the eleventh congress, the only signs the world has had from the GDR leaders have been that *glasnost* and *perestroika* are not needed and not wanted in the GDR. In 1986 Hans-Dieter Schütt, editor-in-chief of the FDJ daily *Junge Welt*, told the West German weekly *Die Zeit* (27 June) that the Soviet

Union was 'not a model for us in terms of technology and progress'. This was a remarkable statement which at an earlier period would have led to instant dismissal and expulsion from the SED (if not worse). Kurt Hager, the SED's chief of ideology, told the West German publication *Stern* (10 April 1987), 'If your neighbour renewed the wallpaper in his flat, would you feel obliged to do the same?'. Hager remembered the German Communist Party's first post-war programme, which had stressed the importance of differing national conditions on the road to Socialism. This was later denounced as an incorrect analysis. More recently, in a speech to SED leaders on 12 February 1988, Honecker took a slightly less hostile view, pointing out that the experiences of other Socialist states would not be ignored. However, the General-Secretary of the SED strongly defended his party's position. The SED leaders have also given other signals such as the way the GDR press played down the visit of Gorbachev to Yugoslavia in March 1988 and the attention given to the new Czechoslovak Communist leader, Miloš Jakeš, a 'conservative', who visited the GDR in March 1988. And were the honours paid to Minister for State Security, General Mielke, on his 80th birthday in December 1987 also a signal?

Whatever the reaction of the Politburo of the SED to Gorbachev's reforms there is no doubt that they are attractive to many both within and outside the SED. There are those SED loyalists who believe the GDR have achieved much in its (nearly) 40 years of existence but who are appalled by its shortcomings. They believe by applying Gorbachev's principles 'creatively' the GDR could become an attractive place to be. Perhaps in some ways they underestimate the difficulties. Some of them take hope from the SED's new contacts with the West-German SPD. Certainly the agreed SED–SPD statement on basic values is entirely compatible with Gorbachev's *glasnost*. The statement maintains that discussion about the two social systems, their successes and failures, must be possible within each system. Both systems must regard each other as capable of reform and development and both should regard each other as capable of peace. Such sentiments break new ground.

However, Otto Reinhold, a ZK member and rector of the SED's own university, warned in *Neues Deutschland* (11 November 1987) that there could be no question of giving up the idea of *Feindbilder* (i.e. the idea that there are definite enemies who must be studied and exposed). Who these are was made clear in *Vom Sinn Des Soldatseins*, a book which is given to young recruits on joining the GDR armed forces. In the edition completed in October 1986 the standard, traditional, Communist view of imperialism was put forward and NATO troops were described as the absolute enemies of humanity. The recruits were warned that the soldiers of West Germany 'would not hesitate a second to shoot on us, if ordered to do so. They would be ready to commit any crime like their US models, who have already left their trail of blood in many countries'. This reveals the distance still to go before the SED–SPD joint statement begins to have real meaning. Nevertheless, the positive developments of even the last 2 years far outweigh the negative ones and would be very difficult to reverse. In the final analysis, what the SED can and cannot do is circumscribed by the Soviet Union and the Federal Republic. It is dependent on their political and economic good will. It remains to be seen whether one day the leaders of these powerful states will feel they trust each other and have enough in common to make the SED superfluous.

2

The SED after two congresses: party policy in the Gorbachev era

Henry Krisch

What is the current political status of the Socialist Unity Party (SED) as the ruling party in a system of 'real socialism'? This question has become more relevant in the wake of two kinds of developments, one long-range, one more immediate.

The long-range question, which has important theoretical implications, refers to the role of the ruling party in a period of rapid social change. This question has become acute for the SED, given the party's own emphasis on 'key technologies' (*Schlüsseltechnologien*) as the motor of social and economic development. What will be the consequences of this emphasis for policies and attitudes regarding the social status, economic rewards, and the political importance of the individuals and strata essential to this development? How might the imperatives of fostering such technologies affect the Party's ability to determine policy regarding such matters as education, industrial investment, or social policy? These developments also call into question the *ideological* basis of the Party's role, as well as the Party's attitude toward economically vital and socially privileged groups.[1]

The more immediate problem for the SED and GDR is that of responding to the Gorbachev era. The urgency of dealing with these trends has been increased by the policies put forth at the CPSU 27th Congress in 1986, and by Gorbachev's subsequent speeches and by CPSU CC resolutions.

What immediate consequences will the SED leadership draw from the Gorbachev initiatives? Two points should be noted here. One is that whatever the SED's immediate responses may be, they will shape the long-term adaption to the forces mentioned above. Second, the decision in Moscow not to bar

Honecker from his long-desired visit to the FRG (in September 1987) indicates that, at the moment, Honecker stands in the Soviet leadership's good graces. This in turn will give him greater leeway in reacting to Soviet pressures and examples.

The GDR's response to Soviet influence is not unitary. There are those issues, such as disarmament and East–West relations generally, where the SED leadership certainly welcomes Gorbachev's initiatives and, by supporting them vigorously, probably hopes to acquire 'credit' in Moscow. With respect to the economy, the SED leadership's reluctance to engage in Soviet-style reforms is clear – and emphasized by the prominence given in the GDR press to laudatory Soviet accounts of GDR economic arrangements.[2]

While 'new thinking' in foreign affairs is welcome, and 'restructuring' (*Perestroika*) in economic matters is warded off as neither relevant to nor necessary for the GDR, proposed Soviet political reforms have been treated very gingerly. This applies particularly to reforms of party structure and processes. As we shall see, there is a striking contrast between the changes made in personnel and, to a lesser extent, practice in the Soviet party since Gorbachev's access to power and parallel developments in the SED.

The SED's 11th Congress (April 1986) was marked by two major trends. On the level of personnel and procedures, there was little or no change from the recent past. For the longer term, however, there were clear, if thus far largely rhetorical indications of an effort to focus party activity into the key economic arenas – the research and development institutions for those *Schlüsseltechnologien* on which the leadership has staked the country's economic future.

Thus, just as the SED's reaction to the Gorbachev *programme* has been marked by different responses to particular policy areas, so also policy regarding the ruling party itself, in comparison to the CPSU, is two-fold. The SED's personnel policy has been a nearly polar opposite from parallel developments in the CPSU, while the efforts to make the ruling party a more relevant and effective guide of a modern society and economy clearly parallels Gorbachev's programme.

In comparing the current status of the SED with that of the CPSU, we will focus on three areas: personnel changes at the leadership level; the structure and composition of the respective parties as reflected in data released in conjunction with the 1986 party congresses (SED 11th and CPSU 27th); and 'new thinking' about the role of the ruling party in the near future.

NEW LEADERSHIPS, OLD LEADERSHIPS

The most striking contrast between the two parties, and the one with the greatest immediate significance, is in the drastic transformation of the CPSU leadership, compared with the relative stability of the SED.

As has been widely noted,[3] the period since Brezhnev's death has been a period of drastic personnel change for the CPSU. This transformation of the Soviet leadership (as well as the middle levels of leadership below the Politburo and Secretariat) has, of course, been facilitated by the advanced age of the Soviet leadership in the late Brezhnev years.

From the death of Kosygin in 1980, through the deaths of Suslov and Brezhnev in 1982, and Andropov and Ustinov in 1984, to that of Chernenko in 1985 (to mention only the most prominent), a natural process has made renewal of the Soviet leadership inescapable. Aside from the physical problem of vacancies, however, it is worth noting that the appointment of new leaders has been shaped to political ends by Andropov and Gorbachev. After years of appointments of Brezhnevite cronies (Bodyul, Chernenko, Tikhonov, etc.), promotions now went to those slighted under the old regime (Solomontsev, Vorotnikov), those associated with blocked reform initiatives (Ryzhkov and other Kirilenko protégés) and, particularly since 1985, associates of Gorbachev (Yakovlev, Eltsin).

The result has been a leadership drastically transformed. For example, aside from Gorbachev himself, only two members of the Politburo (Gromyko and Shcherbitsky) and one member of the Secretariat (Dolgikh) already belonged to those bodies under Brezhnev. Powerful bureaucratic institutions, such as the military, the foreign ministry, and the KGB are headed either by Gorbachev protégés or allies.

At lower levels of Party (and state), there has also been a marked turnover. Thus newcomers accounted for 40 per cent (125 of 307) of the Central Committee elected in 1986. The comparable figure for the SED ZK elected in 1986 is 10 per cent.

In addition Gorbachev, building on the precedent of

Andropov, has developed a powerful tool for advancing his interests throughout the Party *apparat*. This is the practice of rotating local and regional Party officials through a period of service in Moscow, where presumably political as well as performance criteria are used to judge their future suitability.

Moreover, as will be shown below, the Gorbachev years have already seen an unprecedented, high-level, and public questioning of the role of the CPSU in Soviet life in the future.

The stability of the SED leadership during these same post-Brezhnev years is striking. No less than fifteen of the twenty-two full members of the Politburo were already members five years ago (and one of the new members, Defence Minister Heinz Kessler, is a replacement for his deceased predecessor, Heinz Hoffmann). There has been a stable core of the Politburo, which would certainly include, among others, Honecker, Stoph, Mittag, Hager, Mielke, Axen, and Dohlus. The major promotions have been those of Egon Krenz in 1983 and Gunther Schabowski a year later. These two important contenders for the post-Honecker succession replaced two policy rivals of the leader, Paul Verner and Konrad Naumann, respectively. A similar continuity exists at the important *Bezirk* first-secretary level where, of the sixteen leaders (Berlin, fourteen other *Bezirke*, and the Wismut region), no less than four were in their present positions when Honecker became General Secretary in 1971, and seven became first secretary in the first five years of Honecker's tenure. Of the other five, some involved retirement, several (Sindermann, Tiedke, Felfe) promotions to higher positions, and only one, the removal of Konrad Naumann as Berlin first secretary, involved a political demotion. Moreover, only one member of the Secretariat, Inge Lange, is not a full Politburo member (she *does* have Candidate status); this is a most unusual concentration of authority.

Furthermore, unlike the Brezhnev-era CPSU leadership, the SED leadership does not have the dominating group of elderly leaders. While much has been made of the advanced age of several SED leaders, in fact only seven of the thirty-nine members of the leading group are over seventy years old (including of course some key members, such as Honecker, Hager, Stoph, and Mielke); twice as many (fifteen) were born in or after 1928, including Krenz, Felfe, and Schabowski. Nine of them, excluding Honecker, had important FDJ careers, and almost one-third of this group (again not counting Honecker) underwent formal Party-sponsored training in the USSR, either at the CPSU Higher School or, in three cases, at its Komsomol equivalent.[4]

The stability and continuity of leadership has been bound up with the increasing stature of the Party's General Secretary, Erich Honecker; there has been a relatively mild, but none the less unmistakable, spotlighting of the GDR leader.[5] Two significant symptoms of this process are: first, the rehabilitation of Ulbricht-era politicians who had fallen from grace (including Ulbricht himself);[6] and, second, the steady expansion of the Politburo to its present unwieldy twenty-two members. The latter has been a typical tactic of Soviet polity leaders when firmly in power.

Thus, in the wake of its 11th Congress, the SED displays a cohesive leadership that reflects the Party's satisfaction with its record over the past decade and a half. As has been pointed out by close observers,[7] leadership continuity has been accompanied by considerable policy flexibility. Nevertheless, the SED continues to be led by a relatively closed elite of professional politicians, whose receptivity to new ideas or new approaches is likely to be limited. There has as yet been no breakthrough of new thinking, such as that being done by scholars, into the Party's highest councils. (This is less so in foreign policy thinking than in domestic affairs.) As will be seen by comparing the SED with its fraternal Soviet counterpart, there seems to be little conviction on the part of the leadership that the GDR needs a fundamental revision of the way the ruling party operates.

STRUCTURE AND COMPOSITION OF THE TWO PARTIES

Ruling Communist parties have always differed in their structure and contours of membership. This has been true of the SED and the CPSU, and it continues to be so today. For example, the CPSU incorporates about 13 per cent of the over-18 population (9.7 per cent of the whole), while the SED represents some 18 per cent of the over-18 group.[8] The SED, possibly owing to its origins in the 1946 merger with the Soviet-zone SPD, has always had a relatively large membership in proportion to the total population; whereas the CPSU accounts for some 10 per cent of the total population, the corresponding figure for the SED is 14.5 per cent. In the inter-Congress years 1981–6, the SED grew by almost 16 per cent, the CPSU by 9 per cent.

The SED, like the other ruling parties, is dominated by mature males. While in the CPSU, some two-thirds of the members are between 30 and 60 years old, the corresponding figure for the SED is slightly lower (59 per cent).[9] Almost one-fourth of the SED membership is less than 30 years old; the corresponding CPSU figure is 17 per cent.

Women account for 35.6 per cent of the SED membership but only 28.8 per cent of the CPSUs. Neither party has added women to its leadership in significant numbers. The addition of Aleksandra Biryukova to the CPSU CC Secretariat places a woman in the Soviet party and state leadership (the first since Ekaterina Furtseva in the 1960s and only the second since the 1920s). The SED has not had a woman in the top leadership since *its* first decade, except for Ingeborg Lange and Margarete Müller. Lange and Müller are long-time Politburo candidate members (Lange since 1973 and Müller since 1963), and Lange is a ZK Secretary with responsibility for women's affairs. Neither was promoted at the 11th Congress or on other, earlier, and similar occasions.

The social composition of the SED and CPSU are similar and have displayed general continuity over the past quarter century. The SED claims that over half its members are workers, but then states that 37 per cent are *Produktionsarbeiter*. This more meaningful figure corresponds roughly to the (somewhat inflated) 45 per cent of CPSU members said to be workers. A significant difference, reflecting the different social structures of the USSR and GDR, is in the proportion of members who are collective farmers. For the SED the figure is 4.7 per cent; for the CPSU, 11.8 per cent. Both parties are about equal in the number of members with a substantial post-secondary education. For both party leaderships, a key issue is the 'saturation' (in Jerry Hough's word) of technological cadres with reliable party members. In his report to the 11th Congress, Honecker called for strengthening the Party's representation in research and development:[10]

> We regard as very important the establishment of stable party core . . . [wherever] key technologies are developed and applied to production.

Possibly, difficulty in finding enough qualified cadres in these fields, that require lengthy education, lay behind Gorbachev's suggestion (at the January 1987 CC Plenum) that more consideration should be given to the promotion of non-party members to leading positions. Not to do so, he declared, would 'restrict . . . [the party's] possibilities with respect to person-nel'.[11] Clearly both parties have only begun to deal with this issue, which also extends to the social role of skilled persons and their societal-political obligations.

In terms of party structure, little has changed in either party in recent years, nor are there significant differences in practice between them. The CPSU is based upon approximately 440,000 primary party organizations (PPOs), of which about 25 per cent are in industry and 20 per cent in educational, scientific, and cultural institutions. The SED is based on 59,115 *Grund-organisationen* (GO), of which the larger have 23,039 *Abtei-lungsparteiorganisationen* (APO) and 96,104 *Parteigruppen* under them. (I have been unable to find a breakdown of GO by sector.) The ratio of PPOs and GO to total party membership is approximately the same.

THE ROLE OF THE RULING PARTY

The roles of the SED and CPSU, respectively, in leading their societies, have come under intensive and increased scrutiny. The norms of intra-Party behaviour, the relationship of the Party as an institution to its members, and the capacity of the Party effectively to guide social processes have all been subject to review. However, whereas the Soviet version of this review, with its watchwords of 'openness' (*Glasnost*) and 'democratiz-ation', has been dramatic, revealing, and politically challenging, the SED version (in so far as it has taken place at all) has been muted and tentative; it has not challenged the position of national and regional leaders.

The detailed and indeed startling criticisms levelled at the CPSU by Gorbachev and his political allies have come under three headings.[12] First, there was the moral corruption of the party leaders who used their positions for personal gain or for their political advancement, leaders who (to quote just one instance) 'abused their authority, stifled criticism or reaped personal gain . . . [and] became accessories to, or organizers of, criminal actions'. Second, this moral and personal critique was

25

extended to a *political and general* critique of the Party's functioning:

> We have constantly emphasized that the problems that have accumulated in society are connected, to a significant extent, to shortcomings in the activity of the Party itself and in its personnel policy.

Third, practical consequences were drawn from this analysis. There were the replacements and often political and personal disgrace of prominent leaders – for example, several Central Asian Union Republic first secretaries; more significant, however, has been the call for institutional and procedural reform of the CPSU.

The key element here was Gorbachev's call for election of party leaders at all levels of the CPSU and for general democratization of procedures at Party meetings. The CPSU has not yet adopted this proposal for itself; but similar notions have been put into effect in industry and local government. However one would organize such a system, and despite Gorbachev's explicit avowal that the 'decisions of higher agencies are binding on all lower-level Party committees, including decisions on personnel questions', it clearly would produce a major shift in intra-Party power relations.

As Gorbachev has declared, 'some people have difficulty' mastering new approaches in political work, resent criticism, and doubt the value of exposing shortcomings. Undoubtedly this is as true in the GDR as in the Soviet Union, but in one way even more so. The inescapable tendency to push 'openness' into consideration of the past would conjure up not only revised assessments of SED leaders but also, since these leaders (including Honecker!) made crucial decisions on German partition and relations with the FRG, the possibility of 'reopening' the German Question!

It is hardly surprising, therefore, that the SED leadership has shown little enthusiasm for a political restructuring. Nevertheless, there are two factors that have pressed the SED to approach, in a cautious manner, questions of intra-Party procedures. One is, as has been mentioned earlier, the pressure of Soviet example. No matter how much the SED leaders may protest that they are not bound to follow Soviet practice, GDR citizens are aware of the Gorbachev reforms and cannot be kept from asking questions that will go far beyond the 'Gorbachev! Gorbachev!' chants of angry rock music fans.[13]

The other is a publicly little-acknowledged awareness that the same issues of efficiency and control which have been the basis for the Soviet reforms are, at least potentially, important issues for the GDR itself. A growing GDR scholarly literature stresses the role of the subjective factor in maximizing efficient social participation. There is a subtle shift in GDR political culture toward incorporating elitist and performance-oriented values along with the old 'revolutionary' values of participation and self-actualization into a new, system-maintaining amalgam.[14]

Consequently, the SED has stressed the importance of some intra-Party processes, including membership review and party elections, and has given these matters unusual public attention.[15] The published accounts of these matters give an unusual insight into the detailed life of the ruling party.

For example, in the 1985 membership review (*Mitglieder-überprüfung*) over 99 per cent of members participated – but 430 members refused to do so! There were almost 4,000 persons removed from membership, while almost half that number voluntarily left the Party (something not possible in the CPSU). Of those who left or were excluded from the SED, three-fourths 'had no active connection' to the Party, one-fifth did something 'harmful to the Party' (what is unspecified), and 7 per cent advanced their personal interests at the Party's expense.

About three-quarters of the SED secretaries in GO or APO were re-elected. Of the 20,500 who were not, over half changed positions, 5 per cent became students, 33 per cent retired for reasons of age or health. That leaves 6 per cent who were unsatisfactory and almost 2 per cent unaccounted for.

Both the elections and the personal reviews serve mobilizing functions. At the review sessions, members find it difficult not to accept new social obligations. Membership suggestions are actively solicited: 40 per cent dealt with the economy, 30 per cent with Party matters, 20 per cent with local government, and a surprisingly low 10 per cent with conditions of daily life.

Party members are encouraged to participate in these sessions; clearly there is little tradition of lively and meaningful discussion. This may account for the rather odd pride taken in the facts that, for example, the members' *Diskussionsfreudigkeit* rose compared to previous Party elections, and that 70 per cent of those present at meetings of *Parteigruppen*, the smallest

Party unit, spoke at meetings. (At the GO and APO meetings, only one-third of those present spoke in the discussion.)

Party leaderships were urged (in the May 1987 account of Party elections) to make Party meetings more democratic, with more political content and more information for members. 'Many comrades' advocated a system whereby Party leaderships would give regular account of their performance (a favourite Gorbachev theme!), but no specifics were provided.

Reporting on behalf of the SED Politburo to the 5th ZK Plenum in December 1987,[16] Werner Felfe referred briefly to the 'application of the principle of accountability [*Rechenschaftslegung*] and control' as having expanded the circle of 'active Comrades' helping to implement Party decisions, but he gave no details. Felfe's main stress was on cadre development and on the SED's intensified and highly visible ideological training programme. Many accounts describe an ostensible degree of mobilization of SED members almost difficult to believe, if the functions are not carried out *pro forma*. Even trying to eliminate multiple commitments to what is described as 'a growing ability' on the part of SED members to lead mass organizations, one comes up with a total of over one million SED members active in some unpaid (but presumably time-consuming) public activity. (Over 700,000 such commitments relate to the FDGB or the FDJ.)

A comparison of the two Party leaderships' overall assessments of the role played by their respective parties demonstrates a great difference. As has been noted, the CPSU leaders have publicly blamed the Party – its personnel, structure, and processes – for the stagnation of the country. There were, in the phrase used by Gorbachev and Eltsin at the 27th Congress, too many 'zones outside criticism'.

But the SED leaders, whatever their private reservations, have issued no such calls for renewal of the SED and have especially not accepted personal responsibility for mistakes.[17] The contrast between the tone of the speeches at the two Party Congresses was quite blatant, and this contrast has been sharpened as Gorbachev's speeches have grown blunter, more detailed, more critical. The SED leaders' response to Soviet reform efforts has been (with the foreign policy exceptions noted earlier) to deny by omission that the SED needs a restructuring or a democratization of similar proportions.[18]

The nature of this response may be seen in Honecker's

guidelines speech of February 1987.[19] The occasion for this speech was what has become an annual ritual in Honecker's leadership of the party: a formal speech to the gathered SED high command. The audience includes the members of the Politburo and Secretariat, the sixteen *Bezirk* first secretaries, Party secretaries from important industrial *Kombinate*, ZK *Abteilungsleitern*, as well as the formal audience, the 264 first secretaries of the SED *Kriesleitungen*.

Honecker explicitly credited the GDR and SED with conspicuous achievements:

> We have no reason not to mention our progress, indeed I may say our successes . . . We have not the slightest reason to hide the fact that the . . . [socio-economic] course we have followed since the beginning of the 1970s has proven correct . . . we therefore have no reason to hide our light under a bushel.

Moreover, he declared the GDR's socialist democracy to be far superior to bourgeois liberalism; any attempt to contrast socialist economic achievement with a supposed capitalist superiority in individual rights would, of course, be mistaken.

Equally illuminating are the things Honecker did not say. In the section of this speech devoted to the USSR, Honecker neither mentioned Gorbachev by name nor did he mention Gorbachev's programme; indeed, Honecker barely mentioned the 27th CPSU Congress. There was no indication in this passage that the SED, or the people of the GDR generally, had anything special to learn from the USSR.

Furthermore, in the section devoted to the internal development of the Party, there was no criticism of particular leaders, or of a stratum of Party officials, or of corrupt or improper or even merely ineffective practices. A passing reference to improving the conduct of Party meetings is all the reform seemingly needed. This is not to suggest that Honecker is somehow obliged to 'discover' flaws, corrupt officials, or other unwanted phenomena. What seems clear, however, is that as Gorbachev's insistence on reform has grown sharper, Honecker's insistence on continuity and stability, on the validity of past procedures has also become more intense.

CONCLUSIONS

The CPSU 27th Congress and subsequent CC sessions were

marked by frank and detailed self-criticism, while the SED 11th Congress presented a picture of general self-satisfaction. None the less, similar concerns underlie thinking about the future development of both parties. What is at stake is the validity of the Leninist party's social leadership in the age of the 'scientific and technical revolution', or rather its continued relevance to the problems, prospects, collective and individual concerns of a rapidly developing and changing society. While the surface of the SED seems unruffled by serious self-examination, it seems unlikely that younger Party officials and political theorists, both within the Party's own research institutes and elsewhere, are satisfied merely to repeat the standard proposition that the Party is the 'tested and uncontested politically leading force' of socialist society.[20]

One major difficulty lies in the inability or unwillingness of GDR scholarship to deal with the political role of the Party. In a recent, very interesting symposium incorporating contributions by leading GDR social scientists,[21] the question of the Party's role was not addressed directly or in a satisfactory manner. Thus Weichelt[22] maintains that the institutional embodiments of the socialist political system, including the state, all work under the Party's leadership but also describes the socialist state as the 'chief organizer' of the conscious political activity of the masses.

The future development of political life in the GDR, however, must lie in the direction of more self-directing, self-aware political activity of masses of people – if only because such activity is essential to the qualitative economic growth the regime demands, and is important to the self-esteem and satisfaction of the highly qualified personnel needed for such progress. While GDR theorists have produced interesting work on the relationship of masses to state, individual to collective interests, motivation for participation, nature of socialist democracy, and more, they have not dealt adequately with the institution central to all such activity – the Party.[23]

It may well be difficult for the present, relatively long-entrenched SED leadership to sponsor qualitatively new thinking, let alone new forms of Party rule. But surely there were, among the delegates to the 11th Congress and in the GDR at large, both scholars and officials who took to heart Gorbachev's admonition, delivered in his speech to the SED Congress, that 'Marx and Engels taught that a critical attitude toward one's own activity is the essential condition for the success of a revolutionary party'.[24]

NOTES

1. For summaries of recent and growing GDR literature on this subject, see Clemens Burrichter (1986) 'Neue Eliten in der DDR?' and Uwe Ziegler (1986) 'Kommentar', in *DDR-Report 19*, 362–5 and 565–6, respectively. An authoritative, if somewhat defensive GDR statement on this topic is in Wolfgang Weichelt *et al.* (1986) *Der Staat im politischen System der DDR*, Berlin: Staatsverlag der DDR, 74:

> It would be dangerous and mistaken to conclude from the fact that the educational level of the working masses has risen significantly under socialism, from their higher political consciousness . . . that the guidance of society through a Marxist–Leninist party would lose in importance.

2. Two recent examples from *Neues Deutschland* are: Mai Podkljutschnikow, 'Ein Kombinat bietet Lizensen an', July 21, 1987, 3 (reprinted from *Pravda*), and 'Wenn das Kombinat Herr im Hause ist', January 31–February 1, 1987, 2 (reprinted from *Ekonomicheskaya Gazeta*).

3. Sources for this section include: Archie Brown (1985) 'New Man at the Kremlin', *Problems of Communism 34*, 1–23; A. Becker *et al.* (1986) *The 27th Congress of the Communist Party of the Soviet Union: A Report from the Airlie House Conference* (RAND/UCLA and Harriman Institute Study, December 1986), esp. 2–3 and 7–8; Elizabeth Teague, 'Turnover in the Soviet Elite under Gorbachev: Implications for Soviet Politics', *Radio Liberty Research Bulletin RL Supplement 1/86*; own calculations from the Soviet press.

4. Data from files of *Neues Deutschland*, various dates, and *Die Volkskammer der Deutschen Demokratischen Republik, 9, Wahlperiode*, Berlin: Staatsverlag der DDR, 1987.

5. See, for example, the depiction of Honecker's role in setting the party's goals, strategies, and means in Manfred Banaschak (1986) 'Gegenwartsbezogen und Zukunftsorientiert. Zum XI. Parteitag der SED', *Einheit 41*, 482. In the official account of the 1987 party elections, party meetings are described as expressing 'respect and admiration [*Hochachtung und Verehrung*]' for Honecker and his 'tireless striving for peace and socialism'. See 'Parteiwahlen: Angelegenheiten des ganzen Volkes', *Neues Deutschland*, May 6, 1987, 3.

6. For the rehabilitation of Karl Schirdewan, whose fall from political grace in 1958 was an important episode in the rise of Erich Honecker, see *Informationen* (Bundesminister für innerdeutsche Bezeihungen), No. 10 (May 25, 1987), 8. Honecker has quietly revised episodes of his own past: a story on the fortieth anniversary of his leading an FDJ group to the Soviet Union ('Ging in die Geschichte ein – der Friedensflug nach Osten', *Neues Deutschland*, July 18–19, 1987, 3) credits Herbert Geisler as having been a member of the delegation

which, as Heinz Lippmann pointed out in his Honecker biography, was not done in 1967! For one of many stories on Ulbricht, see 'Standhafter Kampfer für die Sache des Sozialismus und des Friedens', *Neues Deutschland*, June 30, 1983, 1–2.

7. Thomas Ammer and Johannes Kuppe (1986) 'XI. Parteitag der SED', *Deutschland Archiv 19*, 616.

8. CPSU: own calculation from Soviet sources; SED calculated from *Statistisches Taschenbuch der DDR 1986* (Berlin: Staatsverlag der DDR, 1986), 3 and *Bericht des Zentralkomitees der Sozialistischen Einheitspartie Deutschlands an den XI. Parteitag (Berichterstatter: Genosse Erich Honecker)* (Berlin: Dietz Verlag, 1986), 84.

9. For this section, in addition to previously cited sources, see 'Bericht über die Entwicklung der Mitgliederbewegung der SED seit dem X. Parteitag und im Jahre 1985', *Neues Deutschland*, January 9, 1986, 3.

10. *Bericht des Zentralkomitees*, 85. For related activities in the GO and at the party higher school, see Uwe Möller (1986) 'Parteiarbeit in der neuen Etappe der wissenschaftlichtechnischen Revolution', *Einheit 41*, 1037–8.

11. As reported in *Pravda*, January 28, 1987; cited from the *Current Digest of the Soviet Press 39*, 5 (March 4, 1987), p. 6.

12. By now the literature on Gorbachev's party reforms is too voluminous to be cited here. Aside from the sources cited in note 4, the best sources are the speeches of Soviet leaders. See, especially, the speeches of Gorbachev and Eltsin at the 27th CPSU Congress (a convenient source is *Current Soviet Policies IX: The Documentary Record of the 27th Congress of the Communist Party of the Soviet Union* (Columbus, OH: CPSP, 1986), and Gorbachev's speech at the January 1987 CC Plenum (a speech *not* fully published in the GDR) and his speech to the CC Plenum of June 1987 (both in *CDSP 39*, 4–5 (February 1987) and *39*, 10 (July 1987). The quoted passages in this section are from these sources.

13. For one of the spate of stories about the GDR fans' reactions to police control measures on the occasion of West Berlin rock concerts at the Wall, see 'Der Ruf "Die Mauer muss" weg wird der SED noch lange in den Ohren klingen', *Frankfurter Allgemeine Zeitung*, June 10, 1987, 2.

14. I have broached some of these issues in an article, 'Political Culture and Political Stability in the German Democratic Republic', *Studies in Comparative Communism 19* (1986), 41–54.

15. Sources for this section (aside from the *Bericht des Zentralkomitees*) include: 'Parteiwahlen: Angelegenheit des ganzen Volkes', *Neues Deutschland*, May 6, 1987, 3; Thomas Ammer (1986) 'Mitglieder und Funktionäre in der SED', *DDR-Report 19*, 497–500; Heinz Mirtscher (1987) 'Parteiwahlen: stärken Kampfkraft und festigen Massenverbundenheit', *Neuer Weg 42*, 307–12; 'Beilage: Stellungnahme zum Bericht der KL der SED Rathenow über Ergebnisse und Erfahrungen der Entwicklung des innerparteilichen Lebens und der Stärkung der Kampfkraft der Grundorganisationen der SED bei

der Verwirklichung der ökonomischen Strategie', *Neuer Weg 40* (1985), 343–46.

16. In *Neues Deutschland*, December 17, 1987.

17. It is noteworthy that whereas incumbent or even deceased CPSU leaders such as Kunaev or Rashidov were singled out for improper acts, no difficulty of the GDR's development or weaknesses in the SED have been blamed publicly on Konrad Naumann.

18. For some early assessments of the SED response to Gorbachev, see Walter Süss (1986) 'Kein Vorbild für die DDR?' *Deutschland Archiv 19*, 965–88, and Heinz Timmermann (1987) 'Gorbatschows Reformansatze – eine Herausforderung für die SED', *DDR-Report 20* 385–8.

20. Erich Honecker (1987) 'Die Aufgaben der Parteiorganizationen bei der weiteren Verwirklichung der Beschlüsse des XI. Parteitages der SED', *Neues Deutschland*, February 7–8, 3–11. The quotations in this section are from this source.

21. Karl-Heinz Röder (ed.) (1986) *Politische Theorie und sozialer Fortschritt*, Berlin: Staatsverlag der DDR.

22. Wolfgang Weichelt (1986) 'Politisches System und Entfaltung der Triebkrafte des Sozialismus bei der weiteren Gestaltung der entwickelten sozialistischen Gesellschaft', in Röder, *op. cit.*, 166–19.

23. See Hartmut Zimmermann (1986) 'Innenpolitische Aspekte des XI. Parteitags der SED', *DDR-Report 19*, 286–90. An example of creative political theorizing and historical analysis in the GDR (but only one of several) is, Uwe-Jen Heuer, 'Zur Geschichte des marxistisch-leninistischen Demokratiebegriffs', in Röder, *op. cit.*, 182–206.

24. *Neues Deutschland*, April 19, 1986.

3

Leadership structures and leadership politics in Hungary and the GDR

Thomas A. Baylis

Two of the senior political figures of Eastern Europe approach their retirement after having achieved a degree of apparent popular approval unparalleled among leaders of those Communist regimes imposed by Soviet force. Hella Pick wrote in the *Guardian* in 1984: 'Today, János Kádár knows that even in free elections against other candidates, he would be certain to emerge the victor'.[1] 'The citizens of the other German state', remarked Theo Sommer in *Die Zeit* in 1986, 'display something almost like quiet reverence' toward Erich Honecker.[2]

Recent reports suggest that Kádár's reputation has suffered a marked decline as Hungary's economic difficulties have grown increasingly acute; the GDR's Honecker appears to have profited domestically from his successful visit to the Federal Republic in September 1987, but his regime now faces growing criticism of its resistance to Gorbachev-style reforms. Even at its height, the popularity of the two leaders, now both 75, undoubtedly rested in part on the reputation of each for mitigating the harshness of an otherwise unloved system. Nevertheless, both can look back upon their years in office with some satisfaction, particularly when they compare the relative political stability and the economic successes of the states they lead to the more parlous condition of most of their Communist neighbours. Both have acquired a reputation for pursuing a course of pragmatic accommodation with their populations; more recently, commentators have observed a surprising degree of convergence in their countries' foreign policy positions. In 1984 and 1985, in particular, the GDR and Hungary risked the ire of the Soviet Union and became the joint target of the invective of the Czech press by asserting the right of small

East European states to act on behalf of their own 'national interest' as well that of the socialist camp as a whole, and to pursue *détente* with West European neighbours even during a period of superpower confrontation.

There remain, to be sure, pronounced differences between the Hungarian and East German versions of 'real socialism'. These were dramatized by the ostentatious military display with which the GDR marked the 25th anniversary of the construction of the Berlin Wall, at a time when Hungarians had become accustomed to exercising their right to travel to the West – and even, every 3 years, to purchase hard currency to do so. The GDR's familiar single candidate elections stand in vivid contrast to the defeat of many of the Hungarian party's preferred nominees in its competitive parliamentary vote of June 1985. In spite of recent measures taken against Hungarian dissidents, the relatively open and critical intellectual atmosphere of Budapest remains quite different from the persistent tension characterizing the relationship between cultural figures and party officials in East Berlin. The initiation of a more daring phase of economic reforms in Hungary in the face of the East European credit crisis at the beginning of this decade contrasts instructively with the relative orthodoxy of the East Germans.

How can we explain both the similarities and the differences? Why is Hungary more adventurous in its economics, culture, and politics than the GDR, and why does it appear to seek and receive greater leeway for such experimentation from the USSR? In this chapter I want to explore one set of variables that may assist us in finding an explanation: leadership structures and leadership practices in the two states. In doing so I do not mean to reject alternative approaches. The differences between the GDR and Hungary are clearly also related to the size, economic importance, and geopolitical position of each country, as well as to the historical relationship of each to the Soviet Union. But as a student of elite politics in Eastern Europe, I have been struck by the frequency with which observers have attributed the distinctiveness of the Hungarian path to the leadership tactics and style of Kádár. Indeed, the term 'Kádárism' (or 'Kádárization')[3] has sometimes been used to signify a particular approach to successful rule in Eastern Europe. In this chapter I will examine precisely what 'Kádárism' has meant in terms of Hungary's leadership structures and practices, and ask how it differs from leadership arrangements in the GDR. I will pursue the comparison in five parts, examining in turn: formal leadership structures; the position and leadership styles of the two General Secretaries; the role, composition, and divisions of the principal leadership 'collectives' – the Politburo and Secretariat; the relations of each set of leaders with the Soviet Union; and the question of leadership succession.

FORMAL STRUCTURES

Although the leading political bodies in both the GDR and Hungary are modelled after those of the USSR, there are some interesting differences between them even in the formal sense. In both countries, the Politburo of the ruling party is the supreme decision-making body, but in Hungary it is considerably more compact (thirteen members) than it is in the GDR (twenty-two members, five candidates)[4] – and thus, one might think, more manageable (small-group theory suggests that seven is about the ideal size for a decision-making committee). Candidate status (said to carry less prestige and not to include the right to vote) no longer exists on the Hungarian Politburo; it has also been abolished on the Central Committee and as a category of party membership.

Until recently, the HSWP Politburo was said to meet only twice a month,[5] while the SED Politburo, like the CPSU's, has for many years met weekly. I am informed that since the late 1970s the Hungarian body has also met each week; its decision-making burdens probably remain lighter than those of its German counterpart, however, owing to the decentralization of economic decisions and the larger policy-making role played by Hungarian government bodies. The Hungarian Party's Central Committee, on the other hand, appears to meet more frequently – some four times a year, as opposed to two for the SED Committee – and is much smaller.[6] At the 13th HSWP Congress in 1985 its size was reduced from 127 to 105, making it the smallest such body in Eastern Europe. The SED Central Committee, by contrast, grew in size – as it has after each Party Congress – from 156 to 165 full members, while keeping the number of candidate members constant at 57; the body as a whole is now twice the size of its Hungarian counterpart. Does this suggest that the Hungarian Committee is more of a working, actively deliberating body, while the SED Committee continues to perform a largely representational function? There are some indications that this is so.[7]

The Central Committee Secretariat of the HSWP is also smaller (nine) than its SED counterpart (eleven). Only four Hungarian Secretaries are simultaneously Politburo members (Kádár, Óvári, Berecz, Lázár), while all eleven SED Secretariat members are either Politburo members or candidates. In this case, the Hungarian practice more closely resembles the Soviet, where such simultaneous membership is taken to be a sign of superior influence. Since the 13th Congress, János Kádár has been designated 'General' rather than 'First' Secretary of the Party, thus bringing his title into conformity with those of other East European bloc leaders, excepting Poland's Jaruzelski; Kádár now also has a 'Deputy' General Secretary, György Lázár, a position that does not formally exist in the GDR, although Egon Krenz appears to fill that role in practice. Until the retirement of Gustav Husak, Kádár was alone among his East European counterparts – with the important exception of Gorbachev – in not simultaneously occupying the position of head of state; neither is he premier. He also does not head a 'National Defence Council', as Gorbachev does.[8] So far as I have been able to ascertain, no such body exists in Hungary, although it does in all the other East European Warsaw Pact states, including Romania.[9]

How important are these differences in formal institutions? At the least, they suggest that the Soviet Union has not found it useful to insist that East European leadership structures be identical with its own, so long as the basic model is followed. The Hungarians, and to a lesser extent the East Germans, have evidently sought to adapt Soviet institutions to fit their own need – and thereby implicitly claimed a small measure of autonomy. More important, differences in formal institutions can have significant practical consequences, a few of which I have already suggested. On the other hand, identical institutions may operate quite differently in practice, and it is to what we know about the actual operation of party leadership bodies in Hungary and the GDR that I now turn.

THE *PRIMUS INTER PARES* IN HUNGARY AND THE GDR

Like the Soviet Union and its other Warsaw Pact allies, both the GDR and Hungary subscribe officially to the doctrine of 'collective leadership'.[10] What sketchy evidence we have of actual decision-making in the two states suggests that major decisions are, indeed, taken collectively in the Politburo (sometimes influenced, to be sure, by Soviet wishes). At the same time, there has been little question that Kádár and Honecker became the dominant figures in their respective parties within a short time of their assumption of the position of First Secretary. A great deal has been written about the purported 'leadership style' of Kádár, and somewhat less about that of Honecker, but the evidence is necessarily anecdotal and comparisons are accordingly somewhat hazardous. Let me nevertheless venture a few remarks centred around the concept of 'authority-building', which has been applied with some success to recent Soviet leaders by writers like George Breslauer, Thane Gustafson, and Dawn Mann.[11]

Both Kádár and Honecker initially took office with the assistance of the Soviet Union, although Honecker assumed his position under considerably more favourable circumstances than Kádár did. Selected by the Russians – purportedly on the recommendation of Yugoslav leaders[12] – to head the Hungarian regime after the crushing of the 1956 revolution, Kádár was inevitably viewed by many of his countrymen as a traitor; yet, as an earlier supporter of Imre Nagy, it is doubtful that he enjoyed the full confidence of the Russians either. Honecker was named to replace the veteran GDR leader Walter Ulbricht shortly before the 8th SED Congress met in 1971. It has been widely assumed that the Russians forced the removal of Ulbricht because of their displeasure over his resistance to their pursuit of East–West agreements over Berlin and inter-German relations, and over his ambitions to stake out a marginally distinctive ideological position for the GDR. But it is also clear that many of Ulbricht's colleagues, long displeased with his autocratic habits, at least welcomed his removal and may have helped initiate it.[13] Honecker's image among East Germans was at best indistinct in 1971 – he was widely viewed as a rather pale bureaucrat and loyal follower of Ulbricht – but he did not face the formidable obstacles to building popular authority that Kádár did.

Building authority in Eastern Europe demands that a leader play successfully to three 'legitimacy audiences' at once: the Soviet leadership, the top and middle-level cadres of the leader's own party (and sometimes different factions among them), and the ordinary citizens of his country. Although the last 'audience' has no direct voice in leadership selection, the *perception* of mass attitudes on the part of the first two can strongly influence their own assessment of the leader's performance.[14] Both Kádár and Honecker can be said to have successfully wooed all three audiences, although Kádár's achievement is the more impressive for having kept him in power for 30 years – twice as long as Honecker – and because of his more difficult starting position.

Students of Hungarian politics show considerable agreement in characterizing Kádár's personality and his decision-making style. He is described as a shy, polite, and self-effacing man who lives modestly and is 'hardly charismatic'.[15] No intellectual himself, although supposedly having many friends among intellectuals, he is said to be given to homely anecdotes and metaphors and to interact easily with ordinary Hungarians; Charles Gati and Sarah Terry have both referred to him as a 'populist'.[16] Commentators stress his personal honesty and tolerance, his candour, and his pragmatism.[17] Characterized by one writer as a 'great compromiser', he is said to be a 'man of the middle', eager to persuade both sides of his sympathy for their views.[18] In Volgyes' words: 'practising the "Kádár csardas" – two steps to the right and two to the left – he has kept the country on an even keel'.[19] His famous slogan, 'whoever is not against us is with us',[20] – a self-conscious reversal of the approach of his Stalinist predecessor Rákosi – seems to reflect not only his efforts to enlist the support of as many Hungarians as possible for his regime, but to characterize his approach to leadership within the HSWP elite.

This quality – and the very fact of his success and his longevity in office – leads observers to praise especially highly his skills as a political tactician. He is said to seek to 'reason with and cajole his opponents, rather than insisting on compliance with his policies'.[21] Ellen Comisso has compared him to a legislative leader who rarely takes initiatives himself, but rather acts as an 'agent' of other, powerful 'principals', and is concerned with 'building winning coalitions and keeping peace in the family'.[22] This metaphor, however, may not do full justice to Kádár's willingness to wield the great personal authority he enjoys. Gati, for example, has written that:

on closer examination, Kádár's most important decisions

suggest . . . that while he is cautious in the first phase of the decision-making process, he is quite prepared to act in a firm and authoritative manner subsequently, at the time when policy decisions are actually finalized, announced, and implemented.[23]

The view of Erich Honecker as a rather grey, conservative figure that prevailed at the time of his appointment as SED First Secretary in 1971 has long since given way to a more positive image in both the West and the GDR itself. Following an interview with Honecker in January 1986, Theo Sommer of *Die Zeit* wrote:

He speaks with a firm, sometimes soft voice. His sentences emerge without adornment or rhetorical flourishes; he formulates them fluently. He is friendly in manner, smiles and laughs, lets himself be interrupted. No embarrassment, but also no feigned joviality. He has his facts at his command. He dispenses with quotations from Marx, Engels, and their successors. He reasons from facts [*aus der Sache*], not from ideology.[24]

As a pragmatist and 'realist' (as Sommer notes, he is particularly fond of the terms 'realism' and 'reason'), Honecker bears a marked resemblance to Kádár. His personal style also resembles Kádár's in so far as he appears to relate easily to his colleagues in the SED leadership and to ordinary comrades, as well as to his frequent Western visitors. In contrast to Ulbricht, on taking office 'he sought and quickly established contacts, in conversation used the personal pronoun "Du", bridged easily – so it appears – the gap between "above" and "below", was more attentive to comradeship than to strict etiquette'.[25] On the other hand, he does not seem to share Kádár's shyness or modesty (or his unpretentious living conditions), and has sometimes been accused of enjoying the small cult of personality that has emerged around him.[26] Unlike Kádár, he has published a lengthy autobiography, which has been widely publicized and translated into several foreign languages,[27] and on the occasion of a recent Leipzig trade fair his picture appeared forty-three times in a single issue of *Neues Deutschland* in the company of various foreign exhibitors and politicians.[28]

To the outside observer, Honecker seems to be more concerned than Kádár with the external trappings of power. He acted quickly and successfully to consolidate his authority after his appointment, moving numerous former colleagues with whom he had worked in the Free German Youth into key party positions and, in 1976, assumed the position of head of state (i.e. Chairman of the State Council). On the basis of frequent personal contacts with him, often in the company of other Politburo members, Günter Gaus, first head of the Federal Republic's diplomatic mission in East Berlin, observed that Honecker came across unambiguously as being 'number one' in the SED leadership.[29] He has sought to identify himself closely and personally with the SED's conciliatory *Westpolitik*, in contrast to Kádár's efforts to remain a 'man of the middle' who maintains some distance from the strong advocates of specific policies. Together with his party, Honecker also seems to be less tolerant of internal disagreement and self-criticism than Kádár and the HSWP. These differences, however, should not obscure what seem to me to remain the overriding similarities in the leadership styles of the two men.

THE COLLECTIVE LEADERSHIP

The symbolic, brokering, and perhaps catalytic leadership roles played by Honecker and Kádár in their respective countries are reinforced by the personal authority both have acquired during their long years in power and through the relationship each has developed with the Soviet leadership (see pp. 47–50). But as I have already remarked, leadership in both the HSWP and SED is officially described as collective, with the parties' Politburos serving as the pivotal decision-making bodies. The domestic reaction against the autocratic practices of Rákosi in Hungary and Ulbricht in the GDR undoubtedly reinforced the dictum laid down by the USSR in the course of destalinization, and again after the fall of Khrushchev: violations of the 'Leninist' norm of collective leadership were not to be tolerated. The proceedings of both Hungarian and East German Politburo meetings are secret, and are not even routinely summarized in the press, as they have been in the USSR beginning with Andropov, and currently are in Poland, Czechoslovakia, and Romania. We do have 'insider' accounts of Politburo operations, however, especially from the GDR.

According to these, the SED Politburo in its weekly meetings goes through a long agenda that mixes important with relatively trivial matters; the agenda and other documents are prepared by the 'Bureau of the Politburo', a body believed to be under the special influence of the General Secretary. The Central Committee Secretariat and its specialized departments furnish, we assume, other discussion materials, and various specialists and functionaries are regularly called to provide information and respond to questions at Politburo meetings. Decisions are usually made by consensus, a procedure that probably also enhances the position of the General Secretary, who must define what the consensus is.[30] There appears to be a high degree of functional specialization among members; one former 'insider' writes that 'each one of the Politburo members is unconditional ruler within his own sphere', and only the General Secretary would venture to intervene in it.[31] This formulation is probably exaggerated, but it is given some confirmation by the lengthy periods during which Politburo members have often remained responsible for the same area of activity.

In both the GDR and Hungarian Politburos – as in most cabinets in Western parliamentary democracies – many decisions appear to be prefigured in informal discussions among key members.[32] In Hungary but not the GDR, Politburo members head two formal committees of the Central Committee – for Economic Policy and for Agitation and Propaganda – and several specialized 'Working Groups'.[33] The two committees, at least, appear to have significant influence over policy-making and implementation.[34] The Hungarian Politburo, as we have already noted, is also smaller than the GDR's and probably deals with a more limited range of questions, but otherwise its operations appear to be similar to those of the East German body. Collective leadership in Hungary, Comisso argues, serves as something of a system of checks and balances, through which 'political leaders control each other'. The HSWP's commitment to collective leadership allows it 'to avoid a political stalemate despite often sharp disagreements within its ranks'; there is a basic 'tolerance for diversity of views'.[35]

The limits of tolerance in both Politburos may be assessed in at least approximate fashion by examining the patterns of turnover and reports of factionalism in the two bodies. Taking 1970, just before the beginning of the Honecker era, as a base point, we find the proportion of Politburo and Secretariat members that has been replaced to be significantly higher in the Hungarian case. Only four of the thirteen members of the

Hungarian Politburo of November 1970 were still on that body in 1987 – Kádár himself, Aczél, Gáspár, and Károly Németh. On the other hand, eleven of the twenty-one SED Politburo members and candidates of 1970 were still members in 1987 – and seven of the other ten had died in office. To be sure, the number of members and candidates in 1987 had grown to twenty-seven, allowing the appointment of more new figures than would otherwise have been possible (see also Table 3.1).

Table 3.1. Turnover in SED and HSWP leadership 1970–87

	Served since 1970	Died in Office	Resigned or Removed		New after 1970	
	N	N	N	%	N	%
Hungary						
Politburo	27	1	13	48.1	14	51.9
Secretariat	21	1	12	57.1	14	66.7
GDR						
Politburo*	40	8	5	12.5	19	47.5
Secretariat	19	3	6	31.5	9	47.4

* Includes both full and candidate members

Only two of the seven HSWP Secretaries of 1970 – Kádár and Óvári – remained Secretaries in 1987, while five of the eleven SED Secretaries of 1970 were still at their posts in 1987 – Honecker, Axen, Hager, Jarowinsky, and Mittag (although Mittag was temporarily shifted out of his position between 1973 and 1976). Not surprisingly, this persistence of high SED functionaries in office means that the average age of Politburo (64) and Secretariat (63) members in the SED exceeds that of their Hungarian counterparts (59 and 56). The differences in average length of service are still more striking (see Table 3.2): nearly 17 years for SED Politburo and 16 for Secretariat members, under 11 and 7 for their HSWP counterparts.

How can we explain this difference, especially given the HSWP's and Kádár's reputation for tolerance? In two ways, I think. First, by a conscious policy of cadre renewal at the highest levels pursued by the Hungarian leadership, in contrast to a principle only infrequently violated by the SED leaders – appointment to the Politburo or Secretariat is normally for life, or at least for 'good behaviour'.[36] Second (and related to the first), by patterns of factionalism in the two parties.

Table 3.2. Age and years in office of present leadership (1987)

	Age		Years in Office	
	Average	Median	Average	Median
Hungary				
Politburo	59	62	10.6	12
Secretariat	56	57	6.6	2
GDR				
Politburo*	64	61	16.8	16
Secretariat	63	60	16.2	14

* Includes both full and candidate members

Kádár, Bennett Kovrig has written:

has shown consummate skill in preserving his centrist program by trimming the leadership to exclude both reformist and dogmatist critics. . . . Kádár's style of rule is to limit the personal power of his associates, leave the management of reform to experts, and redeploy periodically the leading figures both within and between the party and the government.[37]

Kovrig's acute formulation implies that these personnel choices are Kádár's alone to make. In general, we do not know with certainty how appointments to (and demotions from) the Politburo and Secretariat are made in the Soviet bloc; the theory of collective leadership would seem to imply that they must be ratified by the Politburo itself, and we assume that at times the Soviet Union makes its own weight felt in the selection process.

It is reported, however, that in Hungary Kádár makes major personnel decisions himself, acting like a 'chess player' (which he is) manoeuvring pieces on a board.[38] A series of leadership changes in the HSWP beginning in 1974 illustrate the difficulty in interpreting such changes. The removal from the Secretariat of the ardent advocate of the New Economic Mechanism reforms Rezsö Nyers, the agricultural specialist Lajos Fehér, and the cultural functionary György Aczél, all reputedly 'close colleagues' of Kádár, was followed in 1975 by Nyers' departure from the Politburo and the resignation of the prime minister Jenö Fock. At the time, these changes were viewed as a threat to Kádár's own position; if he indeed initiated them, he probably did so as part of a defensive strategy. There were rumours that Kádár might 'be shunted upstairs to some purely ceremonial position', or worse.[39] If so, he apparently recouped his fortunes, and in 1976 the 'conservative' Árpád Pullai was dismissed from the Secretariat, followed in 1978 by Kádár's 'tough' deputy Béla Biszku.[40] In 1980, another prominent advocate of reform, István Huszár, lost his Politburo seat and all his government posts; like Nyers, he was shifted to an 'academic' position – in this case, Director of the Central Committee's Institute of Party History.[41]

Most of these changes, and others, appeared for many years to be related to ongoing disagreements in the Hungarian leadership between the advocates of economic reform and their opponents, who feared excessive decentralization and called attention to the dangers of growing income differences.[42] The NEM was the object of intense controversy when first introduced in 1966, and apparently was approved by only a narrow margin.[43] In part because of Soviet scepticism its scope remained limited throughout the 1970s; at the beginning of the 1980s it moved once again into a bolder phase.[44] Given this history, it is not surprising that factionalism in the HSWP leadership should have revolved for many years around the question of reform. Another factor not present in the GDR is the unusually strong position of the trade unions – headed by Sándor Gáspár – as an advocate of worker interests within the party. Union influence tends to fall on the side of the critics of reform; members have some reason to be unenthusiastic about the social inequalities and possible job insecurities that implementation of such reforms, particularly in a time of austerity, are likely to bring.[45] In a curious sequence of events beginning in late 1983, Gáspár was replaced by Lajos Mehes as Secretary-General of the National Trade Union Council, only to regain his power (albeit without returning to his old position) in March 1985. One interpretation of both his fall and his 'political comeback' linked them directly to the controversies surrounding reform.[46]

Factionalism at the top of the SED has been somewhat less visible than in the HSWP leadership, and appears to be multipolar rather than bipolar. Rumours of divisions in the SED Politburo have often appeared in the Western press, but members of that body appear only rarely to have been expelled from it as a consequence. The GDR's leaders fought their own battles over economic reform in the 1960s (with Honecker reportedly on the side of the critics), but even before Ulbricht left office in 1971 the decision had been made to return to a modified form of a highly centralized system of economic planning and management.[47] Walter Halbritter, a candidate member of the Politburo closely linked to the reforms lost his position in 1973, while Günter Mittag, one of the principal architects of the GDR's 'New Economic System', was replaced as SED Secretary for the economy in 1973 but restored to that position in 1976. During this period Mittag remained a full Politburo member, an instructive contrast to the fate of Nyers in Hungary. Two long-standing candidate members of the Politburo who were also associated with the reform period, Günter Kleiber and Werner Jarowinsky, were promoted to full membership in 1984. The GDR has made a few quiet, limited gestures toward renewed economic reform in the 1980s (avoiding any use of that term, however), but has undertaken nothing that invites comparison with the Hungarian course.[48]

Press reports of Politburo opposition to Honecker's policy of *rapprochement* with the Federal Republic have centred on the Berlin First Secretary Konrad Naumann, the military chieftain Heinz Hoffmann, the head of the State Security Service Erich Mielke, and the Premier Willi Stoph. Naumann – who reportedly had ties with the Soviet Union's Grigory Romanov – was the most open of the critics; in 1982, he had sharply attacked those in the GDR who wanted to 'evade the severity of the international class struggle'.[49] Subsequent challenges to Honecker's policies and a drunken, abusive appearance before academics in East Berlin are said to have led to his departure, for 'health' reasons, from the Politburo in November 1985.[50] Simultaneously, a purported Honecker ally with primary responsibility for West German relations, Herbert Häber, also left the Politburo; his health problems were apparently quite genuine. A short time later Hoffmann died, further diminishing the size of Honecker's purported opposition.

In spite of Honecker's apparent ability to bring allies on to the highest party organs by expanding their size, and by taking advantage of vacancies created by death or ill health, he has not wanted, or been able, to remove possible rivals or presumed opponents. Willi Stoph and Horst Sindermann, who shared the top leadership positions with Honecker after Ulbricht's resignation and were viewed as his potential rivals, were subsequently moved to different positions, but remain on the Politburo and continue to play highly visible roles in the GDR today. The exception, Naumann, had entered the Politburo under Honecker and was initially viewed as one of his supporters. There are several possible explanations of this overall stability. One is that Honecker has followed Brezhnev's example and sought to strengthen his own position by guaranteeing the 'security of cadres'. Another is that the Soviet Union, a pivotal SED Politburo coalition, or some combination of the two has preferred to keep some restraints on his power by resisting attempts to remove his critics. In either case the pattern is quite different from the more frequent 'circulation' of Hungarian elites.

Communist Politburos can also be examined in terms of the 'representation' they afford different institutions and interests in the party, state, and society. A brief comparison of the HSWP and SED Politburos in this respect shows that the first tends to give a greater voice (proportionally) to leading officials of state agencies, the second more to top functionaries of the party organization (a tendency underscored by the inclusion of all eleven party secretaries in the SED Politburo). Both give several seats to leading figures in the economic sphere and the ideological-agitprop-culture establishment, and to the heads of important mass organizations. The East Germans, but not the Hungarians, include the heads of the military and police on their Politburo, and also give the regional party leaderships a number of places (sharply increased at the 11th SED Congress). Quite possibly there are some clues here both to the distribution of power in and to the policy priorities of each regime.

RELATIONS WITH THE SOVIET UNION

The readiness of the Hungarians to embark on bold economic and political experiments, in contrast to the cautious conservatism of the GDR's leaders, is sometimes attributed to the greater leeway allowed the former by the Soviet Union. It is, of course, possible that the GDR's leaders simply have not *sought* greater leeway. However, the supposition that the USSR keeps the GDR on a tighter rein than it does Hungary suggests that possible differences in the pattern of relationships between the leaders of the SED and the HSWP and their Soviet comrades deserve careful scrutiny. The evidence we have about these relationships is meagre, however, and requires the application of the skills of the Kremlinologist and his East German and Hungarian equivalents, skills I do not claim.

Kádár, commentators have noted, has always been highly sensitive to the 'nuances of Soviet politics' and has 'repeatedly' sought to obtain the approval of the CPSU's leader for Hungarian departures from the Soviet example.[51] His 'intimate and trusting' relationship with Khrushchev is said to have alone made it possible for him to overcome domestic opposition during his first years in power.[52] After Khrushchev was removed, however, Kádár 'lost no time in securing the endorsement' of his successors, meeting with Brezhnev seven times in the course of the Soviet leader's first year in office.[53] This did not prevent the Soviet leadership from expressing its reservations about Hungary's reforms;[54] indeed, Soviet scepticism was probably responsible for their stagnation during the 1970s. Kádár gave 'none-too-subtle' support to Yuri Andropov – the Soviet ambassador to Hungary in 1956 – in the struggle to succeed Brezhnev. He persuaded neither Andropov nor his successors, however, to express unqualified approval of the 1980s' expansion of Hungarian reform measures, although they permitted them to proceed. The Hungarians, however, have applauded Gorbachev's reforms and seen in them some confirmation of their own course, even though Kádár is alleged to be uneasy with the Soviet leader's 'dynamic' style.[55]

Although the fulsomeness of SED propagandists' praise for the Soviet model has sometimes reached embarrassing proportions, both Ulbricht and Honecker – unlike Kádár – managed after years of apparently unbending loyalty to find themselves in direct conflict with Soviet wishes. As we saw, resistance to the concessions the Soviet leadership wished to make to further its *détente* policy helped bring Ulbricht down; on the other hand, it was Honecker's essaying of a special East German role in promoting better East–West relations that appears to have led to the outspoken, scarcely veiled attacks on his policy in the Soviet press in July and August, 1984, and the cancellation of his scheduled visit to Bonn.[56] Both the Hungarians and the East Germans evidently sought to use the prolonged Soviet succession crisis to gain greater leeway for themselves in foreign (and, in Hungary, domestic) policy matters, but only the East Germans were reprimanded quite so unambiguously.[57]

Honecker's personal relationships with successive Soviet

General Secretaries appear nevertheless to have been satisfactory. The same cannot be said for his relations with the long-time Soviet ambassador to East Berlin, Piotr Abrassimov. Even after the SED had given every evidence of supporting Chernenko as Brezhnev's successor,[58] Honecker apparently was successful in persuading Andropov to recall Abrassimov.[59] (The very fact, however, that Abrassimov felt able to play the imperious role he did as Soviet ambassador for many years may suggest a lower level of Soviet trust for the East German leadership than for the Hungarians.) Abrassimov's successor, Kochemasov, was apparently unable to resolve the open conflict that broke out between the Soviet leadership and the GDR over Honecker's proposed visit to Bonn; it is reported that Honecker had secured Chernenko's approval for his visit, but the latter was ill during the period in which the conflict peaked. Mikhail Gorbachev, whose selection as CPSU General Secretary was applauded in both Budapest and East Berlin, reportedly continued to monitor and for a time to restrain Honecker's interest in visiting Bonn and further developing warm inter-German ties,[60] although he subsequently endorsed both. At the same time, he singled out the GDR's economic course as a source of inspiration for and possible imitation by the USSR.[61] He has not, as yet, persuaded the GDR to adopt his *glasnost* policies – if indeed he has made any effort to do so. For his part, Honecker has continued to cultivate his image as a German statesman with a special responsibility for promoting reason and understanding in Central Europe. The East German press has played down Gorbachev's domestic reforms, and Honecker has made it clear that the GDR sees no need to emulate them.[62]

It needs to be recalled, of course, that it is not only East European General Secretaries that maintain close ties with their counterparts, and sometimes other high officials, in the Soviet Union. We have already noted the alleged links between Naumann and Romanov, and similar ties existed between Romanov and Hungary's Károly Grósz. The regular professional contacts between bloc defence ministers, secret police officials, ideological functionaries, and so on certainly carry with them the potential for establishing factional linkages across East bloc boundaries. But the evidence of East German–Hungarian differences on this point is too limited to warrant any firm generalizations. One might speculate, however, that the GDR's close military and secret police links with the USSR, coupled with the status of the East German defence and state security ministers as full Politburo members, gives the relevant Soviet officials an avenue of influence over GDR elite decisions that is not present in Hungary.

THE QUESTION OF SUCCESSION

I said at the beginning that both Kádár and Honecker are approaching retirement; perhaps that was incautious. Speculation over the succession to Kádár goes back at least 10 years, and the examples of Mao, Tito, and Brezhnev himself show how long Communist leaders can remain at the helm after Western commentators have pronounced their reigns to be at an end. Still, observers of both Budapest and East Berlin are probably correct in believing that the two leaders have experienced their final Party Congresses while in office. While Honecker's health appears to remain robust, Kádár is said to be suffering from emphysema and to have turned over most of his routine duties to his deputy.[63] In spite of periodic speculation about his imminent retirement,[64] he remained at the head of the Hungarian party as at the end of 1987.[65]

Kádár, is has often been remarked, 'has failed to groom an obvious successor'.[66] The two leading contenders for his mantle are said to be Károly Grósz, named premier in June 1987, and János Berecz, HSWP Secretary for Agitation and Propaganda. Both men are viewed as tough and pragmatic, committed to the present level of economic reform but not to extending it dramatically. Grósz, who reportedly accepted the premiership only at Kádár's urging, has been characterized as a 'hardliner', but perhaps is more precisely described as 'an ambitious careerist with good organizational ability and a penchant for tough oratory'.[67] Berecz was given a Politburo seat at the June 1987 Central Committee meeting and is reported to be Kádár's 'personal favourite'; he has distinguished himself through strong calls for ideological renewal. Figures identified with a more radical reformist course – Ferenc Havasi, the former HSWP Economics Secretary, and Imre Poszgay, the head of the Patriotic People's Front – are judged at the time of writing to be less well positioned.[68]

Honecker has long since put forward his own putative

successor, Egon Krenz, who has followed a career path much like Honecker's own, first as head of the SED's youth organization and then as Central Committee Secretary for security questions.[69] The week-long visit of Gorbachev to the GDR at the time of the 11th Party Congress, however, raised the question of whether the Soviet leader approved of Honecker's choice.[70] Other names have been introduced (or reintroduced) into the succession discussion: for example, Günter Schabowski, the former editor of *Neues Deutschland* who replaced Naumann as First Secretary of the SED's Berlin region; Werner Felfe, SED Secretary for Agriculture; and Hans Modrow, head of the Dresden regional party organization.[71]

The more important question is what the departure of Kádár and Honecker will mean for their respective countries. In each case, the timing of the succession – above all, what the status of Gorbachev and his reforms is at the moment it takes place – will be critical. In general, however, one is tempted to say that it will mean more in Hungary than it will in the GDR. In spite of the tensions between Moscow and East Berlin in 1984 and the present leadership's lack of enthusiasm for Gorbachev's domestic reforms, the GDR's policies do not appear seriously to challenge the evolving Soviet model or Soviet pre-eminence. Moreover, with the departure of Naumann and the death of Hoffman, Honecker's policies appear to enjoy broad, con-sensual support on the Politburo, and it is difficult to imagine any plausible successor dramatically altering them, at least in the short run. Changes in style – a greater effort, say, to emulate Gorbachev's vigour and candour – seem more likely than changes in substance. It is important, however, to note that what is approaching in the GDR is not just the change of one leader but the passing of an entire generation of senior figures who for years have dominated the GDR's leadership.

In Hungary, the course of the regime, and its successes, have been associated more closely with one man.[72] Kádár's successor is not likely to inherit either his stature internally or his special relationship to the Soviet leadership. Once Kádár leaves, the continuing stagnation of Hungarian economic performance is apt to place a review of the regime's current economic policies at the centre of the new leader's agenda, and he may also believe that the continuing debate over political reform demands some sort of resolution. Gorbachev's own commit-ment to reform has given him something of a vested interest in the success of Hungary's economic and political experimentation, but more conservative Soviet leaders might well be tempted to impose restraints – especially if they believe, as seems likely, that Kádár's successor does not have the authority and the skills that have enabled him to keep such changes from getting out of control.

CONCLUSIONS

What does this catalogue of differences – and similarities – between leadership arrangements in the GDR and those in Hungary tell us? In broad terms, it suggests that there is significantly greater flexibility and adaptability at the top of the HSWP than at the head of its East German counterpart. At least prior to the crises of the mid-1980s, the HSWP leadership has been able to respond to changing international and domestic circumstances in ways that – for all their limitations – have been more visible and imaginative than the SED's responses. The greater flexibility of the Hungarian leadership is reflected especially in my most striking finding: the significantly higher level of turnover in membership on the HSWP Politburo and Secretariat. It is also reflected in the greater tolerance for conflict attributed to the Hungarians – in spite of the higher turnover. The candour and breadth of the ongoing Hungarian debate over economic reform and its social consequences, both among specialists and party leaders, have no parallel in the GDR. Leadership flexibility is expressed as well in the superior tactical and other leadership skills attributed to Kádar. It is also expressed in the Hungarians' ability to make significant organizational modifications of the Soviet leadership model; the smaller size of the HSWP Politburo and its greater willingness to delegate decisions to other party organs, state bodies, individual economic enterprises, and even the market is an example.

The SED leadership, by comparison, must be described as more rigid. Personnel turnover at the top of the East German party and state may be lower simply because it appears more threatening to a leadership which has been preoccupied with social (and, by extension, leadership) integration and continuity. The very size of the SED Politburo, and the formal atmosphere said to characterize its meetings, probably inhibits freewheeling debate. Tolerance for open conflict within the leadership and for public discussion of social and economic problems has been consistently low in the GDR, even by East-bloc standards. Also, and more concretely, SED leadership flexibility may be low because Honecker does not share Kádár's apparent authority to undertake leadership changes on his own.

If this assessment is correct, it becomes less surprising that Hungary's economic policies and its treatment of its own population have been more 'liberal', more imaginative, and more generous than the GDR's – even if its economy appears for the moment to be more troubled. To be sure, the precise mechanisms that link leadership flexibility to reformist policies are not always clear, and even the direction of causation may be ambiguous. The Hungarian party's commitment to reform may itself produce, or require, greater flexibility in leadership arrangements. A full explanation of the differences in policy would also require that we take into account the other elements mentioned at the beginning of this essay – geopolitical position, relationship to the USSR, and so on. In identifying the importance of leadership differences we also need to return to our earlier discussion of 'authority-building'.

Extraordinary measures – the parallel that comes to mind is that of the Russian NEP of 1921 – would have been necessary for any Hungarian regime to build a secure base of authority after the events of 1956. That Kádár had – for whatever reasons – collaborated in the Soviet suppression of the Revolution made his task doubly difficult. Nevertheless, his success over the 30 intervening years in creating a firm basis of authority for himself, and in somewhat less certain measure for his party, must be judged as little short of astonishing. Through his conciliatory leadership tactics and his ability to guide economic reform, and a cautious opening to the West between the rocks and shoals of domestic opposition and Soviet scepticism, he has given the Hungarian regime a position which – in spite of growing economic problems and popular discontents – has been the envy of its East European neighbours.[73]

Honecker's task upon becoming SED First Secretary in 1971 was on the whole much easier than Kádár's. But the circumstances of his replacement of Ulbricht (and perhaps the fact that Brezhnev, not Khrushchev, was in power in the USSR) made it very difficult for him to undertake policies that might appear to deviate from the Soviet model. Honecker's own political instincts did not favour innovation, and the veteran, rather conservative majority of the Politburo that he inherited from Ulbricht did not favour it either. Moreover, the very economic success of the GDR – already evident in the late Ulbricht years – made bold experiments seem unnecessary. There is also the factor of age and time. Honecker was nearly 60 – fifteen years older than Kádár – when he took power, and has had only half as many years to build his authority.

This interpretation risks overemphasizing the differences between the two leaders and their states, however. In spite of its leadership rigidities, the GDR has moved a long way in the Honecker era, toward a more relaxed and confident, more pragmatic and generous form of rule. We may justifiably characterize the recent policies of the SED as a cautious form of 'Kadarism' and to that extent as a tribute to the Hungarian example. There is thus a certain irony in the fact that in the twilight of the Kádár era, Hungary finds itself suffering from serious economic difficulties and a profound social malaise, while the GDR, which has followed timorously behind it in its policies, has come to be viewed as the single economic and political success story of the East European bloc.

ACKNOWLEDGEMENTS

I want to express my thanks to Ivan Volgyes and Ellen Comisso for their comments on earlier versions of this chapter.

NOTES

1. Quoted in Bill Lomax (1984) 'Hungary – the quest for legitimacy', in Paul G. Lewis (ed.), *Eastern Europe: Political Crisis and Legitimacy*, 90, New York: St. Martin's. See also Bennett Kovrig (1979) *Communism in Hungary*, 430–1, Stanford: Hoover Institution Press.

2. Theo Sommer (1986) 'Am Staate mäkeln, doch ihn tragen', *Die Zeit* (N. Am. edn), June 27, 8. See also Hendrik Bussiek (1984) *Die real existierende DDR*, 55–6, Hamburg: Fischer Taschenbuch Verlag.

3. See, e.g., Mihaly Vajda (1979) 'Is Kadarism an Alternative?' *Telos*, Spring, 172–9; Ferenc Fehér (1979) 'Kadarism as the model state of Krushchevism', *Telos*, Summer, 19–31.

4. The CPSU Politburo, after the 27th Congress, included twelve members and seven candidate members. Among the East European

parties, the Hungarian Politburo is the smallest and the East German Politburo the largest, except for Romania, which has both a 'political executive committee' (forty-eight members and candidates) and a 'permanent bureau' (eight members).

5. B. Kovrig, *Communism*, 373.

6. The SED Central Committee met eleven times between the Party's 10th and 11th Congresses, the Hungarian Central Committee twenty-three times between the HSWP's 12th and 13th Congresses. The official size of the HSWP Central Committee may be misleading in so far as it is reported that regional First Secretaries and representatives of important state bodies are regularly invited to its meetings. See Maria Huber (1985) 'Der XIII. Partietag der Ungarischen Sozialistischen Arbeiterpartei', *Südosteuropa XXXIV*, 258.

7. Peter Toma and Ivan Volgyes (1977) *Politics in Hungary*, 65, San Francisco: W. H. Freeman; note that 'the influence of the Central Committee has grown considerably since 1968'.

8. See Georg Brunner (1986/1) 'Kommunistische Verfassungsmodelle: Eine typologische Übersicht', *Südosteuropa XXXV*, 30–32.

9. Apart from Romania, Hungary is also the only East European Warsaw Pact member whose top three military leaders are not all graduates of the Voroshilov General Staff Academy in the USSR. See Douglas A. MacGregor (1986) 'Uncertain allies: East European forces in the Warsaw Pact', *Soviet Studies XXXVIII* (April), 227–47. In general, George Schöpflin notes, 'the role of the military in Hungary is uniquely insignificant': Schöpflin (1986), 'Hungary', in Martin McCauley and Stephen Carter (eds), *Leadership and Succession in the Soviet Union, Eastern Europe and China*, 110, Armonk, N.Y.: M.E. Sharpe.

10. See Kovrig, *Communism*, 351, 354; 'Statut der Sozialistischen Einheitspartei Deutschlands', in Eberhard Schneider (ed.), (1977) *SED Programm und Statut um 1976*, 138 (Article 24), Opladen: Leske Verlag & Budrich GmbH, 1977.

11. George Breslauer (1982) *Khrushchev and Brezhnev as Leaders: Building Authority in Soviet Politics*, London: Allen & Unwin; Thane Gustafson and Dawn Mann (1986) 'Gorbachev's first year: building power and authority', *Problems of Communism*, May–June, 1–19; Breslauer (1986) 'The nature of Soviet politics and the Gorbachev leadership', in Alexander Dallin and Condoleeza Rice, *The Gorbachev Era*, 11–29, Stanford, Calif.: Stanford Alumni Association.

12. See Kovrig, *Communism*, 314.

13. For interpretations emphasizing the role of the USSR, see Myron Rush (1974) *How Communist States Change Their Rulers*, 191–219, Ithaca: Cornell University Press; Angela Stent, 'Soviet Policy in the German Democratic Republic', in Sarah Meiklejohn Terry (ed.) (1984), *Soviet Policy in Eastern Europe*, 38–41, New Haven: Yale University Press. An East German writer now in the West reports that Honecker privately told a group of writers that 'we overthrew Ulbricht', see Joachim Seyppl (1982) *Ich bin ein kaputter Typ*, Wiesbaden: Limes Verlag, 16. See also N. Edwina Moreton (1978), *East Germany and the Warsaw Alliance*, Boulder, Colo.: Westview,

182–8. Honecker's remarks at the SED 8th Congress also suggest the depth of Politburo resentments against Ulbricht.

14. To this extent I disagree with those writers who dismiss the importance of popular approval in influencing the behaviour of East European political leaders. See Mark Wright (pseud.), 'Ideology and power in the Czechoslovak political system', in Lewis (ed.) *op. cit.*, 111–20.

15. William Shawcross (1974) *Crime and Compromise: Janos Kadar and the Politics of Hungary Since Revolution*, 237, New York: E.P. Hutton.

16. Charles Gati (1974) 'The Kadar years', *Problems of Communism*, May–June, 25; C. Gati (1986) *Hungary and the Soviet Bloc*, 163, Durham, N.C.: Duke University Press; Sarah M. Terry (1985) 'The implications of economic stringency and political succession for stability in Eastern Europe in the eighties', in 99th Congress, 2nd Session, Joint Economic Committee, *East European Economies: Slow Growth in the 1980s*, 531, Washington: U.S. Government Printing Office.

17. For example: William F. Robinson (1973) *The Pattern of Reform in Hungary*, 72, New York: Praeger; S.M. Terry (1985) 'The Implications', in *East European Economics*, 531.

18. Ivan Volgyes (1982) *Hungary: A Nation of Contradictions*, 29 and 34, Boulder, Colo.: Westview; Ellen Comisso and Paul Marer (1986) 'The Economics and Politics of Reform in Hungary', *International Organization XL* (Spring), 442; Shawcross, 76–77.

19. I. Volgyes, *op. cit.*, 34.

20. See W.F. Robinson, *op. cit.*, 70.

21. P. Toma and I. Volgyes, *op. cit.*, 67.

22. E. Comisso and P. Marer, *op. cit.*, in *International Organization XL*, 442–443.

23. C. Gati, 'Kadar', 27; C. Gati, *Hungary*, 164. See also Volgyes, *op. cit.*, 19.

24. Theo Sommer (1986) 'Ein deutscher Kommunist, ein deutscher Realist', *Die Zeit* (N. Am. edn), February 7, 1. See also Günter Gaus (1987) 'Ein Deutscher und ein Kommunist', *Die Zeit* (N. Am. edn), August 28, 3–4.

25. Dietrich Staritz (1985) *Geschichte der DDR 1949–1985*, 198, Frankfurt am Main: Suhrkamp.

26. For an unusually sharp critique along these lines, see the comments of a former SED ideological functionary: Franz Loeser (1984) *Die unglaubwürdige Gesellschaft: Quo vadis DDR?*, 59, Köln: Bund-Verlag.

27. Erich Honecker (1980) *From My Life*, London: Pergamon.

28. David Childs (1985) 'The GDR and the United States', in Childs (ed.) *Honecker's Germany*, 183, London: Allen & Unwin.

29. Günter Gaus (1983) *Wo Deutschland Liegt – Eine Ortsbestimmung*, 148, Hamburg: Hoffmann und Campe. Elsewhere, Gaus has written that Honecker's status 'rests on an extensively practiced collegiality which, however, never disguises who, if necessary, has the final competence on a question in the ruling body', 'Ein Deutscher', 3.

30. A good summary of these accounts is found in Hermann Weber (1985), *Geschichte der DDR*, 475–482, München: Deutscher Taschenbuch Verlag; see also Thomas A. Baylis, 'Collegial Leadership in East and West Germany' (unpublished paper).

31. F. Loeser, *op. cit.*, 53.

32. H. Weber, *op. cit.*, 478; P. Toma and I. Volgyes, *op. cit.*, 67.

33. Both the committees and the chairpersons of the working groups are formally elected by the Central Committee. See *Nepszabadsag*, March 29, 1985, as translated in Joint Publications Research Service, *Daily Report – Eastern Europe*, JPRS-EPS-85-051, May 17, 1985, 86.

34. P. Toma and I. Volgyes, *op. cit.*, 28. The SED had somewhat similar Politburo 'commissions' earlier in its history, but does not appear to have them now.

35. E. Comisso and P. Marer, *op. cit.*, in *International Organization XL*, 439–41. (In this quotation the original italics have not been reproduced.)

36. See F. Loeser, *op. cit.*, 54–56.

37. Bennett Kovrig, 'Hungary', in Teresa Rakowska-Harmstone (1984), *Communism in Eastern Europe*, 2nd edn, 99, Bloomington: Indiana University Press.

38. C. Gati, *Hungary*, 160, 171. For a brief account of Kadar's earlier success in gradually replacing Stalinists and other conservatives in the leadership with moderates and reformers, see Hans-Georg Heinrich (1986) *Hungary: Politics, Economics and Society*, 46–47, Boulder, Colo.: Lynne Rienner.

39. B. Lomax, in Lewis (ed.) *Eastern Europe*, 91–92; see also C. Gati, 'Kadar', in *Problems of Communism*, May–June, 1974, 33–34.

40. Kovrig, 'Hungary', in Rakowska-Harmstone (ed.) *Communism in Eastern Europe*, 2nd edn, 99.

41. Slobodan Stankovic (1986) 'Hungarian party theorist defends political and economic reforms', *Radio Free Europe Research*, January 3, 12.

42. C. Gati, 'Kadar', in *Problems of Communism*, May–June, 1974, 29. Comisso and Marer speak of two persistent 'informal "wings"' of the leadership on economic policy questions, but suggest that specific leaders may not always align themselves with the same wing (see *op. cit.*, in *International Organization XL*, 441).

43. W.F. Robinson, *op. cit.*, 89–91.

44. See E. Comisso and P. Marer, *op. cit.*, in *International Organization XL*, 425–432, 443–454.

45. See P. Toma and I. Volgyes, *op. cit.*, 67–68; Stephen White, (1986) 'Economic performance and communist legitimacy', *World Politics XXXVIII* (April), 478–479; Bennett Kovrig, 'Hungary', in Richard F. Starr (ed.) (1985) *1985 Yearbook for International Communist Affairs*, 297, Stanford: Hoover Institution Press; Kathrin Sitzler, 'Das Dilemma der Gewerkschaften', *Südosteuropa XXXV* (Nos. 3–4, 1986), 175–183.

46. See Stephen Noti (1987) 'The shifting position of Hungarian

trade unions amidst social and economic reforms', *Soviet Studies* *XXXIX* (January), 75–8.

47. See Thomas A. Baylis (1986) 'Explaining the GDR's economic strategy', *International Organization XL* (Spring) 386–7, 411.

48. See Doris Cornelsen, Manfred Melzer, and Angela Scherzinger (1984) 'DDR-Wirtschaftssystem: Reform in kleinen Schritten', *Vierteljahreshefte zur Wirtschaftsforschung*, no. 2 (1984), 200–20.

49. On the Romanov connection, see William Drozdiak (1985) 'East Germany's rising star is in Gorbachev's galaxy', *Washington Post National Weekly Edition*, December 30, 1985, 14. Naumann's attack is cited in Ilse Spittmann (1983) 'Der Milliardenkredit', *Deutschland Archiv XVI* (August), 785.

50. See *Der Spiegel*, December 2, 1985, 30–32 and December 9, 1985, 14; Eberhard Schneider (1986) 'Die Position des SED-Generalsekretärs 1986 und die Nachfolgefrage in der DDR', *Deutsche Studien XXIV* (March), 68.

51. C. Gati, 'Kadar', 27.

52. W. Shawcross, *op. cit.*, 257–259; Schöpflin, *op. cit.*, in McCauley and Carter (eds) *Leadership*, 105–106. Feher argues that after the 1986 revolution 'not only was the Kadar regime inextricably bound to Khrushchev, but Khrushchev's own political fate depended largely on the outcome of the Hungarian events'. (See F. Feher 'Kadarism' in *Telos*, Summer 1979, 21–22.)

53. Kovrig, *Communism*, 364.

54. *Ibid.*, 392–3.

55. See Rudolf Tökes (1984) 'Hungarian reform imperatives', *Problems of Communism*, Sept.–Oct., 1; Charles Gati (1985) 'The Soviet Empire: alive but not well', *Problems of Communism*, March–April, 85; Vladimir Kusin (1986) 'Gorbachev and Eastern Europe', *Problems of Communism*, Jan.–Feb., 45–47; Vladimir Sobell (1987) 'Eastern European adjustment to Gorbachev's reform program', *Radio Free Europe Research*, March 27, 2 and 5.

56. There are numerous accounts of this episode. See, e.g., Ronald Asmus (1985) 'The dialectic of detente and discord: the Moscow–East Berlin–Bonn Tirangle', *Orbis XXVIII* (Winter), 743–74.

57. The Hungarians, who provided the most explicit justification for distinctive foreign policy ventures by small East European states, were probably the primary target of the Czech attacks, but Kadar did not personally open himself up to Soviet criticism as Honecker did with his West German credit agreement and planned trip to Bonn. See, however, Alfred Reisch and Vladimir V. Kusin, 'National versus international interests', in Mastny, 227–236; Kovrig, 'Hungary', in Starr (ed.) *1985 Yearbook for International Communist Affairs*, 303.

58. Fred Oldenburg (1984) 'Im Dienst der eigenen Sache: Die SED und die Wahl Tschernenkos', *Deutsche Studien XXII* (March), 97–106.

59. See Martin McCauley, 'The German Democratic Republic and the Soviet Union', in Childs (ed.) *Honecker's Germany*, 163.

60. See Kusin, in *Problems of Communism*, Jan.–Feb. 1986, 47–49.

61. Schneider, 73–74.

62. See Sobell; Barbara Donovan, 'Honecker Continues to Reject

Reform', *Radio Free Europe Research*, May 8, 1987. The *Washington Post* (January 3 1988, A25) has cited the assertion of a 'senior' West German government official that (in the newspaper's words) 'on a personal level, Honecker has the worst relationship with Gorbachev of any Warsaw Pact leader'.

63. Ivan Volgyes (1985) 'Hungary: a malaise thinly disguised', *Current History LXXXIV* (November), 367–8.

64. See, e.g. Alfred Reisch (1986) 'Central Committee Meets', *Radio Free Europe Research*, December 23, 3.

65. Kádár was removed from office in May, 1988 and Károly Grósz was appointed as his successor.

66. Kovrig, *Communism*, 373.

67. See *New York Times*, March 31, 1985, 17; Heinrich, 48–51; Kovrig, 'Hungary', *Yearbook for International Communist Affairs 1986* (Stanford: Hoover Institution Press, 1986), 299; Alfred Reisch (1987) 'Major Party and State Leadership Reshuffle', *Radio Free Europe Research*, June 30, 3–7; Ivan Volgyes (1987) 'Hungary: before the storm breaks', *Current History LXXXVI* (November), 375; *Washington Post*, September 28, 1987, A15–A16.

68. See A. Reisch, 'Major'; Volgyes, 'Hungary: before the storm breaks'; Alfred Reisch (1987) 'HSWP Searching for New Ideology', *Radio Free Europe Research*, November 28, 3–8; A. Reisch, 'Imre Pozsgay: the white knight of Hungary's political reform', November 28, 1987, 19–24.

69. See Schneider, 72; Drozdiak, 14.

70. See Peter Jochen Winters (1986) 'Die Ära Honecker geht zu Ende', *Deutschland Archiv XIX* (June), 561–4.

71. See the *Washington Post*, January 3, 1988, A23 and A25.

72. See Volgyes, *Hungary*, 35.

73. It is also arguable that some elements of luck and timing were involved in Hungary's success. Paul Marer, in seeking to explain why Hungary has been in the 'reform forefront', remarks: 'Of considerable importance also has been the lucky coincidence of the right people being at just the right place in crucial periods. For example, Politburo member Lajos Fehér was responsible for agriculture, while Rezsö Nyers, in a similar post, was in charge of economic reforms during crucial decision periods in the 1960s.' Paul Marer (1985) 'Economic reform in Hungary: a summary view and assessment', *Südosteuropa XXXIV* (No. 6) 318.

4

Social courts in the GDR and comrades' courts in the Soviet Union: a comparison

Nancy Travis Wolfe

INTRODUCTION

Under the Marxian concept that in the ultimate Communist society the state would wither away, a principle strongly reaffirmed under Nikita Khrushchev at the 21st and 22nd Party Congresses in the USSR, lay participation in the adjudicatory process is crucial. Lenin had envisioned comrades' courts as a mechanism by which social pressures might reduce antisocial behaviour.[1] Staffed by lay persons of the immediate community, they were to apply and inculcate 'socialist legality'. In the words of one scholar, 'they are courts of the future in the sense that they now operate as an understudy for the regular courts and are intended to replace the regular courts once the society attains full communism'.[2] The German Democratic Republic, in setting up social courts in 1953, drew on the theory and practice of the USSR,[3] but during the following three decades the nature of social courts in the GDR has diverged significantly from the Russian model.

HISTORICAL BACKGROUND

The history of comrades' courts in Russia demonstrates an uneven commitment,[4] whereas that of the social courts of the GDR indicates a steady emphasis.[5] Even though the genesis of comrades' courts in Russia is usually traced to the Leninist period, the concept of popular justice in Russia in the form of village mediation centres predates the Revolution.[6] In 1917 comrades' courts were organized in the Petrograd military district, and by 1919 similar tribunals with jurisdiction over breaches of labour discipline had appeared in enterprises.[7] During the 1920s, however, the trend was reversed, and in the NEP reform period the comrades' courts were further curtailed.[8] In the period before 1961, Kucherov wrote, 'The activity of the comrades' courts came virtually to a standstill'.[9] It was not until Nikita Khrushchev's efforts to increase citizen participation in government gained favour, that comrades' courts were once again stressed. Khrushchev had argued that 'when the social Comrades' Courts are actively operating and the public itself provides people for the ensuring of public order, then it will be considerably easier to fight against offenders'.[10] In the 1963 amendment to the 1961 statute on comrades' courts jurisdiction was extended to include petty cases of hooliganism and theft.[11] Following Khrushchev's fall, the comrades' courts again faded, not to be revived until the Soviet authorities signalled renewed emphasis with a decree on the courts in 1977.[12]

By contrast, extension of the role of social courts in the German Democratic Republic has been consistent.[13] When the Republic was established after World War II, it was necessary to modify the judicial system to incorporate Marxian principles. Germany, too, had an historical institution, the *Schiedsmann* (arbitrator), which could be seen as a precursor of popular justice tribunals.[14] The first social courts were established in state-owned enterprises. Originally these courts, called *Konfliktkommissionen*, had jurisdiction only over labour disputes, but their authority was soon extended to include minor civil matters and petty delicts. As had Khrushchev, Walter Ulbricht called for greater citizen participation in adjudication.[15] When these social courts proved successful, the Council of State in 1964 created similar tribunals, called *Schiedskommissionen*, in residential areas and production associations. In terms of jurisdiction and in types of authorized activity the social courts of the GDR have steadily become an increasingly important part of the judicial system. Recently the People's Assembly approved legislation extending the jurisdiction of the social courts (Paragraphs 13, 14 GGG).[16]

Against this brief historical review of popular justice in Russia and the GDR, the remainder of the discussion will focus on current forms of comrades' courts and social courts. They will be compared in regard to their legal basis, theoretical mission, jurisdiction, composition, procedures, and sanctions.

LEGAL BASIS

The two systems of social courts differ in regard to legal basis, due in part to the fact that the GDR has a unitary form of government while the USSR is a federation. In the GDR the principle of social courts is embedded in the Constitution in Article 92 where the social courts are listed along with the formal state courts as organs of administration of justice (*Rechtspflege*). Two national-level laws govern the social courts: the Court Organization Act of 1974 (*Gerichtsverfassungsgesetz* – GVG) and the Law of Social Courts (*Gesetz über die gesellschaftlichen Gerichte* – GGG) of 1982. In addition, regulations passed by the Council of State in 1982 have the force of law (*Konfliktkommissionsordnung* – KKO and *Schiedskommissionsordnung* – SchKO). Sections of the national criminal procedural code (*Strafprozessordnung* – StPO) include clauses affecting the social courts. Taken together, these legal statements provide a very detailed basis for the operation of social courts in the GDR.

In the USSR, on the other hand, there is no mention of comrades' courts in the federal constitution.[17] An implicit basis for social courts might be seen in Article 9 of the 1977 Constitution, which refers to 'ever broader participation of citizens in managing the affairs of society and the state',[18] but this is tenuous and in no way establishes a federal basis for the comrades' courts. Nor is there any national-level legislation in regard to the operation of comrades' courts in the USSR. The nearest equivalent to the GGG of the GDR is a Model Draft for a statute on comrades' courts, drawn up by the Legislative Proposals Commission of the USSR Supreme Soviet and published in 1959. Even though it was not enacted as an All-Union statute, individual republics did use it as a general pattern, and secondary sources indicate that the variations from the Model Draft are minor in nature.[19]

In 1977 the Presidium of the USSR Supreme Soviet issued a Decree pertaining to improvements in the comrades' courts.[20] Not only did the Presidium tout the advantages of the courts, but it also addressed itself to apparent inadequacies which were to be overcome. Aside from these two documents, the only legal basis for the comrades' courts is to be found in the law of the republics. The RSFSR, for example, incorporated elements of the draft model in its statute of 1961 and later modified the law to reflect the decree of 1977.[21]

If the extent of legislation is a valid indicator, then the role of popular justice in the GDR is greater than in the USSR. In the absence of Russian national law, examination of the comrades' courts in this paper will be based on the RSFSR statute. Unfortunately, there is as yet virtually no empirical literature on the operation of social courts or comrades' courts so the comparison must draw primarily on theoretical sources.

MISSION

Essential consonance can be seen in the stated missions of the two systems; in both, the principal role of the lay tribunals is an educational one. According to Article 1 of the RSFSR statute on comrades' courts (CC):

Comrades' courts are elective social agencies called upon actively to promote the nurturing of citizens in the spirit of a communist attitude toward labour, an attitude of care toward socialist ownership, observance of the rules of socialist community life, the development of a feeling of collectivism and comradely mutual assistance in them, and respect for the dignity and honour of the Soviet people.

The comparable clause of the GGG (Paragraph 3) states that:

the activity of the social courts furthers social activities toward the implementation of social legality and toward the guarantee of order, discipline and security in the combines, businesses, cities and communities. The activity is directed toward protecting the socialist order of the state and society as well as protecting and carrying out the legally-guaranteed rights and interests of the citizen, strengthening the socialistic state and legal consciousness of the citizens, furthering their readiness to voluntarily observe socialist rights and strengthening their intolerance of antisocial behaviour.

As can be seen, teleologically the comrades' court and social courts are virtually identical; they are not established just to decide cases (the normal function of courts in western Europe and the United States) but rather to inculcate socialist principles and to provide practice in self-rule. Clearly, there is as well the intention to effect both specific and general deterrence[22] through 'comradely criticism and assistance'.[23]

Nevertheless, some differences in mission are discernible.

63

Prevention is a stated goal in Russia as it is in the GDR; yet the specificity with which the German law enunciates this principle is significant.[24] The *Konfliktkommissionen* and *Schiedskommissionen* are to make written recommendations for the elimination of causes and conditions conducive to filing of legal actions and commission of infractions of law. As an aid in overcoming deficiencies and illegalities, the recommendations must include factual information concerning the factors which predispose toward criminality and offer suggestions concerning means by which these may be ameliorated (Paragraph 16 (1) SchKO). The social courts have the right to monitor the realization of the recommendations. Those to whom the recommendations are directed must respond in writing within two weeks, explaining steps taken or reasons why the recommendation was not followed.

Article 17 of the RSFSR statute (CC) similarly calls upon the comrades' courts to inform 'social organizations and officials of the causes and conditions uncovered by them which furthered the commission of the violation of the law'. The impact of such recommendations has been strengthened. Although the 1961 statute did not make response obligatory,[25] under current law the comrades' court is to be notified within a month about measures taken to rectify the situation.

POSITION WITHIN JUDICIAL SYSTEM

The exact status of comrades' courts and social courts is one which is much debated in the literature. The first difficulty is to define 'court': in part, of course, the definition turns on such factors as mission, jurisdictional boundaries, the legal effect of decisions, the possibility and routes of appeal, as well as the procedures followed. More critical perhaps in determining the status of the tribunals is the perception of them held by the government. Boiter refers to the official theory 'that a comrades' court is a voluntary creation of the entire group at any of these locations and is accordingly a public or social organization rather than a part of the state apparatus'.[26] Savickij states that despite their being called courts, they are 'outside' the judicial system and do not 'administer law'.[27] It cannot be denied, however, that their function is judicial, in that they make decisions over cases which fall within the jurisdiction of state courts.[28]

The GDR social courts, while having a mission similar to that of the comrades' courts, are accorded the status of quasi-courts, as mentioned above.[29] They are organs of administration of justice and as such are held to be unitary with the ordinary courts.[30] Comparison of charts of court systems in the two countries gives visible evidence of the difference in position of social courts.[31]

A strong indicator that both comrades' courts and social courts are intrinsically different from ordinary courts is the use of a special vocabulary to refer to their scope and activities. As Berman and Spindler note, the person charged in a comrades' court with an offence is referred to as a 'person brought before the Comrades' Court'; if held responsible, he is an 'offender'. The court does not 'punish' but instead administers 'measures of social pressure'.[32] A special vocabulary is also used for GDR social courts: to begin with, the tribunal is called a 'commission' (only when referred to collectively are they called 'courts'), and the sessions are labelled 'deliberations' (*Beratungen*). The person called to answer for a criminal offence is addressed as the 'inculpated' (*Beschuldigte*), and if he is found responsible, he is subjected to 'educational measures' (*Erziehungsmassnahmen*).

FORMS OF SOCIAL COURTS

Differentiation between popular tribunals established at places of work and places of residence is sharper in the GDR than in the RSFSR. Article 2 (CC) calls for the establishment of comrades' courts in 'enterprises and in institutions, organizations, and higher and secondary specialized educational institutions . . . at collective farms and in houses served by housing operations offices, housing administrations, or united in street committees, as well as in rural population centres and settlements'. Reference is later made to comrades' courts in the place of work, study or residence (Article 9 CC).

In the GDR, however, there are entirely separate bodies of law (*Ordnungen*) governing social courts in the workplace and in residential areas which distinguish jurisdiction, initiation, selection of members, oversight, etc. While many of the same points are covered throughout the RSFSR law, occupational comrades' courts are treated separately from residential ones.

Further evidence of the divergent nature of comrades' courts

65

and social courts can be seen in regard to scheduling and the composition of the tribunals. Article 11 (CC) stipulates that 'the time and place of considering the case shall be determined by the chairman of the comrades' court and shall be publicized widely to citizens', and Article 13 adds that the sessions are to be held during non-working hours. Sessions are scheduled *ad hoc*; the chairman summons members only when a case is filed with the court.[33]

In the GDR, on the other hand, social courts have regularly scheduled meeting times. Each social court is to select a time and inform the authorities; then it is to make itself available at the appointed time for consultation or for a hearing when a case has been presented to it. Notices of scheduled meetings are displayed in prominent places such as post offices or buildings for services. When necessary, the social court can hold an *ad hoc* meeting to consider a case. Like the comrades' courts, social courts meet after hours in the residential areas. Those within enterprises or businesses may, however, convene during working time.

Inasmuch as training in adjudication of members of the community is a primary goal, the extent to which citizens are involved and the patterns of service are important factors. There are fewer members in a tribunal in Russia than in the GDR. According to Article 5 (CC), the number of members in an individual comrades' court is to be established by the meeting which elects them. It is not to be less than five; a quorum consists of three members (Article 13 CC). In the GDR, social courts in the enterprises or businesses are to have between six and fifteen members. For both, the number necessary for a quorum is four.

Given this difference in numbers of members, it is difficult to compare the degree to which community members gain experience in adjudication. In the GDR repeated tenure is usual, and often the chairman of a social court is a person who has served for many years. Fewer persons are elected to serve as members of comrades' courts, but the *ad hoc* nature of these tribunals may mean that the frequent selection of new members results in participation as wide as that in the GDR.

JURISDICTION

Jurisdiction of the comrades' courts and the social courts is limited to minor anti-social acts, both civil and criminal. A specific statement of jurisdiction is to be found in Article 7 of the Russian statute. Boiter[34] has categorized the jurisdiction of comrades' courts into three groups as follows: (1) cases in which the comrades' courts have exclusive jurisdiction because the charge preferred concerns moral standards or communal rules rather than a formal violation of law; (2) cases of crimes committed for the first time; (3) cases already begun in a people's court which the presiding judge may elect to 'transfer' for hearing in a comrades' court.

The GDR statute for social courts designates jurisdiction of the *Konfliktkommissionen* over labour matters and petty crimes, over violations of administrative rules and crimes when the case is referred to the court, over transgression of school responsibility, and over civil disputes (Paragraph 13 GGG). Jurisdiction of the residential social courts, *Schiedskommissionen*, is similar, except that they do not usually hear labour cases. Overlapping jurisdiction between the two types of tribunals exists in Russia as well as in the GDR, since a person can be called before a tribunal on the basis of his work affiliation or his residence.

While the laws of both countries mention specific types of behaviour to be sanctioned in the popular tribunals (for example: truancy, damage to state or social property, unauthorized use of means of transport, hooliganism, slander, insult, violation of housing regulations, property disputes), emphasis on particular offences may vary. For example, the Russian statute has a quite detailed statement concerning alcoholic beverages, even listing types of beverage use to be sanctioned and possible compulsory treatment (Articles 7 (5), 18 CC).[35] Also there is a clause authorizing sanction for the 'failure to fulfill or the improper fulfilment by parents, guardians, or curators of duties relating to the nurturing of children; an unworthy attitude toward parents; unworthy conduct in the family; an unworthy attitude toward women' (Article 7 (8) CC).

Under the original statute in the RSFSR, comrades' courts were given jurisdiction over 'parasitical' behaviour. Even though the 1959 Draft Model suggested that trial of parasitic elements should continue to take place in comrades' courts, the new RSFSR statute did not include this jurisdiction.[36] Concern about the vagueness of the law and its delegation of functions to the tribunals which had previously been reserved to the ordinary courts resulted in removal of this jurisdiction from the comrades' courts.[37]

SELECTION OF MEMBERS

The theoretical basis of popular justice tribunals would dictate that the process for selection of members be democratic. Service is on a voluntary basis, and methods of selection of tribunal members are, in general, similar in the two countries. The steps are more precisely specified in the GDR, but there is as much effort in the USSR to ensure that persons in the immediate working or residential area serve as members.

The Russian statute provides for open ballot election at general meetings of labour collectives or gatherings of citizens at the place of residence (Article 5 CC). The meetings are to be convoked by the trade union committee or by the executive committees of local soviets of people's deputies. There is a right of challenge, and members who 'have not justified the trust placed in them' (Article 6, 13 CC) are subject to recall. Apparently there is no fixed term of service; a clause in the 1961 statute had set a term of 2 years,[38] but this was omitted from the 1982 statute.

Election procedure in the GDR varies according to the type of tribunal. For selection of members of the *Konflikt-kommission*, the union has a constitutionally granted role which involves its leadership at all stages (Paragraph 7 GGG). With regard to the *Schiedskommissionen*, the Minister of Justice has a parallel function (Paragraph 10 (1) GGG). The law (Paragraph 6 (2) GGG) stipulates that members of the social Courts be elected either directly by citizens (*Konfliktkommissionen*) or by local representative bodies (*Schiedskommissionen*). Election is by secret ballot, and there is a right to challenge members of the social courts.

As in all socialist societies, the critical stage is not the election but the nomination process which precedes it.[39] Under Article 4 (CC), candidates are to be 'nominated by Party, trade union, Komsomol, and other social organizations, as well as by individual citizens'. Los found that in Russia 'the selection of judges takes place under considerable pressure from the party and trade unions', and she noted that in the early 1960s every third member of the comrades' courts was a party member.[40]

GDR statistics indicate that at least half of the social court members are in the SED.[41] In the GDR, candidates for *Konfliktkommissionen* are nominated in the union groups and by leaders of the union in a gathering of the workers. To gauge the influence of the SED in member selection, one would have to know the degree to which union leadership is controlled. For *Schiedskommissionen* members, suggestions for nomination are to be solicited from the mass organizations; a nomination list is to be assembled through committees of the National Front. Again the question is the degree to which the National Front is under the direct influence of the party when making nominations.

PROCEDURES

It is, of course, a stated principle that proceedings in the tribunals, though informal, are to follow the law of the country (Articles 3, 15 CC, Articles 92, 96 Verf., Paragraph 2 (3) GGG). Because the comrades' courts and social courts are composed of lay persons, the law stipulates guidance from formal state organs. According to Kucherov, there is some indication that in Russia this aid is in some jurisdictions insufficient: he writes that a basic defect of the courts is the lack of legal knowledge of the members.[42]

Procedures in the popular courts are to be informal and quick, and they are to involve the public in the process to the greatest extent possible. A more casual approach, it is hoped, may avoid exacerbation of the dispute or criminal tendency and open the way toward mediation, conciliation or rehabilitation.[43] One way to foster an aura of informality is to avoid the use of courtrooms.[44] Instead, hearings are held in the meeting rooms of an enterprise or a community building, in locations that are easily accessible and familiar to the participants. Furthermore, the seating arrangement is often one which plays down the authoritative role of the members of the court in order to encourage interaction. Exclusion of legal counsel contributes to the atmosphere of informality.[45] Rather than being adversarial, hearings of the tribunals are inquisitorial in style.[46] It is the responsibility of the social courts to seek out all necessary information prior to and during the hearings (Paragraphs 8 (1) KKO, Paragraph 8 (1) SchKO).

Celerity in comrades' courts is guaranteed by the rule that they are to consider cases within 15 days of receipt, within 10 days if the case concerns petty hooliganism, petty stealing or petty speculation (Article 11 CC). Although the social courts of the GDR are not held to such a tight time-frame, they too are forced to react quickly. Within 4 weeks of receipt of the cases, the social court must hold a hearing (Paragraph 2 (3) KKO, Paragraph 2 (3) SchKO), and the decision of the court must be formally communicated to the participants, to the prosecutor, and to the appropriate authorities within 2 weeks (Paragraph 13 (2) KKO, Paragraph 13 (2) SchKO).

Central to the mission of the tribunals is extensive public participation.[47] This takes many forms: presentation of evidence, interrogation by spectators, offers of assistance in the resocialization of the accused. Article 12 of the Russian statute provides for the involvement of a representative of the collective where the offender works. Following the hearing, decisions are to be made known to the general public. In fact, in the GDR, even the deliberation subsequent to the taking of evidence is held in public.

Despite the effort to keep the tribunals informal, minimal rules are necessary for effective functioning. In Russia, a person summoned before the comrades' court is obliged to appear (Article 14 CC). Should he fail to appear, the court must try to determine why and schedule a second hearing. Failure to appear a second time without valid reason opens the way for consideration of the case *in absentia*. The rule in the GDR is slightly different. A person is not legally obligated to appear in a social court, not even the accused person or a party to a civil dispute. Failure to appear, however, in some circumstances does not preclude the court from hearing a civil case. Repeated failure to respond to the invitation of a social court in the GDR will result in transferral of the matter to the ordinary courts.

Some, but not all, of the due-process rights, customary in ordinary courts, exist in the popular tribunals. Article 13 of the RSFSR statute stipulates that 'the person brought before the court, the victim, and participants in a civil law dispute shall enjoy equal rights'. Often, though, the tribunals are criticized for failing to provide adequate legal protection. Berman and Spindler[48] noted the lack of procedural safeguards in comrades' courts: 'there is a danger that the people who participate in these quasi-judicial proceedings will identify them with law, and that their sense of such basic legal principles as the right to counsel, the presumption of innocence, the precise formulation of issues, and the like, will thereby become dulled'. Presumption of innocence[49] does apply in the social courts of the GDR, but it is questioned whether it can be assured in the absence of specific due process rights. The usual response to charges of insufficient protection is that there is review of the decisions by higher authorities or courts.

Related to this issue is that of double jeopardy. Given the fact that the Russian tribunals are not classified as true courts, the obvious inference is that challenge on the grounds of double jeopardy is not valid. The situation in the GDR is more complex; the social courts are an integral part of the judicial system; yet the possibility exists that a person could be tried by an ordinary court subsequent to a hearing in a social court. Inasmuch as social courts do not 'convict' or 'punish', a trial would not technically constitute 'double jeopardy' as the term is used in Western law. Nevertheless, the criminal procedural code contains a clause which allows trial in a state court only when it later becomes known that the act was substantially more antisocial or dangerous to the society than at first believed (14 (3) StPO). This must occur within 6 months of the decision of the social body.

SANCTIONS

Despite being labelled 'courts', neither the comrades' courts nor the social courts function as do the ordinary courts. Their mission is not to settle cases but to educate.[50] In other words, their goal is not responsibility and penalty assignment in the classic sense; instead they are to aid the parties (including the defendant) in recognizing their responsibility in a socialist system.[51] This goal is to be achieved through persuasion rather than by coercion. The educative role of the popular justice tribunals extends to the general public as well, and to achieve this purpose, sessions of comrades' courts or social courts are sometimes held in special locations, chosen by the chairman, to increase community awareness (Article 11 CC).[52]

Neither the comrades' court nor the social court is considered a 'criminal' proceeding.[53] Legally speaking, their decisions are not 'punishment' even in instances where a person is found responsible for an act which is defined as criminal, and there is no 'criminal record' (Paragraph 37 (3) StGB). The tribunals are to achieve their purpose through persuasion rather than through negative reinforcement.[54] In a sense, then, the tribunals represent a decriminalization, in that a finding of responsibility for an offence is not entered as a 'criminal record'.[55] The 'measures of social pressure' imposed in Russia are intended to be persuasive rather than coercive.[56] Kucherov spoke of the 'decrease in punitive character', noting that in the 1961 law the following punishments were removed: forced labour, concentration camps, loss of job.[57] It was still possible, however, to raise the question of eviction, when it was not possible to live with the offender or when he behaved violently (Article 15 (7) of the 1961 Statute of Comrades' Courts). GDR statutes distinguish between 'educational measures' which can be imposed and those which can merely be confirmed (that is, where there is voluntary agreement to the measure). Specific measures to be imposed include the usual types of sanctions, such as fines, economic deprivation, compensation, etc. In addition, however, in line with socialist theory, the tribunals are able to require that an apology be made, to the victim and/or to the collective (Article 16 CC, Paragraph 20 GGG).

A highly controversial aspect of the tribunals is their ability to make a social condemnation. The comrades' courts are authorized to announce a warning, a social censure or a social reprimand, with or without publication in the press (Article 16 CC); these remain valid for a year (Article 21 CC). There is an expungement clause; should the person not commit a violation of the law or an anti-social offence in this period, he shall be considered as not having been subjected to measures of social pressure (Article 21 CC).[58] Similarly, in the GDR, the social courts have authority to pronounce censure (Paragraph 20 (1) GGG); this can be confined to the session or it can result in public notice in the workplace or place of residence.

Control over execution of decisions is provided by statute (Articles 20, 22 CC); decisions are to be carried out by 'the district, city, district in city, rural village, and settlement soviets of people's deputies'. Statutes of the GDR (Paragraph 57 (4) KKO, Paragraph 53 (4) SchKO) provide the social courts with a similar ability to monitor compliance with their decisions. In the event of non-compliance, both systems invoke the authority of the ordinary court; following investigation of the legality of the decision, the judge can issue a writ of execution.

CONCLUSION

The foregoing discussion, based primarily on a comparison of statutory prescription in Russia and the GDR does not, alas, give much insight regarding the really crucial questions concerning the *actual* function and effect of comrades' courts and social courts. There is little published information concerning the operation of comrades' courts; most of it is either a description based on the statute of the RSFSR or repetition of comments made by early writers. The only extensive discussion of actual practice is to be found in Feifer, but this account was written in the early 1960s.[59] An attempt to evaluate the popular tribunals, therefore, founders on a lack of empirical data.[60] Secondary statements, like that of Berman, that the comrades' courts 'in action have impressed outside observers by the good spirit with which they are received' can hardly be taken at face value;[61] nor can one generalize on the basis of information in accounts written by members of the courts or by governmental agencies published in a society where there is a controlled press and where repercussions for unpopular statements may be serious.[62]

Do the tribunals foster adherence to socialist legality and enhance social cohesiveness or do they, as some analysts fear, alienate those brought before them through a painful exposure to members of their work or residential community? Writers refer to the potentially detrimental effect of the high degree of embarrassment; Berman and Spindler spoke of offenders who choose to have their cases heard by the ordinary court rather than to be tried before their collective.[63] Kucherov quotes a Kolkhoz woman who pleaded that she be punished with any fine but not submitted to the shame of a comrades' court.[64] One author contended that only a few of the persons whose offences had been handled by comrades' courts betrayed 'the trust placed in them by committing further offences'.[65] Savickij supports his contention that the comrades' courts were effective by saying that 63 per cent of the offenders did not recidivate, but he gives no date or citation for the figure.[66] There is the possibility, too, that the tribunals will be used as a means of settling scores or expressing resentment against a loner.[67] Similar questions are raised in the literature on GDR social courts.[68] Schroeder, for instance, suggests that there is a kind of 'extortion' in that the accused person is led to accept the 'unpleasant' session in the social court, in order to avoid a criminal trial and to avoid prejudicing the ordinary court judges in such a trial.[69]

Are the popular tribunals the wave of the future in socialist legal systems? Given the uneven history of comrades' courts and the lack of emphasis on them in the literature, the answer in regard to the USSR is probably no, though Russian authors continue to support the principle of informal justice by lay members of the community. There is remarkably little discussion regarding comrades' courts, even in official publications.[70] Whether this can be taken as evidence that the government does not place much value on them is uncertain. At the end of his favourable evaluation of comrades' courts, Kucherov refers to the Russian view that the courts lead toward the 'paradisical conditions of the future when, under communism, legal coercion will not be necessary and people will act righteously not from fear of punishment but directed by rules of communist morality, as Lenin taught', adding that this 'is, of course, pure utopia!'[71]

In the GDR the incorporation of the social courts into the formal court system may signal a divergence from the Marxian goal of a non-state judiciary. On the other hand, through continual expansion of the jurisdiction of the social courts, the role of lay persons in adjudication is increasing. Statistics concerning court operation indicate that social courts are relieving the formal courts of some of their case-load.

In both countries there is a clear tendency to create more law, more rules, more regulations, a situation which would appear to call for expert interpretation and application, thus complicating the role of the lay person in adjudication. Berman and Spindler speak of the inherent contradiction evident in the concurrent hope for a communist society, where there will be no need for law and the stress on socialist legality. They wrote, 'Despite all the praises heaped upon socialist legality, it is sometimes viewed theoretically as a negative phenomenon, a necessary evil destined to disappear, and this negative side of law has been emphasized particularly in connection with the positive virtues of informal, spontaneous correction of errant citizens by the collective itself'.[72]

Toeplitz finds the GDR system highly interesting from the theoretical point of view because of the merging of the two seemingly contradictory trends: while official duties of jurisdiction are being transferred to the competence of social bodies, the social courts are at the same time being integrated into the overall system of law courts.[73] The necessity to insure that the law is properly applied requires that the social courts be subordinated to the control and direction of official law courts and that the parties to the case have a right of appeal in the state court. Also concerned about uniform application of law, Wünsche writes, 'what matters is the process of the further socialization of the judiciary in the sense of Lenin's remark that we must be judges ourselves and that the citizens in general must take part in the judiciary and the administration of the country'.[74]

ACKNOWLEDGEMENTS

The author wishes to express her appreciation to the International Research and Exchanges Board which provided funding for this research.

ABBREVIATIONS

CC   Statute on Comrades' Courts in the RSFSR (11 March 1977, Amended 3 December 1982 (Vedomosti RSFSR (1977), no. 12, item 254; (1982), no. 49, item 1822, 16 May 1985). See: Butler, W.E. (Compiler, Translater). 'Statute on Comrades' Courts in the RSFSR,' in: *Basic Documents on the Soviet Legal System*. New York: Oceana Publications, 1983.

GGG   Gesetz über die gesellschaftlichen Gerichte (Law on Social Courts in the GDR) (GB1. I 1982 Nr. 13 S. 269).

GVG   Gerichtsverfassungsgesetz (Law on Construction of Courts of the GDR) (GB1. I 1974 Nr. 48 S. 457).

KKO   Konfliktkommissionsordnung (Law on Conflict Commissions of the German Democratic Republic) (GB1.

I 1982 Nr. 13 S. 274; Ber. GB1. I 1983, Nr. 28 S. 276).

SchKO Schiedskommissionsordnung (Law on Dispute Commissions of the German Democratic Republic) (GB1. I 1982 Nr. 13 S. 283; Ber. GB1. I 1983 Nr. 28 S. 276).

StPO Strafprozessordnung (Criminal Procedural Code of the GDR) (GB1. I 1975 Nr. 4 S. 62, GB1. I 1977 Nr. 10 S. 100, GB1 I 1979 Nr. 17 S. 139).

StGB Strafgesetzbuch (Criminal Law Code of the GDR) (GB1. I 1975 Nr. 3 S. 14, GB1. I 1977 Nr. 10 S. 100, GB1. I 1979 Nr. 17 S. 139, GB1. I 1982 Nr. 13 S. 269, GB1. I 1985 Nr. 31 S. 345).

Verf Verfassung (Constitution of the GDR) (6 April 1968, GB1. I 1974 Nr. 47 S. 432).

NOTES

1. John N. Hazard (1969) *Communists and Their Law*, 117, Chicago: University of Chicago Press.

2. Mary Ann Glendon, Michael W. Gordon, and Christopher Osakwe (1982) *Comparative Legal Traditions*, 309, St. Paul, Minnesota: West Publishing Company.

3. Erich Buchholz (1986) 'Gesellschaftliche Gerichte in der DDR – Organe der Strafrechtspflege', *Zeitschrift für die gesamte Strafrechtswissenschaft*, 98 (4), 952.

4. Heinz Wolf (1976) *Zur Praxis der Kameradschaftsgerichte in der UdSSR*, 7ff, Potsdam-Babelsberg: Akademie für Staats- und Rechtswissenschaft der DDR; Albert Boiter (1973), 'Comrades' Courts', *Encyclopedia of Soviet Law* vol. 1, 145.

5. Kurt Wunsche (1969) 'The social courts – development and legal character', in Lawyers Association of the GDR, *Law and Legislation in the German Democratic Republic 2*, 35–40; Udo Krause (1983) '30 Years of social courts', in Lawyers Association of the GDR, *Law and Legislation in the German Democratic Republic*, Berlin: Lawyers Association of the GDR, *1–2*, 34–37.

6. Hans-Theodor Schmidt (1969) *Die sowjetischen Gesellschaftsgerichte: am Beispiel der RSFSR*, 9, Köln: Verlag Wissenschaft und Politik; Peter Solomon, 'Criminalization and decriminalization in Soviet criminal policy', *Law and Society Review* 16, 1981–2, 27.

7. Samuel Kucherov (1970) *The Organs of Soviet Administration of Justice: Their History and Operation*, 156–7, Leiden: E.J. Brill; W.E. Butler (1983) *Soviet Law*, 128, London: Butterworths.

8. Maria Los (1984) 'Ideology and "popular justice" under Communism' (unpublished paper), 15.

9. Kucherov, *op. cit.*, 166.

10. Harold J. Berman and James W. Spindler (1963) 'Soviet comrades' courts', *Washington Law Review 38*, 854–5.

11. Kucherov, *op. cit.*, 191.

12. Frits Gorlé (1982) 'The latest developments in the area of comradely justice', in F.J.M. Feldbrugge, and William B. Simons, *Perspectives on Soviet Law for 1980s*, 171, The Hague: Martinus Nijhoff.

13. For the early history of the comrades' courts, see Kucherov, *op. cit.*; Peter Solomon, *op. cit.*, 19–37; Valerij Savickij (1982) 'Die Kameradengerichte in der UdSSR', *Jahrbuch für Ostrecht 24*, 263–73; and Bette D. Fox, 'Comrades' Courts in Bulgaria', paper presented at the Annual Meeting of the American Society of Criminology, San Diego, 1985.

14. Gustav-Adolf Lübchen (1983) 'Social Courts in the German Democratic Republic', in Lawyers Association of the GDR, *Law and Legislation in the German Demoratic*, Berlin: Lawyers Association of the GDR, 1983, *1–2*, 22; Buchholz (1986) in *Z.g. Strafrechtswissenschaft 98* (4), 952.

15. Hartmut Zimmermann (ed.) (1985) *DDR Handbuch*, 549 Köln: Verlag Wissenschaft und Politik.

16. Explanation of abbreviations is given at the end of the chapter. Herbert Kern (1986) Zur gesellschaftlichen Wirksamkeit der Schiedskommissionen und zur Stellung und zu den Aufgaben der Beiräte für Schiedskommissionen, *Der Schoeffe 33* (1), 1–2; Helmut Grieger and Frohmut Müller (1983) *Die Erweiterung der Rechte der gesellschaftlichen Gerichte und ihr Zusammenwirken mit örtlichen Staatsorganen, Betrieben und gesellschaftlichen Organisationen*, Potsdam-Babelsberg: Akademie für Staats- und Rechtswissenschaft der DDR.

17. Gorlé *op. cit.*, 172.

18. S.E. Finer (1979) *Five Constitutions: Contrasts and Comparisons*, New York: Penguin Books.

19. Boiter, *op. cit.* in *Encyclopedia of Soviet Law*, vol. 1, 1973, 146.

20. Gorlé, *op. cit.*, in Feldbrugge and Simons, *Perspectives on Soviet Law for the 1980s*, 171.

21. An English version of the statute is to be found in W.E. Butler (1972) 'Comradely justice in eastern Europe', *Current Legal Problems 25*, London: Stevens & Son, 238–46. For changes in the law since this date, see I. Grischin (1986) 'Das Statut uber die Kameradschaftsgerichte', *Der Schöffe 33* (9), 203–4.

22. Leon Lipson (1964) 'Extrajudicial institutions in Soviet justice: comrades' courts and anti-parasite tribunals', A.B.A. Section of *International and Comparative Law*, August 7–12, 1964, 286.

23. Berman and Spindler, *op. cit.* in *Washington Law Review 38*, 1963, 844.

24. Rudolf Winkler (Leiter) (1985) *Leitfaden für Schiedskommissionen*, 53, Berlin: Staatsverlag der Deutschen Demokratischen Republik.

25. Henry J. Abraham (1980) *The Judicial Process*, 289, New York: Oxford University Press.

26. Boiter, *op. cit.*, in *Encyclopedia of Soviet Law*, vol. 1, 1973.

27. Savickij, 264–65.
28. W.E. Butler (1972) 'Comradely justice in eastern Europe', *Current Legal Problems 25*, 214, London: Stevens & Sons.
29. Reiland compares the social courts of the GDR with the system of Betriebsjustiz in the Federal Republic of Germany, Werner Reiland, *Die gesellschaftliche Gerichte der DDR*. Tübingen: Horst Erdmann Verlag, 1971, 202ff.
30. Kurt Wünsche (Leiter). *Grundlagen der Rechtspflege: Lehrbuch*. Berlin: Staatsverlag der Deutschen Demokratischen Republik, 1983, 77–78.
31. Abraham, *op. cit.*, 288; Wünsche, *op. cit.*, 101.
32. Berman and Spindler, *op. cit.*, 843.
33. Boiter, *op. cit.*, 146.
34. Ibid., 147.
35. W. Iwannikow, 'Die Kameradschaftsgerichte des Rayons Arbeiten', *Der Schöffe*, 1986, 33 (No. 11), 244–246.
36. Boiter *op. cit.*, 147.
37. Peter H. Solomon, *Soviet Criminologists and Criminal Policy*. New York: Columbia University Press, 1978, 68–69.
38. Berman and Spindler, *op. cit.*, 860.
39. George Feifer (1964) *Justice in Moscow*, 125, New York: Simon & Schuster.
40. Los, *op. cit.*, 33. In regard to training for members of comrades' courts, see Louise Shelley (1978) 'Soviet Crime Prevention: Theory and Results', *Prison Journal 58* (2), 62.
41. Erhart Körting (1981) 'Grundtendenzen in der Entwicklung der gesellschaftlichen Gerichte der DDR', *Jahrbuch für Ostrecht, 21*, 115.
42. Kucherov, *op. cit.*, 190–191, 196.
43. Buchholz, *op. cit.* in *Z.g. Strafrechtswissenschaft 98*, 1986, 962.
44. For accounts of individual cases, see Feifer, *op. cit.*; John N. Hazard (1969) *The Soviet Legal System*, Dobbs Ferry: Oceana Publications; Roy Turner, *Law in the USSR* (1981), Moscow: Novosti Press Agency Publishing House.
45. John N. Hazard (1983) *Managing Change in the USSR*, 161, Cambridge: Cambridge University Press.
46. Glendon *et al.*, *op. cit.*, Erhmann refers to the comrades' courts as 'revivalist-type tribunals', Henry W. Erhmann (1976) *Comparative Legal Cultures*, 104, Englewood Cliffs, New Jersey: Prentice-Hall.
47. Bodo Müller (1985) 'The problem of criminality in the German Democratic Republic (GDR) with special emphasis given to social courts', unpublished paper, 1.
48. Berman and Spindler, *op. cit.* in *Washington Law Review 38*, 1963, 846.
49. Horst Luther (Leiter) (1977) *Strafverfahrensrecht*, 83–4, Berlin: Staatsverlag der Deutschen Demokratischen Republik.
50. Wolf, 10; Inga Markovits (1986) 'Pursuing one's rights under socialism', *Stanford Law Review 38* (3), Feb., 710.
51. Zimmermann (ed.) *op. cit.*, 548.
52. For example, a hearing of a juvenile case may be taken to a

classroom in order to reinforce the character-building aspect of the school.

53. Glendon *et al.*, *op. cit.*; Buchholz, *op. cit.* in *Z.g. Strafrechts-wissenschaft 98*, 1986, 969.

54. Kucherov, *op. cit.*, 189.

55. In the GDR, however, the offence remains part of criminal statistics.

56. Berman and Spindler, *op. cit.*, in *Washington Law Review 38*, 1963, 842.

57. Kucherov, *op. cit.*, 172.

58. Formerly, the comrades' courts were able to raise the question of eviction (Article 15 of the 1961 statute).

59. See also Friedrich-Christian Schroeder (1984) 'Send her to a kolkhoz!': a comrades' court proceeding in Moscow', *Soviet Union 11* (3), 290–292.

60. Berman and Spindler, *op. cit.*, 894, 907; Boiter, *op. cit.*, 148; Gorlé *op. cit.*, 173; Theodore L. Becker (1970) *Comparative Judicial Politics*, 331, Chicago: Rand McNally, 1970, 331; Los, *op. cit.*, 20; Peter Sperlich (1985) 'The incentive structure of lay adjucation in two legal cultures', 16, paper presented at the 13th World Congress of the International Political Science Association.

61. Harold J. Berman (1980) 'Justice in the USSR', in Samuel Hendel (ed.), *The Soviet Crucible: The Soviet System in Theory and Practice*, 240, North Scituate, Massachusetts: Duxbury Press.

62. Barghoorn writes that: 'incomplete data suggest that the anxiety expressed by some Soviet and Western jurists when the people's guards and comrades' courts began their activities around 1959 was only partially justified', Frederick C. Barghoorn (1972) *Politics in the USSR*, 300, Boston: Little Brown and Company.

63. Berman and Spindler, *op. cit.*, 895.

64. Kucherov, *op. cit.*, 196.

65. Boris Alekseevich Victorov (1969) 'Public Participation and Crime Prevention in the Union of Soviet Socialist Republics', *International Review of Criminal Law 27*, 39.

66. Savickij, *op. cit.*, 271.

67. Lipson, *op. cit.*, 286.

68. Erika Lieser-Triebnigg (1982) 'Ein neues Gesetz für die gesell-schaftliche Gerichte', *Deutschland Archiv 15*, Juni, 571.

69. Friedrich-Christian Schroeder (1983) *Das Strafrecht des realen Sozialismus*, 137, Opladen: Westdeutscher Verlag.

70. The description of the legal system in the Novosty Press Agency Yearbook for 1981, for instance, mentions them only once (Novosti Press Agency, *'81 Yearbook: USSR*, Moscow: Novosti Press Agency. Bassiouni and Savitski allocated only one paragraph to comrades' courts in their book on the criminal justice system of the USSR, see M. Cherif Bassiouni and V.M. Savitski (1976) *The Criminal Justice System of the USSR*, Springfield, Illinois: Charles C. Thomas.

71. Kucherov, *op. cit.*, 197.

72. Berman and Spindler, *op. cit.*, 901.

73. Heinrich Toeplitz (1973) 'Problems of the social courts in the

German Democratic Republic', in Lawyers Association of the GDR, *Law and Legislation in the German Democratic Republic*, 1, 5, Berlin: Lawyers Association of the GDR.

74. Kurt Wünsche (1983) 'On the Legal Nature of the Social Courts and their Jurisdiction', in Lawyers Association of the GDR, *Law and Legislation in the German Democratic Republic*, 29, Berlin: Lawyers Association of the GDR.

5

Socialist transformation and gender inequality: women in the GDR and in Hungary

Marilyn Rueschemeyer and Szonja Szelényi

The socialist transformation in Eastern Europe shook the foundation of traditional family life. Within years of the revolution, women entered the workforce in large numbers and began to occupy positions which had been previously reserved for men. Never before in the history of gender relations has there been such an *overnight* transformation in the situation of women. The fact of these changes goes undisputed. There is disagreement, however, about whether their impact was limited to the creation of formal equality between the sexes, or whether they had a much deeper influence on gender relations.

Feminists have approached these questions from two opposing perspectives, one emphasizing the achievements that have been made, the other expressing disappointment with the inequalities which have remained. According to the first position, socialist states have made major advances in emancipating women: they have introduced progressive family policies, enlarged women's educational and occupational opportunities, and sponsored the establishment of socialized domestic services.[1] Practical measures like these helped liberate women from their traditional bondage to the home and allowed them to compete for jobs on broadly similar terms with men. This position is able to account for the importance of structural changes in the lives of East European women. It is less successful, however, in explaining the continued existence of gender stereotypes.

The second perspective minimizes the salience of the new opportunities which have opened up to women and emphasizes the role of tradition in the structuring of gender relations.[2] These feminists point to the persistence of long-established norms in the allocation of domestic chores, criticize the gender segregation of the labour force, and lament the absence of an independent women's movement in contemporary socialist societies. Contrary to the first position, advocates of this view are able to account for the continued importance of tradition in Eastern Europe. However, they tend to underestimate the significance of structural changes and, therefore, misjudge the magnitude of the improvements which have been made since the Second World War.

These different perspectives leave us with apparently contradictory accounts of the impact of socialism on gender relations. At the same time, they also raise several interesting questions. Does the socialist transformation, indeed, have a negligible impact on the position of women? What is the reason for the persistence of gender stereotypes? Are present dilemmas concerning women's emancipation equally shared by all socialist societies, or are those with traditional pasts more deeply affected?

To address these questions, this chapter compares gender relations in two socialist societies: the German Democratic Republic and Hungary. These East European countries simultaneously experienced the transition to socialism in 1949, but they arrived there from diverse historical and cultural backgrounds. Prior to the Second World War, Hungary was economically less developed than Germany, with a much higher percentage of its population employed in agriculture. In addition, Hungary was also more traditional; more people adhered to old religious patterns and social forms as well as a division of roles in the family which was gender-specific. There had been a much shorter exposure to socialist thought.

The GDR–Hungary comparison is interesting because it illustrates the way in which socialist economic development had a standardizing effect on the structure of opportunities which are currently available to women. At the same time, it also shows that historical and cultural factors exert a lasting influence on gender arrangements; this greatly inhibits and modifies change. To demonstrate these, we will briefly outline the history of women's labour-force participation in the two countries and will describe their present socio-economic condition. Here, we will sketch both the advances that have been made in emancipating women by socialist states and the extent of the inequality which has remained. Finally, we will explore some of the new problems which have emerged from recent structural changes, and will point to the absence of a new comprehensive model for gender relationships which takes into account the implications of female employment for gender relations as a whole.

DEVELOPMENTS IN THE GERMAN DEMOCRATIC REPUBLIC

That part of Germany that is now the GDR was occupied by the Soviet Union at the end of the Second World War. At that time, both Germanys were in a crisis: there were food shortages, cities were in ruin, and the great industrial capacity of pre-war Germany was devastated. Workers were desperately needed to rebuild the country. In 1945, there were approximately 3 million more women than men in the GDR; hence it was not long before the new East German government called on women to contribute their labour to the massive reconstruction task.[3]

In addition to stark economic need, there were other pressures on the GDR government which encouraged women's labour-force participation. Socialist ideology, for example, was a major driving force behind the attempt to integrate women into economic life. The re-emergence of the German Left and the formation of anti-fascist women's commissions at the end of the Second World War both served, either by way of example or through their egalitarian ideologies, to obtain the economic co-operation of women. In this process, the exemplary work lives of prominent socialist women (especially those of Rosa Luxemburg and Clara Zetkin) provided the government with an important reference point in the attempt to legitimize women's newly-enhanced economic role. Rather immediately, the Soviet military administration introduced regulations to ensure equal pay for equal work and, in 1949, the new East German constitution proudly heralded the legal equality of the sexes.

At the time women were entering the workforce in large numbers, the social supports that developed later in the GDR were virtually non-existent. During the 1950s, therefore, women had to organize nurseries and kindergartens on their own, through the women's committees at their factories. It was not until the late 1960s, when the GDR further consolidated and centralized its institutions and economic life, that the system of *Krippen* (for children under 3) and *Kindergarten* (for children between the ages of 3 and 6) were developed. By the time of the 8th Party Congress in 1971, however, it became clear to the GDR leadership that even more concrete supports for working women would have to be introduced if they were to remain active in economic life *and* continue to raise more than one child. Appropriately, as soon as the number of children born fell below replacement level,[4] the government introduced a large number of social supports to co-ordinate women's productive and reproductive lives. Some of these included: a reduction of working hours for women with two or more children, a monthly 'household day' for working mothers, paid leave for women to take care of ill children, and a generous loan programme to help establish young couples. Also in this period, the 26 weeks pregnancy leave and the 20 weeks post-natal leave for women were extended to a full year with pay, with the return to a job at the same or similar level guaranteed. (There is now an option for fathers to take this leave as well, but, so far, this has only rarely been used.) These supports were additions to an already existing programme of heavily subsidized food and rents, as well as to the provision of education and health care. Finally, the GDR government also made a commitment to ensure that, in an economy pervaded by chronic housing shortages, young couples, families with children, and single-parent families would be among the first to receive newly-built, state-subsidized apartments.[5]

Largely as a result of these measures, today 87 per cent of all GDR women capable of working do so, a third of them being employed part-time.[6] In addition, approximately 50 per cent of all infants are in *Krippen*, 90 per cent of all children between the ages of 3 and 6 attend *Kindergarten*, and about 75 per cent of all school-age children in grades 1–4 rely on the afternoon day-care services which are provided by the government.[7] Finally, a large number of adults and nearly all children take their main meal at their respective workplace or school.[8]

HISTORICAL CHANGES IN HUNGARY

Hungary before the Second World War was a more traditional and agrarian society than the GDR. At the turn of the century, for example, over three-quarters of its working population was still engaged in agricultural work, which placed Hungary among the least industrialized nations of Europe at the time.[9] In this country of 'landlord and peasant', agricultural property was highly concentrated in the hands of a few aristocrats, and most people worked for wages either as tenant farmers, landless labourers, or estate servants.[10]

Due to the semi-feudal nature of Hungarian social structure, as well as the country's dependence on foreign capital, industrialization progressed at a very slow rate. Fearful of the effects of rapid modernization, proprietors chose to invest their capital in small entrepreneurial firms, rather than in labour-intensive workshops or large-scale manufacturing industries.[11] Of course, factory organizations did develop in certain areas of economic life (i.e., in iron-, machine-, and food-manufacturing); however, even well into the twentieth century, these were outnumbered by small-scale productive establishments.[12] As late as 1930, therefore, well over 50 per cent of the Hungarian workforce was still employed in agriculture.[13]

For a brief period in the early 1940s, industrial development received a special boost because of the country's involvement in the Second World War. In the last few years of the war, however, battle destruction was so complete, that, by 1949, Hungary's industrial capacity was back at its outdated pre-war state: bridges were blown up, streets were demolished, railway tracks were torn up, and warehouses were robbed.[14] What the fleeing Hungarian fascists (*nyilasok*) did not manage to destroy, angry proprietors on their way out of the country either demolished or exported. More than half the country's livestock, almost 30 per cent of its agricultural machinery, and most of its industrial equipment had thus disappeared by the end of the war.[15]

In the post-war era, Hungary entered a path of economic development similar to the GDR. Between 1949 and 1968, large estates were broken up, agriculture was collectivized, and all major industrial enterprises were nationalized.[16] In addition, a concerted effort was made by the Hungarian state to speed up the transition to a modern economy by heavy investments in labour-intensive industries, as well as by a massive transfer of manpower from agriculture to manufacturing. As a result of these changes, the proportion of those engaged in agricultural production declined considerably, from 53.8 per cent in 1949 to 20.2 per cent by 1986.[17] In this period of extensive economic growth, the demand for industrial labour was so great that it quickly exhausted its predominantly male supply. To fill remaining vacancies, as well as to overcome recurring labour shortages, the Hungarian government, much like its GDR counterpart, began a large-scale campaign to recruit women into the labour force.

Women's participation in economic life, of course, did not begin in 1949. Women played an important role in the maintenance of pre-industrial households, and some even worked for wages as domestics or agricultural servants on the large aristocratic estates.[18] Their entry into the *waged* labour force, however, did not begin on a noticeable scale until the onset of industrialization, when textile, food, and tobacco factories began to recruit them in large numbers.[19] By the turn of the century, women were finding jobs in the trade, service, and health industries, as well as in administrative and clerical occupations. Additionally, due to the expansion of educational opportunities in this period,[20] women also entered a select number of professional jobs, such as nursing, midwifery and teaching.[21]

By the early decades of the twentieth century, the image of the working woman was no longer an unheard of phenomenon. Nevertheless, fundamental changes in women's labour force participation did not take place until the end of the Second World War, when the transition to a socialist economy greatly accelerated their entry into the workforce. After 1949, the demand for female labour rapidly increased and the percentage of economically active women skyrocketed, rising from 34.6 per cent in 1949 to 70.8 per cent by 1980 (see Table 5.1).

Since the end of the Second World War, the Hungarian state

Table 5.1. Distribution of women between the ages of 15 and 54 by economic activity in Hungary 1949–80 (in percentages)

Economic activity	1949	1960	1970	1980
Economically Active	34.6	49.9	63.7	70.8
Inactive Earners	1.3	0.7	6.1	12.3
Of which on child-care leave	–	–	4.8	9.0
Dependants	64.1	49.4	30.2	16.9
Of which pupils, students	2.1	3.6	6.9	6.0
Other dependants	62.0	45.8	23.3	10.9

Source: Barnabás Barta, András Klinger, Károly Miltényi, and György Vukovich (1984) *Fertility, Female Employment, and Policy Measures in Hungary*, 24, Geneva: International Labour Organisation.

has maintained a formally egalitarian attitude toward the sexes. Much as in the GDR, it guarantees the sexes equal opportunities in social, economic, and political life, assuring them not only equal rights to education and employment, but also equal pay for equal amounts of work performed.[22] Economic necessity, combined with the mandates of socialist ideology, pushed the Hungarian state not only to establish the formal equality of the sexes, but also to create favourable conditions which would ensure women's continued participation in economic life.

In the immediate post-revolutionary years, the social supports necessary to assist working women in their domestic tasks were largely undeveloped. To be sure, kindergarten (*kisdedóvódák*) and day-time shelters (*menedékházak*) for children between the ages of 3 and 5 had been in existence since 1928 and crèches (*bölcsödék*) had also been available to, at least, some women since 1908.[23] These services, however, were not sufficiently widespread by 1949 to meet the extensive child-care needs of the growing number of working women. As early as 1953, therefore, the Hungarian government introduced several policies both to facilitate the full-time participation of women in the workforce, as well as to attempt to influence their future fertility.[24] Just as in the GDR, the state expanded child-care facilities, socialized many domestic responsibilities, and introduced a set of progressive family policies.

As a result of these changes, working women today are entitled to 20 weeks of fully paid maternity leave, extra paid holidays to take care of their families, and several days of leave to nurse ailing children. Moreover, since the introduction of the child-care grant (GYES, or *Gyerek Eltartási Segély*) in 1967, nursing women have been able to take an extended leave with pay from the end of the maternity leave until their youngest child is three years old, in order to care for their young children. Similarly to the GDR, women receiving this grant are able to retain their position at work, so that at the completion of the nurturing years they can return to a similar (if not exactly the same) position to that which they held prior to giving birth.[25] In addition to these benefits, families with children are also provided with a monthly 'family allowance' and a variety of state-supported services, such as highly subsidized paediatric care, free education, discount rates on medicine, and low-cost child-care facilities. Finally, the Hungarian state also created a multitude of subsidized domestic services, such as day-care and meals for children at school, low-cost eating facilities for adults at work, and inexpensive public laundromats. By 1980, state provision of these supports was so extensive that it amounted to as much as 9 per cent of the net national product in Hungary, which affirms the strong commitment of the Hungarian leadership to the assistance of working women.[26]

GDR WOMEN: EDUCATION, WORK, POLITICS

The encouragement given to women to study and enter the workforce had dramatic results in the GDR, even taking into account some of the obstacles and regressions along the way. During the 1950s, for example, the overwhelming majority of women still worked in unskilled jobs. By 1971, already 80 per cent of all women under 30 years of age had skilled workers' training or post-secondary education, while, in the same year, only 22 per cent of those over 60 had studied at all. More recent statistics on women's educational attainment in the GDR indicate that, in 1980, as many as 80.3 per cent of all women under 30 had completed vocational school: 57.5 per cent of these graduated as skilled workers, 21.9 per cent had higher specialized training, while the remaining 0.9 per cent possessed other vocational skills.[27] At present, approximately half of all university students are women (see Table 5.2); and women under 35 have the same level of education as men.[28]

There are lifelong opportunities in the GDR for further education although these have been reduced somewhat in recent years. Factory women over 35, for example, have the opportunity to be classified as skilled workers (even without taking an exam) simply by demonstrating that they have been successful at their jobs for over 3 years. In addition, a large number of companies today offer on-the-job training programmes for women, which have been designed with their special needs in mind.[29] Provisions like these have been extremely helpful to both men and women in changing their occupation or in increasing their skill level in the later years of their life.

New opportunities have also been created for women in the occupational structure. Whereas in 1955 approximately a quarter of all working women were employed in agriculture, by 1980 less than 10 per cent of them were so employed.[30] Today,

Table 5.2. Female students in higher education in the GDR, 1951–83 (in percentages)

Year	All students	Students in residence	Correspondence students
1951	21.3	23.4	5.2
1960	25.3	31.4	8.2
1970	35.4	43.2	15.9
1975	48.2	56.0	21.4
1980	48.7	52.8	26.5
1983	50.0	53.0	28.5

Source: Statistisches Jahrbuch der DDR, 1984, 303, Berlin: Staatsverlag der Deutschen Demokratischen Republik. (Evening study not shown).

about 30 per cent of all women work in manufacturing industries. In addition, women comprise 46 per cent of doctors, 45.8 per cent of dentists, 61 per cent of pharmacists, 30 per cent of lawyers, and 76 per cent of teachers.[31] Finally, they have also managed to enter such traditionally male fields as metallurgy, engineering, and construction work.

Notwithstanding these changes, major differences between men and women in the occupational structure have remained. Women continue to be heavily employed in trade and light industry, the lower-paid sectors of the economy, and remain dominant in education and the social services (see Table 5.3). In addition, while government regulations formally ensure

Table 5.3. The share of female members of the labour force in different economic sectors in the GDR, 1970–84 (in percentages)

Economic sector	1970	1975	1980	1984
Industry	42.5	43.7	43.3	41.9
Crafts	40.1	38.7	38.0	37.4
Construction	13.3	14.9	16.2	16.3
Agriculture and forestry	45.8	42.9	41.5	39.4
Transportation	28.5	27.3	27.4	27.0
Post and telecommunications	68.8	70.5	70.0	69.3
Trade	69.2	71.4	72.8	72.8
Other productive sectors	53.7	54.2	55.1	55.0
Non-productive sectors	70.2	72.3	72.8	73.2
Total	48.3	49.6	49.9	49.4

Source: Gerd Meyer (1986) 'Frauen in den Machthierarchien der DDR'. Deutschland Archiv 3, 305.

equal pay for equal work, it is not unusual for women to be excluded from heavy industry, mining, and many construction jobs, which are considered high risk and are, accordingly, well paid.[32] Also, because opportunities for work are still behind the advances that have been in education and in training, a number of educated and highly skilled women continue to be forced into accepted jobs for which they are over-qualified.

Women's political representation is similarly riddled with contradictions. Although one-third of all leadership positions are held by women (see Panel A, Table 5.4), the higher the position at work, in government, or in the mass organizations,

---

Table 5.4. Percentage of women in occupation leadership positions in the GDR (percentage of female employees in the sectors is shown inside the brackets)

A. *In all Sectors of Society – about one-third*

B. *In the Economy* 1950: 8–10% 1970: 20% 1982: 30% (1983: 49.4%)
    a. Industry all sectors 1979: every fifth 1983: every sixth (1983: 42.4%)
       in 1979 Top positions in Kombinaten: 2.3%
               Deputy Directors: 12%
               Leading Positions at the third level: 19.7%
       Light Industry: 1983: about 50%
    b. Agriculture 1976: 16.2%
               1979 and 1983: every sixth (1983: 39.9%)
    c. Services: Altogether 1983: about 50%
       Trade: 1984: 58% (1983: 72.8%)
       Post and telecommunications: 1983: about 50% (1983: 69.3%)

C. *Cultural and Social Sectors*:
    Education, Science, Culture: 1983: 56.6%
    Education: Teachers: 1970: 58.1% 1982: 70.1%
            Principals: 1970: 23.3% 1982: 32.0%
                     (1983: together 76.7%)

    Higher Education including
    Technical Higher Education: 1983: about one third

    Of these, professors and
    instructors: 1981: 7.5%

D. *Health Care: 1983: 56.6% (1983: 83.8%)*
             Doctors: 1982: 52% Dentists: 1982: 57%
             Pharmacists: 1982: 68%
             Doctors in Local Public Health 1978: 20% 1983: about 50%

Source: Gerd Meyer (1986) 'Frauen in den Machthierarchien der DDR', *Deutschland Archiv 3*, 306.

the lower the percentage of women. In 1985, for example, while women comprised 35.5 per cent of all members in the Socialist Unity Party, fewer than 5 per cent of the first secretaries at the country level and none of the first secretaries at the district level were women. Likewise, while at the national level women constituted 13.5 per cent of all members in the Central Committee, no woman has yet become a full member of the Politburo.[33] Finally, while 30 per cent of all city mayors, and 10 to 20 per cent of executive councils at the district level were women, only one out of the forty-five members of the Council of Ministers was a woman. Regrettably, women's representation in the National Front shows identical patterns.[34]

Such detailing of differences between men and women is not meant to negate the real advances that have been made to eradicate gender inequality in the GDR. In fact, women are very active in the middle levels of the occupational hierarchy, their representation in the parliament is considerable, and they comprise half of all union functionaries. Nevertheless, a large proportion of them continue to be employed in traditionally female occupations and their absence from the highest levels of industry, the professions, and political life is still highly visible.

HUNGARIAN WOMEN IN THE WORKFORCE

As in the GDR, major steps have been taken by the Hungarian state in providing women with equal access to educational,

Table 5.5. Proportion of men and women at selected levels of schooling completed in Hungary 1949–80

	No schooling completed		8 or more years		High school or more		Some tertiary education	
Years	men	women	men	women	men	women	men	women
	%	%	%	%	%	%	%	%
1949	4.1	5.5	21.9	19.5	8.6	3.6	3.5	0.6
1960	2.6	3.7	34.5	31.3	12.0	6.6	4.7	1.2
1970	1.5	1.9	55.1	48.0	18.2	13.9	6.5	2.4
1980	0.7	1.5	71.1	61.6	24.4	22.4	8.6	4.6
1984	0.8	1.3	77.2	67.9	27.3	26.6	10.1	5.9

Source: Hungarian Central Statistical Office (1985) Statisztikai Évkönyv 1985 (Statistical Yearbook 1985), 32, Budapest: Központi Statisztikai Hivatal.

occupational, and political opportunities. Largely because of this, the educational gap between the sexes has closed considerably over the past 20 years. Table 5.5 shows, for example, that the proportion of women completing 8 or more years of schooling nearly doubled, while the percentage of those finishing high school or college has more than tripled between 1960 and 1980.

Whereas in terms of *years of schooling* equality between the sexes has almost been attained, significant differences in *type of training* have remained. Recent studies have shown, for example, that women are still outnumbered in technical colleges and industrial apprenticeships, while in vocational schools they continue to be channelled into courses (e.g., hairdressing, kindergarten teaching, and catering) which are associated with the nurturing role.[35] Even in tertiary institutions, where women have made their greatest advances since the Second World War, they remain *under-represented* in so-called 'masculine' courses on engineering, agriculture, and veterinary

Table 5.6. The percentage of women among those attending tertiary institutions in Hungary by type of studies, in 1985.

Type of studies	Percentage of women	Total number attending
	%	
Technical and engineering	16.9	16,806
Agricultural sciences	33.4	4,057
Veterinary medicine	16.8	524
Medical sciences	55.6	7,422
Health	95.1	1,044
Economics	66.8	5,692
Law and administration	57.7	3,090
Liberal arts	76.8	3,916
Natural sciences	47.9	3,671
Education	72.4	8,457
Physical therapy	93.3	433
Physical education	45.7	422
Teachers' colleges	87.6	5,436
Kindergarten teaching	99.2	1,394
Fine arts	54.1	1,826
All studies combined	52.3	64,190

Source: Hungarian Central Statistical Office (1986) *Statisztikai Évkönyv 1985* (Statistical Yearbook 1985), 290, Budapest: Központi Statisztikai Hivatal.

science, and are *over-represented* in the more 'feminine' fields of pharmacy, education, and health care (see Table 5.6).

This 'odd combination of emancipation and bondage' characterizes not only patterns of educational attainment, but also women's occupational opportunities in Hungary.[36] As in the GDR, women's involvement in the waged labour force has skyrocketed over the past 20 years (see Table 5.1). Home and employment are now officially recognized as harmonious spheres, and women's participation in the workforce is regarded as a normal and expected part of their adult life. Consequently, most women work full-time, a large number stay in the labour force on a continuous basis, and some have attained positions of importance in economic life.

Due to greater educational opportunities, as well as the provision of social supports by the state, there have been tremendous changes in the quality of women's employment since the Second World War. The proportion of female skilled manual workers, for example, has increased from 4 per cent in 1943 to 17.8 per cent by 1980 (see Table 5.7).[37] In addition, women have entered previously male-dominated fields and are today present in industrial sectors which, several decades ago, were simply not open to them: women today may be seen sweeping streets, working on construction sites, building homes, or carrying heavy loads in industrial occupations. An increasing number of them also work in mining and manufacturing industries, in building and construction, as well as in transportation and telecommunications (see Table 5.8). Perhaps the greatest improvements made by women, however, are in the professions. As Table 5.9 indicates, there has been a

Table 5.7. Distribution of women employed in manual occupations by skill level in Hungary 1970–80 (in percentages)

Skill level	1970	1980
	%	%
Skilled workers	13.8	17.8
Semiskilled workers	41.9	58.7
Unskilled workers	37.3	18.8
Agricultural helping family members	7.0	7.7
Total	100.0	100.0

Source: Árpád Olajos, (ed.) (1983) *Tanulmányok a Nöi Munkáról*, 28, Budapest: Kossuth Könyvkiadó, 1983).

Table 5.8. Percentage of economically active women among economically active persons in the major divisions on national economy in Hungary 1949–80 (in percentages)

Major division of national economy	1949	1960	1970	1980
	%	%	%	%
Mining and manufacturing	23.1	33.0	41.7	43.9
Building and construction	3.7	10.6	15.5	18.0
Agriculture and forestry	29.7	38.2	38.5	36.2
Transportation and communications	9.4	16.9	22.1	24.4
Trade	35.9	52.0	61.0	63.3
Water works and supply	24.1	24.4	19.3	23.2
Non-material branches (of service character)	43.0	45.1	57.0	59.7
Total, all branches	29.2	35.5	41.2	43.4

Source: Barnabás Barta, András Klinger, Károly Miltényi, and György Vukovich (1984) *Fertility, Female Employment, and Policy Measures in Hungary*, 31, Geneva: International Labour Organisation.

Table 5.9. Proportion of women employed in selected non-manual occupations in Hungary 1960–80 (in percentages)

Occupation	1960	1980
	%	%
Doctors and dentists	20.9	43.6
Pharmacists	50.3	75.4
University teachers	20.5	31.5
High school teachers	40.2	56.7
Primary school teachers	63.9	78.8
Draughtsmen	66.7	86.9
Chief accountants	21.0	48.9
Company managers	7.4	15.5
Managers of agricultural co-operatives	2.4	.7.4
Administrative managers and council leaders	8.1	16.4

Source: Árpád Olajos, ed., *Tanulmányok a Nöi Munkáról*, (Budapest: Kossuth Könyvkiadó, 1983), p. 108.

dramatic increase in the proportion of women doctors, dentists, lawyers, pharmacists, university teachers, draughtsmen, and chief accountants, and they have also made great strides in supervisory roles and in leadership positions.

These data indicate that major steps have been taken by the Hungarian state in emancipating women from their traditional bondage to the home. Irrespective of these changes, however, gender-segregation of occupations continues on a large scale. Women are still heavily concentrated in semi-skilled and unskilled occupations (see Table 5.7), they are considerably over-represented in the service sector of the economy (see Table 5.8), and they continue to earn 20 to 30 per cent less than their male co-workers.[38] Furthermore, while their position has improved significantly in the professions, their opportunities for top-level leadership posts still leave a lot to be desired. Only 28.7 per cent of the members of the Hungarian Socialist Workers' Party are women,[39] and they are rarely appointed to high-level administrative posts.[40]

PROBLEMS AND TENSIONS FACED BY WOMEN IN THE GDR

Contemporary problems of GDR women stem from remaining traditional stereotypes and expectations, from contradictory goals and inconsistent state policies, from a series of occupational pressures, as well as from rapidly changing gender roles. Unlike in the West, biological explanations are still popularly used in the GDR to justify the special relationship of mothers to their children, as well as to legitimize women's greater involvement in domestic life. As Helga Hortz (an East German philosopher) was once quoted as saying about the GDR: 'There are hardly any objections to be raised about the social emancipation of women; but the other side of oppression, the subjugation of women by men is generally considered unproblematic or natural.'[41]

In this context, it is not surprising to find that women in the GDR continue to bear almost all of the burdens of household tasks. There are women, of course, who enjoy some aspects of this role. However, when they work full-time, they neither have the time nor the inclination to prepare elaborate dinners during the week, nor to welcome guests in the more traditional manner. As a result, an increasing number of women are beginning to demand some help from their husbands. According to a recent survey, these demands are slowly being satisfied: a few men have taken the 'baby year' leave, and some have even stayed home from work in order to take care of ill children. In addition, the results also indicated that younger and educated men are becoming more willing to assist in domestic life.[42] Consequently, while the average German woman still has little free time on her hands and performs over three-quarters of all household chores, younger and educated women now do 60 per cent of these tasks.[43]

Educational practices in the GDR reflect similar patterns of gender arrangements. In schools, for example, boys and girls learn from the same curriculum, yet they are exposed to text books in which women are typically portrayed as primary caretakers. Moreover, children are encouraged, at home as well as in school, to become involved in gender-typed activities. Thus, in their free time, girls join artistic and people-oriented groups, while boys spend longer periods of time in sports and participate in activities which prepare them for a technical and scientific future. Later career choices of children reflect these gender-differentiated socialization practices; this has led a number of GDR sociologists to worry about the role of early childhood experiences in maintaining gender inequality.[44]

In addition to these contradictory educational practices, state goals show many other inconsistencies in trying to co-ordinate work and family life. For instance, while in its Family Law (*Familiengesetzbuch*) the GDR government continues to defend the nuclear family as the 'smallest cell of society',[45] its work regulations reflect a primary concern with economic efficiency, rather than an attempt to bridge the difference between public and private lives. To be sure, there is some recognition on the part of the state that certain types of economic organization have a negative impact on family lives. State responses to the difficulties of shift workers, for example, illustrate that steps *are* being taken to compensate them for their irregular work schedules. They are granted additional holidays and reduced work hours, they are supplied with transportation to their apartments, they are offered many opportunities for exercise, and they are also provided with warm meals at their workplace. However, the necessity of shift work itself is never questioned in the GDR; hence, shift workers must resort to *private* solutions in the practical task of organizing their dual work and family demands.[46]

Not only are state policies inconsistent, but GDR citizens also have contradictory goals and expectations where the family is concerned. Nowhere is this seen more clearly than in the duality of their commitment to work and their oft-publicized concern with family life. Even with all the state supports available to working families today, both parents are away from home during the day and they return in the evening to find that there are additional chores that need to be completed. To ease the double burden of their work and family lives, GDR women often accept jobs which are below their qualifications, in order to remain close to their apartments or to be near their children's day-care facilities. Increasingly, however, professional highly skilled women are less willing to make such compromises. A series of private interviews with professional women has revealed, for example, that the longer they are involved in professional life, the more reluctant they are to trade work for family life.[47] Their absorption in work and their close involvement with their collective thus frequently leads to many of the complications that dual career families in the West are now beginning to experience.[48] Based on current rates, in fact, one in three marriages in the GDR is expected to end in divorce.[49]

Women's reactions to these problems are documented in newspapers and magazines and in the new genre of women's novels as well as in ethnographic studies and academic research articles. These sources indicate that women in the GDR are currently reassessing not only the number of children they wish to have, given their difficult circumstances, but also the expectations they have for their relationships with men. In addition, many of them are also beginning to reconsider the nature of their commitment to work. Recruiters of women for higher level positions at universities thus frequently observe that while women are urged to take their second doctorate, or are encouraged to assume leadership positions at work, they often refuse.[50] These refusals reflect not only women's primary concern with their family responsibilities and their continued reluctance to compete with men in the public sphere, but also their desire to do well in their professional career *while maintaining a satisfying personal life*.[51]

Although few women would willingly remain at home without work, it seems many women in the GDR are increasingly disappointed with what had been sold to them as 'The Great Career'.[52] They are dissatisfied with their restricted opportunities at work, their continued disadvantages with respect to men, and the inability of the GDR leadership to provide satisfactory domestic services. Lacking a viable public medium through which to express these ideas, women have learned to cope with these contemporary dilemmas in their own way. Thus, they often refuse to take on additional responsibilities at work, they decline offers to advance their educational careers, and, whenever possible, they opt for part-time work or reduced work hours. Although each one of these options place women at further disadvantage with respect to men, many still choose these solutions and subsequently express relief at not having to negotiate work and family demands.

Observers of family life in the GDR often conclude that nothing much has changed since the Second World War: women have only added work outside the home to their traditional domestic responsibilities. Others maintain, however, that everything has changed, as traditional family mores have been replaced by decadent ways of life in the wake of women's labour-force participation. While a large proportion of women still marry early in the GDR (in 1979, the average age at first marriage was 23.3 years for men and 21.3 years for women), it is true that a sizeable number of young couples now live together without marrying.[53] In 1979, for example, 28 per cent of those between the ages of 18 and 40 lived in such *de facto* arrangements (*Lebensgemeinschaften*). At the same time, more than half of these couples claimed that they planned to marry later,[54] which indicates that they regarded this form of living arrangement merely as a temporary testing period, rather than a viable alternative to traditional married life. As in the West, single-parent families are also on the rise. To some extent, this is largely due to increasing divorce rates, but even more importantly, to the growing number of unwed mothers.[55]

In spite of recent changes in living arrangements, the traditional family model (consisting of two parents and children living together in a separate household) still described 56.4 per cent of all existing households in 1981 (the other 12.4 per cent were single-parent families with children, and the remaining 31.2 per cent were childless couples).[56] Interviews with professional women indicate, however, that inside these traditional family structures, highly skilled and professional women no longer identify themselves merely as mothers and wives,[57] while the emotional atmosphere as well as the power arrangements in these families are slowly being transformed.[58]

HUNGARIAN FAMILY LIFE

Women's increased labour-force participation in Hungary has

prompted heated arguments over work and family issues. Over the last 40 years, three fairly well-defined positions have emerged out of these publicly-waged debates. According to the first position, it is unlikely that socialism will be able to expand women's current rate of labour-force participation. Consequently, protagonists of this view maintain that what is needed today is not so much further attempts to integrate women into the workforce, but sustained policies which allow women to harmonize their work and family lives. Towards this end, these theorists encourage the introduction of part-time work and flexible hours for working mothers, as well as the development of existing household services to assist women in their domestic tasks.[59] In a similar vein, some have suggested that the most efficient way to deal with women's double burden today is to literally 'increase the freedom of choice between a job and the household' by increasing the amount of the family allowance and the baby-care benefit, as well as by paying housewives for their contributions to economic life.[60] Interestingly, while proponents of this position have evidently accepted women's new economic role, their suggestions for labour reforms are still imbued with the stereotypical idea that only women are responsible for domestic tasks.

By contrast, the second position maintains that formal measures helping women integrate work and family life are necessary, but not sufficient for their full emancipation under socialism. These feminists argue that as long as traditional gender roles are retained as an integral part of socialist culture, it will not be possible to arrange work and family lives efficiently, because the burdens of household chores will continue to fall exclusively on the shoulders of women. They maintain that while men continue to be excused from participation in domestic life, and so long as this excuse is publicly supported, women's integration into the labour force will continue to fall short of pronounced socialist ideals.[61]

Finally, on the neo-conservative side of the work–family debate, several authors have lately argued for a complete return to traditional gender stereotypes. They have accused working women of breaking up the family, disrupting children's early socialization, and creating major social problems by not providing the elderly with the necessary care when the need arrives. Moreover, they have also suggested that working women are the main cause of Hungary's low birth rate, the heightened competition among spouses, and men's deteriorating health. According to these authors, the solution to these problems lies not in helping women cope with their double burden, but in eliminating its presence altogether. Hence, they advocate the re-establishment of traditional gender roles, by which they mean, of course, the return of women to their kitchens and the reinstitution of men as their families' primary breadwinner.[62]

The reliability of these positions in reflecting general public opinion in Hungary is, of course, unclear because we derived them from academic articles, not from nation-wide public opinion polls. At any rate, they highlight many of the dilemmas which accompanied changing gender roles by raising these issues in public debates. In this context, it is interesting to note that two of the three positions demonstrate a strong attachment to traditional stereotypes, in so far as they assume that domestic labour is essentially a woman's task. Given the nature of our sources, one could argue that this reflects merely the peculiar attachment of some academics to gender stereotypes. As it turns out, however, survey data indicated that these long-established norms are also shared by the Hungarian public at large. According to the results of a 1977 opinion poll, for example, a representative sample of the population agreed that the most important character traits in men were *political understanding, firmness*, and *intelligence*, while in women they were *thrift, common sense*, and *skills in child rearing*.[63]

Along similar lines, other studies have shown that little has changed in the strength of tradition over the allocation of domestic responsibilities. Housework continues to be regarded as a typically female occupation and men still obstinately refuse to share domestic tasks. In 1977, women spent an average of 4.28 hours per day on household chores, while men contributed merely 1.63 hours of their time.[64] Certainly, there have been some changes in the division of domestic work since the Second World War. Recent household statistics indicate, for example, that educated and higher-status men, as well as those living in urban areas, are slightly more likely than others to help their wives around the home.[65] However, these results need to be interpreted with extreme caution: because these changes are recent and also very small, their reliability in terms of predicting men's future domestic involvement still stands on highly questionable ground.

Meanwhile, in most Hungarian families, tolerance of women's labour-force participation and an acceptance of the attendant need for new domestic arrangements are not easily obtained. On the contrary, marital conflicts have risen steeply since couples were made to balance two careers and one family under a single roof.[66] Changing gender roles and women's new opportunities in the public sphere soon clashed head on with traditional stereotypes, and this, in turn, placed tremendous strains on contemporary family life.[67] According to recent figures, 30 per cent of all marriages in Hungary are expected to fail,[68] as working women today are less willing to tolerate unsatisfying family lives than were home-bound women in the past.[69] The growing divorce rate and a steady increase in the number of single-parent families are only two indicators of the lack of fit between women's new economic role and the persistence of old stereotypes.[70]

THE IMPACT OF THE SECOND ECONOMY ON GENDER INEQUALITY

Since 1968, the second economy has formed an integral part of Hungarian economic life. In fact, its presence is so overbearing today that it constitutes a significant source of income for about three-quarters of all Hungarian families.[71] There are four types of second economy activities in Hungary.[72] First, there are legalized activities for which an operation licence from the state is required. These include: full-time mini-farming, part-time farming, and organized sub-contracting inside socialist firms.[73] Second, there are a fair number of people in Hungary who earn extra cash from tips and bribes. Unlike in the West, however, not only hairdressers, barbers and waiters are able to participate in these activities. So-called 'thank you' monies are also given for medical and dental care, automobile repair, home maintenance, and machine repair services. Third, there are semi-legal activities (moonlighting jobs of all sorts) which individuals perform in addition to their full-time job with the state. Professionals and craftsmen, for example, can offer their highly valued skills and services on the market without necessarily obtaining a formal operation licence from the state.[74] Finally, there are also a number of recalcitrant market arrangements, which range from illegal use of state-owned property to unlawful monetary transactions. These, however, are difficult to monitor because they operate mostly on the black market. As a result, the remaining discussion will, generally, not pertain to them.

The second economy offers workers numerous benefits. The most obvious of these is, of course, the extra cash, which in the case of the illegal or semi-legal activities is not subject to taxation. More importantly, however, workers employed in the second economy have enhanced bargaining power with state management. In an economy that suffers from chronic labour shortages, but one in which the second economy offers an alternative source of employment, workers participating in the second economy are able to negotiate their wages and working conditions with state management, using their second economy employment as a weapon at the bargaining table.[75]

With the exception of the agricultural sector, women's involvement in the second economy is strictly limited. Even here, however, while a significant proportion of mini-farmers are women, little recognition is given to their market activities.[76] In census calculations as well as in survey data, they continue to be recorded merely as 'housewives', and the money they earn from their farming activities is typically classified as 'family income'. Moreover, while they certainly share the benefits of the additional income with their husbands, they do not enjoy the added bargaining power that their husbands have with respect to state management.

Women's participation in the non-agricultural sector of the second economy is even less prominent. This is not surprising, given that most of these activities are centred in the upper echelons of professional work, as well as in highly skilled manual occupations,[77] where women are vastly under-represented. Yet even in those second-economy activities which are located in industries and at skill levels where women are relatively well represented, they are excluded from market-oriented production. For example, they are routinely excluded from 'enterprise business work partnerships' (*vállalati gazdasági munkaközösségek*, or VGMs) because these operate after regular work hours and it is generally assumed that women are obliged to spend this time looking after families.

In all probability, the strengthening of the second economy in Hungary will lead to undesirable outcomes where the position of women is concerned. It will contribute to the maintenance of a sex-segregated labour force, because it creates new opportunities primarily in those areas of economic life where women are largely under-represented. In addition, it will augment the already existing power of men in families, as it will render it increasingly difficult for women to demand the sharing of domestic tasks from men who, similarly to themselves, carry two jobs at a time. This, in turn, will help preserve traditional norms in the allocation of household tasks and will maintain women's disadvantages in the public sphere by excluding them from the most profitable activities of Hungarian economic life.

CONCLUSIONS

This brief overview of gender relations in Hungary and GDR reveals an interesting feature of the socialist transformation, namely its standardizing effect of systems on gender stratification. As our discussion illustrates, cross-national similarities in socialist economic development have resulted in the creation of parallel opportunity structures for women. Largely as a result of economic pressures, women in both countries were urged to upgrade their educational credentials, encouraged to enter political life, and motivated to assume occupational roles which had been previously reserved for men. Overlapping with these economic needs, cross-national similarities in governing ideology also inspired the two countries' states to introduce equivalent legislation with respect to the labour of women. To lighten the burdens of domestic life, for example, both countries launched a series of progressive family policies, extended their child-care facilities, and provided women with a variety of state-supported domestic services.

The introduction of these measures suggests that Hungary and the GDR have made major advances in emancipating women from their traditional bondage to the home. At the same time, because these changes took place virtually overnight, men and women in both countries were left behind in having to cope with the psychological consequences of their newly established gender roles. At first glance, it appears that socialist theory, with its putatively egalitarian sentiments towards the sexes, provided an orienting ideology in these difficult times of change. As our discussion reveals, however, it had little to say about the appropriate gender arrangements which should accompany the new division of labour. Consequently, while established roles were beginning to crumble, *new gender conceptions* which involve a more comprehensive reworking of old patterns failed to emerge. This resulted in the unique situation whereby men and women, in both countries, continued to hold on to their long-established gender norms, yet lived in an environment wherein the structural conditions necessary for the emancipation of women were already present. Throughout this paper, we have tried to capture this lack of congruence between existing gender norms and the newly established structural arrangements by summarizing the available literature on the reflections of women themselves, on the inconsistent policies of socialist states, as well as on public debates over work and family life.

Notwithstanding the significance of these cross-national similarities in the position of women, the fact remains that present contradictions and dilemmas over gender roles are handled quite differently in the two countries. Thus, in the GDR, men and women are somewhat less tradition-bound, with a higher percentage of women more fully integrated into economic life and a greater willingness among certain groups of men to share domestic tasks. By comparison, Hungarians are still very much entangled in the web of traditional stereotypes. Men in this country are far less willing to participate in domestic life and women carry an even heavier workload than their GDR counterparts. Contemporary dialogues over work and family life are also suggestive of major cross-national differences in gender attitudes. In Hungary, there is more talk about the negative consequences of women's labour-force participation and there is longer-lasting reminiscence of the days that have passed. While there is some evidence that similar sentiments are also expressed in the GDR, only in Hungary have we observed an emergent (and vocal) neo-conservative side in these public debates.

Greater resistance to changing gender roles in Hungary is undoubtedly due to this country's more traditional past, as well as its weaker legacy of socialist ideas. Unlike the GDR, where traditional stereotypes are beginning to show signs of erosion, in Hungary they continue to withstand the passing of time. Tradition, however, is not wholly accountable for this. Indeed, recent trends in gender relations indicate that the re-emergence of private property, rather than allowing men and women to break with the ways of the past, will render the 'tenacious hold of men' even more difficult to shake off.[78]

To predict the future of socialist gender relations from the evidence that we presented in this paper would be an ambitious task. Our objective was far more modest. Using published documents and the available literature as well as our own research, we wished merely to chronicle the developments thus far, as well as to make some speculative remarks about cross-national trends over the past 40 years. Any attempt to go beyond this simple comparison would require better data and measurements with a greater degree of comparability. We hope, however, that our ideas will encourage further research on women in these societies, so that we may come to a better understanding of the effects of socialist policies on gender relations.

ACKNOWLEDGEMENTS

During the preparation of this manuscript both Rueschemeyer and Szelényi were supported by a grant from the Joint Committee on Eastern Europe of the American Council of Learned Societies and the Social Science Research Council.

NOTES

1. Maxine Molyneux (1981) 'Women in socialist societies', in Kate Young, Carol Wolkowitz, and Roslyn McCullagh (eds) *Of Marriage and the Market*, pp. 61–3, London: Routledge & Kegan Paul; Christel Lane (1983) 'Women in Socialist Society With Special Reference to the German Democratic Republic', *Sociology 17*, 501; see also Barbara Holland (ed.) (1985) *Soviet Sisterhood*, Bloomington: Indiana University Press.

2. Mária Márkus, 'Women and work: emancipation at a dead end', in András Hegedüs, Ágnes Heller, Mária Márkus, and Mihály Vajda (eds), *The Humanisation of Socialism*, 87–8, London: Allison & Busby; see also Hilda Scott (1974), *Does Socialism Liberate Women?* Boston: Beacon Press.

3. Christiane Lemke (1985) 'Women and politics in East Germany', *Socialist Review 15*, 123.

4. Peter C. Ludz and Ursula Ludz (1985) 'Bevölkerung', in *DDR Handbuch*, 217–18, Wissenschaftliche Leitung: Hartmut Zimmer-

mann, under Mitarbeit von Horst Ulrich and Michael Fehlauer, Koln: Verlag Wissenscheft und Politik.

5. Marilyn Rueschemeyer, 'New towns in the German Democratic Republic', in Marily Rueschemeyer and Christiane Lemke (eds) *The Quality of Life in the German Democratic Republic: Changes and Developments in a State Socialist Society*, New York: M.E. Sharpe (forthcoming).

6. Jutta Gysi and Wulfram Speigner (1983) *Changes in the Life Patterns of Families in the German Democratic Republic*, 38, Berlin: Academy of Sciences of the GDR, Institute of Sociology and Social Policy.

7. Ibid., 48.

8. Marilyn Rueschemeyer (1981) *Professional Work and Marriage: An East–West Comparison*, 134, London: Macmillan.

9. Katalin Koncz, (1984) 'A Nök Foglalkoztatásának Demográfiai, Gazdasági Körülményei Magyarországon az Ipari Forradalom Kibontakozásától az Elsö Világháborúig' (Demographic and Economic Conditions of Women's Employment in Hungary from the Beginning of the Industrial Revolution to the First World War), *Demográfia 27* (2–3), 277–8.

10. Walter Connor (1979) *Socialism, Politics and Equality*, 35, New York: Columbia University Press.

11. Ibid., 36.

12. Koncz, *op. cit.* in *Demográfia 27* (2–3), 278.

13. Connor, *Socialism, Politics, and Equality*, 36.

14. Mátyás Unger and Ottó Szabolcs (1979) *Magyarország Története* (The History of Hungary), 359, Budapest: Gondolat.

15. Ibid., 359–60.

16. Albert Simkus (1984) 'Structural Transformation and Social Mobility: Hungary 1938–1973', *American Sociological Review 7* (June), 295.

17. Hungarian Central Statistical Office (1986) *Statisztikai Évkönyv 1985* (Statistical Yearbook 1985), 23, Budapest: Központi Statisztikai Hivatal.

18. Koncz, *op. cit.* in *Demográfia 27* (2–3), 285, 288.

19. Ibid., 288.

20. Ibid., 281–3.

21. Ibid., 289.

22. Julia Turgonyi and Zsuzsa Ferge (1969) *Az Ipari Munkásnök Munkaés Életkörülményei* (The Work- and Life-Situations of Female Industrial Workers), 38, Budapest: Kossuth Könyvkiadó.

23. Koncz, *op. cit.* in *Demográfia 27* (2–3), 283–4.

24. Barnabás Barta, András Klinger, Károly Miltényi, and György Vukovich (1985) 'Hungary' in Valentina Bodrova and Richard Anker (eds) *Working Women in Socialist Countries*, 32, Geneva: International Labour Organisation.

25. Barta *et al.*, 'Hungary', 44–5.

26. Ibid., 42.

27. Irene Dölling, 'Culture and Gender', in Rueschemeyer and Lemki (eds) *The Quality of Life in the German Democratic Republic*.

28. Christel Lane, 'Women in Socialist Society', 492.

29. Ibid., 495.

30. *Statistisches Jahrbuch der DDR 1984*, 109, Berlin: Staatsverlag der Deutschen Demokratischen Republik; see also Gerd Meyer (1986) 'Frauen in den Machthierarchien der DDR', *Deutschland Archiv 3*, 305.

31. Christel Lane, 'Women in Socialist Society', 496.

32. Ibid., 496.

33. Christel Sudau, 'Women in the GDR' (1978) *New German Critique 13*, 71.

34. Meyer, 'Frauen in den Machthierarchien der DDR', 307.

35. Zsuzsa Ferge (1983) 'Változik-e manapság a nők helyzete?' (Have there been Changes Lately in the Position of Women?) in Arpad Olajos (ed.), *Tanulmányok a Nöi Munkáról* (Studies on Women's Work), 233–8 Budapest: Kossuth Könykiadó.

36. This phrase belongs to Harold L. Wilensky; see his 'Women's work: economic growth, ideology, structure', *Industrial Relations 7* (May 1968), 243.

37. Katalin Koncz (1984) 'A Nök Foglalkoztatásának Demográfiai, Gazdasági Körülményei Magyarországon a Két Világháború Alatt' (Demographic and Economic Conditions of Women's Employment in Hungary Between the Two World Wars), *Demográfia 27* (4), 430.

38. Róbert Manchin (1983) 'A Férfi-Nöi Keresetek Külömbségéröl' (On the Difference between Male and Female Earnings), in Árpad Olajos (ed.) *Tanulmányok a Nöi Munkáról*, 170.

39. Tamás Kolosi and Ágnes Bokor (1985) 'A Párttagság és a Társadalmi Rétegzödés' (Party Membership and Social Stratification) in Várnai Gyorgi (ed.), *A Társadalmi Struktura, az Életmód, és a Tudat Alakulása Magyarországon*, 78–9, (The Formation of Social Structure, Life Style, and Knowledge in Hungary), Budapest: MSZMP KB Társadalomtudományi Intézete.

40. Júlia Molnárné Venyige, 'Nök a Vezetésben' (Women in Leadership) in Olajos (ed.) *Tanulmányok a Nöi Munkáról*, 42.

41. Quoted in Christel Sudau, 'Women in the GDR', 72.

42. Christel Lane, 'Women in Socialist society', 500.

43. Marilyn Rueschemeyer (1983) 'Integrating work and personal life: an analysis of three professional work collectives in the German Democratic Republic', *GDR Monitor* (Winter), 33.

44. Hildegard Maria Nickel, 'Gender socialization and relationships as a function of the social division of labor – a sociological explanation for the reproduction of gender differences', in Rueschemeyer and Lemke (eds) *The Quality of Life in the GDR*.

45. Christel Sudau, 'Women in the GDR', 78.

46. Michael Dennis, 'Individual burden – social requirement: human and social aspects of shiftwork in the GDR'. In Rueschemeyer and Lemke (eds) *The Quality of Life in the GDR*.

47. Marilyn Rueschemeyer, 'Integrating Work and Personal Life', 32.

48. Rueschemeyer, *Professional Work and Marriage*.

49. *Statistisches Jahrbuch der DDR 1984*, 369 and 345; see also Ludz and Ludz, 'Bevölkerung', 218.

50. Rueschemeyer, 'Integrating Work and Personal Life', 32.

51. Rueschemeyer, *Professional Work and Marriage*, 135–164.

52. Christel Sudau, 'Women in the GDR', 77.

53. *Statistisches Jahrbuch der DDR 1984*, 369.

54. Jutta Gysi (1983) 'Zur Lebensweise der Familie in der DDR', *Demographie Seminar*, Akademie der Wissenschaftern Der DDR, 4.

55. Ibid., 4.

56. Ibid., 3. (Individuals living alone were not included in these 'household' figures.)

57. Christel Lane, 'Women in Socialist Society', 493.

58. See, for example, Marilyn Rueschemeyer, 'Integrating Work and Personal Life', 34.

59. See Ferge, 'Változik-e Manapság a Nök Helyzete?', 251; János Kovács (1985) 'A Nöi foglalkoztatás Perspektívái' (Perspective on women's employment), in Árpád Olajos (ed.), *Tanulmányok a Nöi Munkáról*, 18–19; and Gábor Vági (1985) 'Az Otthoni Munka és a Szolgáltatások Kapcsolata – Fejlödési Tendenciák' (The Relationship Between Domestic Work and Social Supports-Developmental Tendencies), in Katalin Koncz (ed.) *Nök és Férfiak* (Women and Men), 226–31, Budapest: Kossuth Könyvkiadó.

60. J. Tímár (1983) 'Problems of Full Employment', *Acta Oeconomica 31* (3–4) 220.

61. Ágnes Heller and Mihály Vajda, 'Communism and the Family', in András Hegedüs *et al.*, (eds), *The Humanisation of Socialism*, 7–17; see also Mária Márkus, 'Women and Work: Emancipation at a Dead End', 78.

62. See Dávid Bíró (1982) 'A Teremtés Koronái és a Gyengébb Nem' (The Crowns of Creation and the Weaker Sex), *Valóság 9* (September) 62–70; Löcsei Pál (1985) 'A Nöi Munkavállalás és a Hagyományos Magyar Család' (Women's Employment and the Traditional Hungarian Family), *Kortárs 10*, 86–90.

63. Zsuzsa Ferge (1979) *A Society in the Making*, White Plains, New York: M.E. Sharpe, Inc., 106.

64. Koncz, *Nök és Férfiak*, 270.

65. See Vági, 'Az Otthoni Munka és a Szolgáltatások Kapcsolata', 222; Turgonyi and Ferge, *Az Ipari Munkásnök Munka- és Életkörülményei*, 67; and Zsuzsa Orolin, 'A Nök Foglalkoztatásának Szociálpolitikai Vonatkozásai' (The Social Policy Implications of Women's Employment), in Olajos (ed.) *Tanulmányok a Nöi Munkáról*, 64.

66. Bíró, 'A Teremtés Koronái', 65.

67. Júlia Molnárné Venyige, 'Nöi Muka és a Társadalmi Munkaszervezet' (Women's Work and the Social Organisation of Work), in Koncz (ed.) *Nök es Férfiak*, 187.

68. Lászlo Cseh-Szombathy (1985) *A Háztartási Konfliktusok Szociológiája* (The Sociology of Family Conflicts), 73–5, Gondolat: Budapest.

69. Bíró, 'A Teremtés Koronái', 65.

70. Hungarian Central Statistical Office, *Statisztikai Évköny 1985*, 36 and 40.

71. Péter Galasi (1985) 'Extra income and labor market position' in Péter Galasi and György Sziraczki (eds) *Market and Second Economy in Hungary*, 296, Budapest: Kossuth Könyvkiadó.

72. For an extended review of these, see Robert M. Jenkins, 'Social inequality in the state Socialist division of labor: earnings determination in contemporary Hungary', unpublished doctoral dissertation, University of Wisconsin-Madison, Chapter 2.

73. See Róbert Manchin and Iván Szelényi (1985) 'Theories of family agricultural production in collectivized economies', *Sociologia Ruralis 25* (3–4), 250–51 and 261–62; and David Stark (1986) 'Rethinking internal labor markets: new insights from a comparative perspective', *American Sociological Review 51* (August), 496.

74. Janos Kornai (1985) *Contradictions and Dilemmas*, 100, Budapest: Corvina, 100.

75. Manchin and Szelényi, 'Theories of Family Agricultural Production', 261.

76. Erzsébet Örszigeti (1986) *Asszonyok Férfisorban* (Women in the Role of Men) 99–158, Budapest: Szépirodalmi Könyvkiadó.

77. David Stark, 'Rethinking Internal Labor Markets', 497.

78. This phrase was borrowed from Harold L. Wilensky; see his 'Women's Work', 241.

6

Is the GDR the future of Hungary and the Baltics? Dissent and the Lutheran Church in Eastern Europe

Robert F. Goeckel

My present study cannot claim to be as theoretically insightful as the article to which the title refers, Melvin Croan's analysis of the evolution of stable one-party systems.[1] My purpose is more modest – to investigate to what extent the relationship between the state and the Evangelical Lutheran Church in other Soviet bloc settings resembles that in the GDR. As various studies have shown, the relationship in the GDR has moved from one of confrontation in the 1940s and 1950s to one of increasing co-operation and *rapprochement* in the 1970s and 1980s, symbolized by church–state summits in 1978 and 1985 and marked by the heavy publicity accorded the Luther anniversary in 1983.[2] In this chapter, I inquire whether this political change is unique to the GDR or has occurred in other Communist systems, in particular Hungary and the Baltics, and to offer tentative explanations of empirical differences in the churches' role.

The study focuses on the Lutheran Church in the three systems. The *rapprochement* between the church and state in the GDR has involved primarily the Lutheran church; official relations with the Catholic church have remained cooler. It would appear reasonable to propose that confession plays a role in *rapprochement* with the state and to test this hypothesis by looking at Lutheranism in three different Communist systems.

My analysis further delineates this topic by looking not at church–state relations in general, but rather at the churches' relationships to non-religious dissent. An extremely significant development in the GDR context has been the extent to which the Lutheran church has served as a catalyst and umbrella for non-religious dissent, in a narrow sense. In particular, on the relatively new issues of peace and the environment, the church has articulated independent positions and provided 'free space' for the blossoming of policy-oriented dissent. It would seem reasonable to hypothesize that the church might play a similar role in other settings, to the extent that such issues are the object of dissent.

My analysis indicates that the differences between the role of the Lutheran churches in the three settings outweigh the similarities. Widespread dissent exists in Hungary but is primarily based in the intelligentsia and the youth; the Lutheran Church has abstained from non-religious dissent, as well as public religious dissent, for that matter. In Estonia and Latvia, dissent seems much more limited and centres largely around the nationality question; again the Lutheran church has played little apparent role, particularly in Latvia. The differences between the role of the church in the systems, I argue, are related to differences in theology, in institutional autonomy of the churches, in internal democracy in the churches, in political significance to the respective regime of the church, and the experience of Stalinism.

The 'GDR model', which will serve as the basis for comparison, is one that has developed only in recent years. Prior to the organizational separation of the East German churches from the West German churches in 1969, the relationship with the state tended to be dominated by the unresolved German question. Particularly in the 1960s, the still all-German church organizations occasioned considerable conflict in the relationship. The organizational independence from the West German churches served as a precondition for the *rapprochement* which has developed in the 1970s. The church has increasingly articulated a position as a 'church within socialism' and the state has responded by curtailing atheistic propaganda and making concessions to the churches' institutional interests. Despite the continuing problems posed by discrimination of individual Christians by the ideological state and the activist role *vis-à-vis* non-religious dissent, the church now enjoys a relatively harmonious relationship with the state. The Hungarian church, to which I shall turn first, also enjoys harmonious relations with the state, yet seemingly at the expense of a voice in dissent.

HUNGARY

For the most part, the 'social contract' propounded by Kádár since 1956 has brought about social quiescence in Hungary.[3] The massive emigration of opponents of the regime in 1956, combined with repression coincident with the restoration of communist control, produced a disillusioned and depoliticized populace, eventually willing to co-operate with the regime in exchange for the material benefits to be had from Kádár's 'goulasch communism'. Kádár's slogan – 'those who are not against us, are for us' – provided the basis for a minimal consensus through the 1960s and much of the 1970s. The churches have also joined in this consensus. They have enjoyed liberal treatment under Kádár, although the abdication of Cardinal Mindszenty in 1974 was an important prerequisite in the case of the Catholics. Anti-religious propaganda has been reduced to a minimum and church institutional interests protected. Kádár has particularly courted the small Lutheran church.

In recent years, however, Kádár's societal consensus has frayed, if not eroded, and new sources of dissent have arisen, casting doubt on the future of Kádárism. In marked contrast to the GDR, however, the Lutheran church has played a peripheral role in this new dissent. It has avoided direct support of this non-religious dissent and disciplined those church leaders critical of the state. Nor has it played an indirect role in terms of serving as an umbrella for non-religious dissent; the new dissenters have chosen other vehicles for expressing their opposition. Indeed, as will be seen, the church has acted increasingly as a pillar of support for the regime.

The increasing dissent takes various forms. Ironically, one of the more serious forms, given the history of dissent and political stability in the Soviet bloc, is dissent on economic issues. After producing remarkable results for several years after its introduction in 1968, the Hungarian model has encountered increasing difficulties in the 1980s.[4] The increased reliance on material incentives has produced larger income differences, leading some to question whether these are consistent with the goals of socialism. Moreover, the economic reforms have left some social groups behind, in particular the aged and young married couples. Their pensions and salaries have not kept pace with price increases which have resulted from increasing consumer demand. To compensate, increasing numbers of pensioners have resorted to employment after retirement; young couples are reluctant to have children, contributing to an alarming stagnation, even decline, in the population. The crass materialism has also produced undesirable side-effects, such as corruption. Corruption is certainly not unique to Hungary; indeed one could argue that it is more widespread in the more orthodox centrally planned economies. However, the manifestations of successful corruption are more extreme and potentially destabilizing in a society that offers greater opportunities for conspicuous consumption, as in Hungary. Finally workers have been increasingly anxious regarding the issues of job security in enterprises which prove less competitive than others. These various negative effects of the economic reform have been compounded by the poor international economic climate of the 1980s, which inordinately affects an economy as dependent on foreign trade as Hungary. These concerns have not remained merely latent, but have manifested themselves in increasing criticism and debate within the party and state bodies. The 1985 congress of the Hungarian Socialist Workers Party (HWSP) saw official admission of numerous economic problems and, more importantly, intense debate and criticism by the delegates. Similarly, at the trade union congress in 1986, delegates expressed concern regarding the enterprise councils proposed by the government and demanded that job guarantees be provided.[5] Although this criticism has occurred primarily within official organizations and been contained by them, the formation of an unofficial organization to advocate the interests of the poor – Foundation for Assistance to the Poor – bodes ill for the regime's attempt to confine this dissent to official forums.[6]

Another source of increasing dissent, perhaps more aptly labelled disaffection, is youth alienation. Hungary has exhibited social problems common to advanced industrial societies in both East and West. However, the *extent* of the problems, as well as the greater official openness regarding them, has contributed to a sense of social crisis. This alienation manifests itself in various ways – the widespread abuse of alcohol and incidence of alcoholism, the high suicide rate, the high divorce rate, and the low birth rate. These social problems are by no means new to Hungary, nor is Hungary unique in the Soviet bloc in expressing them. However, in recent times, the regime has been forced to admit that it also faces an incipient drug problem, a social problem long held to affect only the West. Oppositional figures blame this deterioration in the country's social and moral health on the 'quasiculture' inflicted on

113

Hungary since 1956, a culture of a 'defeatist, agonizing, self-exploiting, and neurotic society' which had left nihilism as the major current of Hungarian life.[7] Such dissidents see a remedy to this malaise in the small core of intellectuals which might promote 'self-development' among open-minded youth. A further symptom of youth alienation, as well as a response to it, is the increasing interest of youth in religion. The state acknowledges this renewed interest, but ascribes it to the natural curiosity of youth regarding those things which are unknown to them.[8]

A third dimension of dissent involves political and nationalist dissent.[9] Those advocating political change in the regime focus on the issues of democratization of the political process and respect for human rights. Centring on such prominent intellectuals as Lazlo Rajk and Andrus Hegedus, the democratic opposition has argued that economic liberalization must be extended to the political realm as well. It has tended to use *samizdat* as the primary means of expressing its dissent, avoiding more open demonstrations of protest. Recently, however, they have allied at international forums, such as UNESCO meetings, with those supporting the cultural rights of minority Hungarians in Romania, Czechoslovakia, and the USSR. This nationalist dissent protests against the systematic campaign against Hungarian language and culture, particularly in Romania, and the strictures placed on travel and contacts with the minorities. It alleges that in seeking to avoid tension with its socialist neighbours, Hungary's diplomatic approach has actually facilitated a deterioration of the situation of the minority Hungarians. Sandor Csoori, a leading nationalist dissenter, calls on Hungary to expose the situation to the world community.

In recent years Hungary has also seen an increase in dissent over the issue of the environment. Unlike the GDR, in which the environmental dissent has grown almost exclusively within the context of the church, in Hungary this movement has developed outside traditional institutions. Known as the Danube Circle, the environmental movement was formed in 1983 and collected 10,000 signatures in opposition to the hydro-electric power project to be built jointly by Hungary and Czechoslovakia on the Danube River.[10] They charge that the dam would pollute drinking water, would be vulnerable to earthquakes, would be too expensive to construct, and would cede territory to Czechoslovakia as a result of the altered stream-bed. The environmentalists, also known as the 'Blues', have established contacts with the 'Greens' in Austria and West Germany and attempted to mobilize the Austrian 'Greens' to block the Austrian banks from providing credits for the dam's construction. The Chernobyl disaster raises questions regarding the safety of nuclear power, but the 'Blues' have not as yet reacted publicly.[11]

Finally, Hungary has experienced dissent focusing on questions of peace and militarization. In 1981, students at the University of Budapest formed Dialog, an autonomous non-official peace group which planned to hold a march on behalf of multilateral disarmament.[12] Its goals were to provide a balanced criticism of the arms race and militarization in East and West. Contacts with Western peace groups were initiated, as well as with the GDR churches. Dialog failed to gain the popular support which these other groups enjoyed, and disbanded in 1984. The leaders of the movement explained its failure as the result of the dominance of economic issues in the public debate and the public's scepticism regarding peace due to the regime's propagandistic use of the term. Some continue to register their dissent by refusing to serve in the military, serving 30–36 months in prison instead.[13]

Given this wide spectrum of dissent in Hungary and the ideological conflict between Marxism–Leninism and religion, one would expect the Lutheran Church also to play a role as dissenter. Indeed, the relatively liberal policy of the regime towards dissent, and the fact that contacts among the various groupings seem to be increasing, would seem to suggest co-operation between the church and other forms of dissent, as one finds in the GDR. Such has not been the case. The Lutheran church, indeed all churches in Hungary, have experienced very little dissent internally in this period of the late 1970s/early 1980s. To the extent that dissent has developed in the churches, it has occurred in the Catholic church in the form of so-called 'basis communities' similar to the grass-roots Catholic groups in Latin America.[14] These groups have sprouted up, to a certain extent, in opposition to the Catholic hierarchy which they perceive as too accommodationist toward the regime. They have challenged the church doctrinally and politically, in particular on the issue of militarization and peace. Some 'basis communities' have advocated pacifism and conscientious objection to military service. Rome and the Hungarian church leadership have disciplined certain priests involved in the movement and reined it in.

Apart from this nominal Catholic dissent, however, the absence of dissent in the Lutheran church and ties to the various dissent groupings is striking. The various groups tend to be composed of intellectuals; church or religious leaders have not been involved. Nor is there evidence that the church has provided organizational assistance (meeting locations, etc.). When the state responds with repression against dissenters (for example, administrative measures and force against the peace and environmental movements, or arrests, jailings, and house searches of political dissenters) the church does not appear to intercede publicly or privately on their behalf. For instance, the introduction of labour camps to 'rehabilitate' so-called labour 'shirkers' met with no apparent protest from the church. Indeed it remained for the secular *samizdat* publication *Beszelo* to argue for the rights of those 'on the fringe of society'.[15] Unlike in the GDR, in Hungary the secular dissenters are more likely to intercede on behalf of religious liberty for the churches than vice versa.

In fact, under the leadership of the recently-deceased Archbishop Zoltan Kaldy, the Lutheran church has co-operated quite closely with the regime since 1958.[16] Kaldy replaced the deposed Bishop Lajos Ordass in that year as the leading figure in the Hungarian Lutheran church. Unlike Ordass, who resisted the state's confiscation of church schools and its attempts to control church appointments, Kaldy co-operated with the state on these matters. Kaldy was very active in state bodies, such as the parliament, the Peoples Patriotic Front, and the National Peace Council.

Moreover, to justify this co-operation with the Marxist state, he articulated a theological position known as *diakonia* theology, or theology of service. Despite his early pietistic Lutheran position favouring distance from the state and political affairs, Kaldy adopted a position favouring *diakonia*, 'Service to those endeavours which struggle for the attainment of peace and happiness of mankind', based on the love of God for mankind. He pursued the 'purification of the theology of the church from those non-theological elements which want to bind the axle of the church's wagon to political reaction'. Like certain groups in the GDR church, Kaldy criticized the church's historically privileged status and greeted the secularizing tendencies of socialism.

According to Kaldy, the 'contemporary Hungarian Lutheran regards the present-day Hungarian state authority as a servant of God'. Thus the church cannot be neutral between socialism and capitalism, but stands on the side of socialism as 'a morally higher and more pure social order'. In practice this was reflected in Kaldy's strong support for the state's official peace policy and opposition to 'endeavours directed by the United States towards world domination'. He viewed Third World problems as resulting from neo-colonialism by the West. In domestic matters this 'service theology' has focused on moral issues, such as support for the family, on which traditional views of the church coincide with the views of the state. Quite in contrast to the GDR church – which in its formula of 'church within socialism' has sought to exercise 'critical solidarity' with the regime and yet also gives support for those 'on the edge of society' – the Hungarian church has assumed a position of 'church for socialism'.

This 'theology of service' has encountered some opposition, both within the church as well as abroad. However, Kaldy ensconced it in the constitution of the church. The commitment to this theology is thus binding on pastors, who are subject to discipline by the church authorities. In 1984 in a letter to the General Assembly of the Lutheran World Federation (LWF) meeting in Budapest, Pastor Zoltan Doka criticized the theology of service as yielding a 'servile church' and attacked Kaldy's autocratic methods. Kaldy's attempt to remove Doka from his position for this breach of discipline was checked only as a result of the glare of international publicity surrounding the assembly and Kaldy's election as head of the LWF. Criticism of Kaldy as overly conformist to the regime has likewise arisen in international circles, resulting in not inconsiderable opposition to his election as president of the LWF. The stifling of discussion of church affairs strikes many as un-Lutheran. Various GDR church leaders have indicated that they see little in the political *diakonia* in the Hungarian model which they would imitate in the GDR.[17] None the less, the LWF's desire to gain greater access to the Eastern European churches has led to a dampening of foreign criticism of Kaldy's policy.

The co-operative policy of the churches, Catholic and Reformed as well as Lutheran, has conditioned and facilitated the state's response to the rising chorus of dissent in recent years. On the one hand, the state has used measured doses of repression to limit the dissenters' activities. House searches and harrassment, selective arrests and jailings, use of force against public expressions of protest, the euphemistic 'administrative measures' have all been employed on a more frequent basis than in the past.[18] Purges of the writer's union and editorial staff of non-conformist journals have also been part of the tool-kit of the regime. Unlike the GDR, Hungary has not been reluctant to crack down on conscientious objectors, meting out sentences of 30–36 months.

On the other hand, the state has also sought to reduce dissent by expanding economic reforms and extending the reform into the political and cultural area.[19] The new 5-year plan calls for greater decentralization of the economic decision-making process and increased use of incentives. The regime has recognized 'the multiplicity of interests' in society and now attempts to integrate them via the official organizations. For example, to heighten attention on low commitment of youth to the system, the emphasis of the party's youth work has shifted to newly-created sub-units of the trade union. Institutions of continued education patterned on the German *Volkshochschule*, closed in the Stalinist period, are being resurrected. The new election law of 1985 mandated competitive elections to the parliament, albeit among candidates required to pledge adherence to the HSWP's programme. Finally, the relatively greater information and openness regarding Chernobyl, as well as the plan to compensate some farmers for lost earnings due to the effects of Chernobyl – Hungary was the only country in the bloc to do so – indicate the regime's attempts to adjust policy in order to defuse discontent.

The state's attempts to defuse dissent have also taken the form of increased support for the institutional churches. In various forums, state spokesmen have lauded the churches' role in Hungary. The state has reassured the churches and Christians that religiousness is not viewed as 'open or covert antisocialism' and greeted the heightened 'curiosity' of the youth about religion. The regime has found that religious people possess 'moral values which encourage participation in the furthering of socialism'.[20] This has resulted in increased publicity for church activities, support for church construction, and permission for increased numbers of publications by the church. The state's forthcomingness was also indicated by its increased receptiveness to international church contacts, as revealed by the first-time meeting of such a large body as the LWF in a Soviet bloc country. Thus the state has recognized the usefulness of the 'serving church' in combating certain social problems. Moreover, it hopes thereby to limit dissent within the church, as well as church ties to other dissenters.

ESTONIA AND LATVIA

The situation in the Baltic republics of the USSR differs quite considerably from that in the GDR and Hungary.[21] After 22 years of independence in the inter-war period, these states fell prey to the Molotov–Ribbentrop agreement of 1939, were occupied by the Soviet Union in June 1940 and then reoccupied by them after the German interregnum. The memories of czarist Russian rule and concomitant 'russification', as well as the relatively high standard of living and freedom of the independence period, caused considerable opposition to Soviet rule, even to the point of armed resistance for several years. In contrast to Eastern Europe, rule by Moscow-based 'russified' factions in the Communist party has continued long after de-Stalinization. Policies aimed at the socialist transformation of the economy and the cultural-ethnic russification of society have continued throughout, albeit somewhat less successfully in Estonia than in Latvia. Despite the relatively high standard of living the two republics enjoy compared with the rest of the USSR, a Kádár-like social contract between regime and populace has been impossible due to the rather obvious manifestations of Russian control of the republican party, state, and economic organizations and the resultant national resentment. In this context, practically all forms of dissent take on national overtones and threaten Russian national control. As a result, such dissent has called forth considerably greater repression than in the GDR and Hungary. The Lutheran churches constitute the major dimension of religious life in both republics, but have been decimated by the emigration during the Second World War and the imprisonment of large numbers of clergy under Soviet rule. More recently, anti-religious campaigns and russification have taken a toll on church strength. This intimidation has left the churches reluctant to engage in dissent or support non-religious dissenters.

Evidence of overt dissent on economic issues has been limited, despite the basis for such dissent. Much of Estonian and Latvian industry is subordinated directly to the control of Moscow ministries. The abandonment of the decentralizing economic policy of Khrushchev resulted in greater integration of the Baltic economies. Despite its relatively productive agricultural sector, the Baltics have been forced to deliver food to other areas of the USSR to compensate for shortfalls of production, resulting in periodic food shortages in the former since the mid-1970s. None the less, dissent on this issue has been rare. In the wake of Solidarity, in 1980–82 several strikes and protests occurred in Estonia, in some cases involving several thousands of people.[22] Protesters demanded improved living conditions as well as political freedom. An attempt to organize a strike movement met with little success, however. More recently, certain state officials have sought limited economic change to deal with consumer dissatisfaction, successfully urging Moscow to allow private enterprise in the service sector. Gorbachev has targeted the Baltics for limited economic reforms.

Youth alienation has also manifested itself, again tending to merge with nationalist dissent. Western cultural influences – for example, punk music and drug addiction – have affected the youth, deriving partly from Estonia's exposure to Finnish television and Finnish 'punk' tourists. During a 1980 demonstration, several thousand school children rampaged through Tallinn, declaring their opposition to the increased use of Russian in the schools.[23] Youth dissent has also been manifested in exit from the system: the number of defectors to the West has increased, including even ranking leaders of the party youth organization.

Cultural and national dissent has been considerably more prevalent, taking the form of public protest and underground samizdat-based organizations. Although the most dramatic mass protests have occurred in Lithuania, where the dissent movement is better organized, Estonia and, to a lesser extent, Latvia have also seen public demonstrations (e.g. in 1972 and 1976 in Estonia, 1977 in Latvia). These have apparently been rather well-organized protests involving workers and youth, not simply the intelligentsia, in marked contrast with dissent in the GDR and Hungary. Samizdat movements, such as the Estonian National Front, have arisen, demanding independence and free elections for Estonia, as well as an end to russification. Regime attempts to crush these movements have been much more intense than in Hungary, but have met with mixed success.

Environmentalism has been an increasing source of dissent in recent times, although it too has tended to spill over into national dissent. Environmental concerns have a strong tradition in Estonia.[24] Several issues have highlighted this dissent in recent times. The construction of a massive new port a Muugu has led to protests to the regime against the environmental damage as well as the importation of large numbers of non-Estonians in order to construct and maintain the port. The opponents have unsuccessfully appealed to Finland in attempts to block the port. Environmentalists have charged that the Soviet nuclear submarine base in Estonia has already polluted drinking water in the area. Finally, the increased exploitation of oil shale and phosphorite in north-east Estonia, in the context of declining Soviet oil production, has aroused considerable opposition. Opponents claim that the mining devastates the land and pollutes the water table. Particularly significant is the fact that the government itself has promoted ecological awareness by: broadcasting radio programmes; objectively reporting the activities of the West German 'Greens' in the press; and discussing the issue rather openly. In 1985 the party went so far as to blame industries under Moscow's control for the phosphorite-related pollution and pleaded with Moscow bureaucracies to limit the damage.

The peace movement in the Baltics has been rather limited in its efforts, tending toward traditional nationalist dissent.[25] An open letter protesting the invasion of Afghanistan was publicized in 1980. In a 1981 letter a number of dissidents urged that a proposed Nordic nuclear weapons-free zone be extended to include the Baltic republics, citing the effects of the Second World War on the 'independent Baltic republics'. In a 1983 letter to the Stockholm conference, the dissidents went even further, decrying the militarization of youth in the Baltics and the repression of the independent peace movement. They demanded the 'decolonization of the Baltics' and protested against the Soviet arms build-up in the region. Arrest of the signers has led to a diminution of peace activity since 1984.

As in Hungary, open expressions of religious dissent in Estonia and Latvia have been few and tended not to involve the Lutheran churches. Dissent has occurred among Baptists, as in other parts of the Soviet Union. Isolated cases of Lutheran pastors who have criticized the regime are also known. In one case, an Estonian minister, Harry Motsnik, spoke out in sermons on behalf of human rights and criticized the Soviet actions in Afghanistan and Poland.[26] His dissent also focused on national concerns, such as the russification campaign and censorship, as well as religious concerns, such as the ban on religious instruction of children. Motsnik blamed the 'world-wide threat of war and our fear for our future . . . on the evil that abides in our laws'. The church hierarchy forced him to resign his position; shortly thereafter he was arrested and later 'recanted' his ideas. As this case demonstrates, the church has shown itself willing to control dissent in its own ranks but unable to protect its own clergy, much less non-religious dissenters from repression. It is not surprising that, as in Hungary, the church hierarchy actively supports Soviet policy, particularly on issues of foreign policy. The heads of both the Estonian and Latvian churches have been active in the official peace movement. The late Bishop Janis Matulis of Latvia indicated that 'it is our duty to support the humanitarian steps taken by the Soviet Union and all peace forces for peace, for the prohibition of disastrous nuclear weapons, and for general and complete disarmanent'.[27] Unlike Hungary, however, the Baltic Lutheran churches have not developed a theology to explain their co-operation with the regime.

The reaction of the state to various forms of dissent, most of which seem to lead to national dissent, contrasts considerably with that of the Hungarian regime. It has relied, for the most party, on heightened repression – increased house searches and interrogations, arrests, detention, and imprisonment. The prison terms have been harsh, usually combined with years of internal exile. Administrative measures have been used to curtail contact with Western influences; changes in republican *komsomol* leadership indicate the party's concern. Rather than make policy adjustments which might defuse nationalist dissent, the russification programme has been intensified (for example, increased emphasis on Russian language in schools and the media). Most importantly for the purposes of this analysis, there is no evidence of an opening to the Lutheran church, such as has occurred in the GDR, and, to a lesser extent, in Hungary. International ecumenical contacts have eased some-what in recent years, particularly with the World Council of

Churches and the Lutheran World Federation. But the regime has not been forthcoming on either the institutional needs of the church (e.g. training of new clergy, increased church publications, etc.) or the treatment of Christians in society.

THE GDR

It is not my purpose in this chapter to discuss either the absolute levels of dissent in the GDR or the relative levels compared with Hungary and Estonia/Latvia.[28] Rather it is my intention to review the role which the Lutheran church has played in the various forms of dissent. My argument is that, with the possible exception of dissent on economic issues, the church has been more active in support of dissent than the Lutheran churches in Hungary or the Baltics, either through direct pronouncements or by serving as a forum and catalyst for non-church dissent.

In the realm of economic policy, the church has become subdued in recent years. During the process of socialist transformation, it was more vocal, supporting the land reform in 1946 but opposing the excesses of collectivization later. During the early Honecker period, it spoke up for the small businesses which were being nationalized. In recent times the church has limited itself to criticizing certain socially question-able side-effects of modern society, for example certain social activists have criticized the consumerism and performance orientation of GDR society. Recently the alleged materialism of those leaving for the West has come under fire. However, these criticisms represent quite modest dissent. Bahro's system-immanent criticism of 'real existing socialism' found no echo in the church. Indeed, the church has often praised the achieve-ments of socialism, for example on the occasion of the thirtieth anniversary of the founding of the GDR. The state earlier rejected the church's claims to 'improve socialism', but has not needed to do so in recent years. The relative success of the GDR's economic strategy has reduced dissent on this issue compared with other Soviet bloc states.[29]

Youth alienation is perhaps even more prevalent in the GDR than Hungary and the Baltics. The church has addressed itself increasingly to the 'growing number of youth who are opting out under pressure to conform to norms, who are individually and socially "homeless" and turn to the church in their search to find personal meaning'.[30] The church recognizes the need for increased 'free space' for youth to develop in an open atmosphere, which would be more 'democratic' than the FDJ. The church has organized 'blues masses' and retreats to attract these youth. This so-called 'open youth work' of the church with problem youth has challenged the traditional conception of the church and church members, leading to conflict within the church. For example, recently the increasingly vocal presence of homosexuals in the church and their demands on the church have caused considerable controversy in the church leadership.[31] Tabooed by society at large, they have turned to the church in their quest for an ersatz for the social respect which society denies them. The 'free space' in the church provides them with the voice they lack in society, but the demands they make on the church (e.g. ordination of homosexuals) cause controversy in and challenge to the church. The state feels threatened by any so-called 'asocial behaviour' – witness the rampage at a rock concert on Alexanderplatz in 1977 – and, despite occasional conflict with the church over its youth work, has tacitly accepted a greater role for the church in dealing with such youth. As a result, social conflicts are played out, writ small, within the church.

In terms of political-cultural dissent, the GDR church in the early post-war period viewed the GDR, and hence the political system, as provisional. By 1958, hoping to limit conflict with the regime, the church pledged to 'respect the development of socialism'. Not until the Berlin Wall sealed the division of Germany, however, did the church begin to formulate its political orientation as a 'church within socialism'. It has gradually yielded its claim to being a 'guardian office' with regard to the state, a role which many veterans of the Nazi period claimed for the church vis-à-vis the totalitarian state. Today the church recognizes the leading role of the Communist party and no longer calls for free elections. However, it has consistently exercised measured political criticism of certain conditions. For example, it has often called for greater freedom of movement, most recently in the context of the massive emigration in 1984–5.[32] It has frequently insisted that the regime provide greater information to its citizens, for example in the context of the Polish crisis, and criticized the censorship of church publications and denial of visas to Western reporters to attend church meetings. The church has often provided a forum for dissident writers and musicians, although the state has at times used pressure to prevent this collaboration.

The church has moved from a position embodying nationalist dissent to its current ambiguous stance. The apocalypse of the Third Reich delegitimized German nationalism in much of German society, including the church. However, as an all-German institution until 1969, the German Lutheran church kept alive hopes of German reunification and restoration of lost territories. The East German church reconciled itself in the 1950s to the loss of the territories east of the Oder–Neisse line and increasingly accepted the division of Germany. On the occasion of the fortieth anniversary of the end of the Second World War, the GDR church, in co-operation with the West German church, called upon Germans to 'not demand the restoration of earlier relationships, which are not be to had, . . . to understand the current borders as, above all, the consequences of the Second World War and to ponder them as the consequences of our guilt'.[33] None the less, the church remains an implicit defender of the German historical and cultural nation, as the above and previous joint statements reveal. The Luther Year demonstrated that the church remains a very important part of a diffuse, yet extant German cultural nation.[34] The regime seems to have accepted the latent 'special relationship' between the two German churches, which had continued despite their organizational separation in 1969.

A novel dimension of dissent in the GDR is the environmental movement. Certainly stimulated in part by the rise of the 'Greens' in the FRG, the environmental movement has nevertheless developed and flourished within the context of the Lutheran church. The church has established its own environmental institute in Wittenberg which conducts studies and holds periodic conferences. The church has instigated actions demonstrative of its concern for environmental deterioration, for example tree-planting projects and foregoing the use of automobiles on certain Sundays. Certain demonstrations of environmental concern have gone beyond the permissible, such as the bicycle protest in Halle in 1983, and occasioned state repression. By and large, however, the environmentalists have avoided sensitive subjects, such as nuclear power, and activities which might engender confrontation with the state. The state's sensitivity to the dissent and the problem is revealed by its discussion with church officials, as well as by its negotiation of regional treaties limiting pollution. However, the response to Chernobyl may test the state's relative tolerance of the environmental movement and the church's role in it. The church leadership called the disaster 'an urgent occasion to rethink again the social responsibility of atomic energy' and asserted diplomatically that 'in our opinion there is no longer reason for an optimistic evaluation of this technology after Chernobyl'. The independent ecology movement was less diplomatic, collecting petitions calling for a national referendum on nuclear power and publicizing information regarding radiation levels.[35]

Perhaps the issue which best demonstrates the church's active role in dissent in recent years is that of peace. It is in fact not a new issue for the church. Major figures in the then all-German church opposed the rearmament of West Germany and its membership in NATO, just as earlier voices were raised in opposition to the permanent quartering of police units in the GDR. The church's efforts were responsible for the creation in 1964 of an alternative to armed military service in the GDR, namely construction brigades whose members are often called *Bausoldaten*. The GDR church has consistently supported equal treatment of those opting for *Bausoldat* status and petitioned the regime on behalf of those 'total resisters' to either form of service. As early as 1965, in a prophetic statement, the GDR church interpreted unarmed service as 'the clearer signal of peace service'.[36] Thus, the dissent on this issue dates from the earliest days following the war.

The issue of peace took on a new urgency in the later 1970s, due to international developments as well as GDR policy. The heightened conflict over the issue of INF modernization threatened the warming relations between the two Germanys. Domestic policies of the GDR contributed to this tension (for example, the introduction of military training in the high schools in 1978 and the heightened legal and party-based restrictions on Western contacts in 1979). The church has itself served as an initiator of peace efforts: the church's support for the Eastern treaties and the Helsinki conference come to mind; the educational programme to counteract the growing militarization, introduced in 1979, is another example.

By the early 1980s, however, the church was overtaken by the rising tide of public opposition to the military build-up.[37] To a certain extent, the church became an umbrella for the peace groups' activities; it lost the initiative to them and often found itself reacting to their initiatives. The Dresden memorial rallies – the 'swords into plowshares' imbroglio, the 'social peace service' proposal (another Dresden initiative, puzzling given the fact that Dresden cannot receive West German television and the presumption that all dissidents live in Prenzlauer Berg!) – all were initiatives of 'basic communities' which confronted the church hierarchy with tough choices. Each time it was forced to make concessions to the state, but managed to demonstrate its autonomy and remain an umbrella for the independent peace movement. In such quasi-institutions as the annual Berlin Peace Workshops and the GDR-wide Ten Days of Peace, the peace movement lives on, despite the discouragement of INF deployment and the emigration to the West.

In the context of the ebb of the unofficial peace movement, the official expressions of the church resume their catalytic role. The church has denounced the 'logic, spirit, and practice of nuclear deterrence' and called for replacing it with a 'security partnership' between the two Germanys, a formulation employed by Honecker and the SPD in recent years. The church has lent its support to proposals such as a nuclear-weapon-free zone in central Europe, and in 1985 it rejected the strategic defence initiatives of the US and the USSR.[38]

Perhaps more significant than these pronouncements on foreign policy issues is the church's support for alternatives to military service as the church continues to tilt toward pacifism.[39] The continued propaganda attacks ('the *Bausoldaten* share nothing of the spirit of peace service') and increased arrests of 'total resisters' in recent months signal the state's sensitivity to this trend.[40] This tilt toward pacifism is likely to be braked somewhat by the new head of the Church Federation, conservative Lutheran Bishop Werner Leich of Thuringia, but the long-term tendency (rooted in generational change in the clergy, and in grass-roots and other church leaders) is likely to remain in force.

A most interesting dimension of the peace issue is the convergence of interest between church and state since late 1983. The much-vaunted attempts at 'damage limitation' by Honecker following the INF deployment were paralleled by attempts by the church to keep the lines of communication open between the two Germanys. As the Soviet–GDR fissures regarding the inter-German *détente* became more open and the Soviets forced the cancellation of Honecker's visit to the FRG, the increase in sympathy and support for him was almost palpable. This was reflected in the church leadership's September 1984 characterization of the relationship with the state as one of 'basic trust'. Speaking for the church, Bishop Hempel gave the state a vote of confidence during his summit with Honecker in February 1985, declaring the church's 'readiness to let all open questions between church and state recede behind the task of maintaining peace'.[41] To be sure, relations have cooled somewhat since then, due largely to the continuing conflicts over the discrimination against Christians in the educational system and in career opportunities, as well as the related issue of dealing with the causes of East Germans' desire to emigrate. None the less, the recent SED–SPD initiatives certainly register approval in the church, indeed even parallel the church's long-standing warm ties to SPD leaders such as Wehner, Brandt, and Rau.

EXPLANATION AND SUMMARY

This study has found that significant levels of dissent exist in all three systems studied, particularly in the GDR and Hungary. However, despite the common confessional heritage of the Lutheran churches in these three settings, the differences among them in terms of the churches' role *vis-à-vis* non-religious dissent outweigh the similarities. In the GDR, the Lutheran church, by its pronouncements and facilitation of dissent, has played a significant role in the increase of dissent. Widespread dissent also exists in Hungary but is based in the intelligentsia and the youth; the Lutheran church has abstained from non-religious dissent, as well as public religious dissent. In the Baltics, dissent is more limited and tends to centre on the nationality question; again the Lutheran churches have played little apparent role, particularly in Latvia.

One possible explanation of these different outcomes might be the obvious differences in the size of the respective Lutheran churches: the small size of the Hungarian and Baltic churches may predispose them to avoid dissent from the political system, in contrast to the larger GDR church. The confessional distribution of the areas under study undeniably varies: Lutherans are the dominant denomination in the GDR and a distant third behind the Catholic and Reformed denominations in Hungary. In Estonia, Lutherans again represent the major denomination; in Latvia they are roughly equal in strength with the Catholic church. All things being equal, a regime will be more solicitous of the larger church than the smaller one.

Yet the empirical evidence of this study suggests that size, while important in the state's calculations, is less important than other factors in explaining the churches' relationship to non-religious dissent. On the basis of size alone, one would expect an activist church in the Estonian case as well, which the study did not find to be the case. Moreover, the case of the predominant, yet relatively passive, Hungarian Catholic church demonstrates that size alone does not explain a church's involvement in non-religious dissent, a conclusion confirmed by the politically-loyal dominant Orthodox churches in Bulgaria and Romania. As Table 6.1 indicates, all the churches under study have experienced drastic declines in church adherence since the onset of Communism. Thus, decline in size does not seem correlated with involvement in dissent either: the decline in adherence has been less severe in the case of the servile Hungarian Lutheran church than in the case of the activist GDR church.

A more adequate explanation of the variation requires that several additional factors be considered. First, differences in theology have led the GDR church to be more critical than the others. Despite the common confession, there exists no theological consensus among the churches because historical experience has influenced their theological positions. I would argue that theology is not merely derivative from other interests. It sets the framework for the relationship with the regime. Policies of the church must be legitimized in terms of it, even if taken for other reasons, and this process may constrain the church. The church's theology is strongly influenced by the traditional Lutheran deference to the state, but the experience of the Third Reich has introduced strong elements of Barth and Bonhoeffer into its thought.[42] Their ideas, favouring criticism of secular authority and a conception of 'church for others', have led the church to assume a more dissenting posture. As in Hungary, there has been a stream of thought advocating strict deference to the regime and abandonment of social influence,

Table 6.1. Confessional distribution and institutional strength

	Membership (Adults and Affiliated)	% of Population	Clergy
GDR			
Lutheran (1946)	14,963,000	80.0	5,300
Lutheran (1970)	10,096,077	59.0	4,220
Lutheran (1978)	7,895,000	47.0	4,000
Catholic (1980)	1,344,266	7.8	1,336
Estonia			
Lutheran (1938)	874,000		200
Lutheran (1980)	300,000	22.0	
Lutheran (1984)	250,000	18.0	125
Russian Orthodox (1980)	200,000	14.7	
Catholic (1980)	2,500	0.2	2
Latvia			
Lutheran (1941)	1,000,000		288
Lutheran (1970)	350,000	14.8	100
Lutheran (1980)	350,000	14.8	100
Russian Orthodox (1980)	500,000	21.0	
Catholic (1980)	260,000	11.0	134
Hungary			
Lutheran (1945)	450,000		430
Lutheran (1980)	450,000	4.4	
Lutheran (1982)	400,000	4.0	400
Catholic (1980)	6,124,328	59.0	3,678
Reformed (1980)	1,950,000	19.0	1,650

Sources:
GDR: Henkys, pp. 424, 449; Alfred Reinhold, 'Jeder dritte Mitteldeutsche ohne Konfession', *Deutschland Archiv* v. 2, n. 10 (October 1969), p. 1119.
Estonia and Latvia: Salo, in Parming and Jarvasoo, 209–10; Duin, 115.
Hungary: Kurt Hutten (1967) *Iron Curtain Christians*, 119–200 Minneapolis: Augsburg, 1967; Beeson 263.
Non-Lutheran Denominations: David B. Barrett (ed.) (1982), *World Christian Encyclopedia*, Oxford: Oxford University Press, 695–96, 313, 367.

as part of a radical interpretation of Luther's 'two kingdoms' doctrine; however, it has always remained a distinctly isolated and compromised minority. In Hungary, on the other hand, this radical interpretation has been in the ascendant – perhaps in part because the church's experiences with fascism was less searing – and in the form of Káldy's 'theology of service' has made the church more pliable to the state's wishes and less likely to advocate unpopular causes. The Baltic churches seem to have little theological profile; survival seems to have supplanted theology in their concerns.

A second factor in explaining the differences is the level of institutional autonomy.[43] Along several dimensions, the GDR church enjoys greater autonomy than its brethren in Hungary and the Baltics. In terms of financial strength the churches vary considerably. All four have been weakened by loss of members and the church tax; all receive subventions from the state. However, the dependence in the GDR is less – it depends on the state for only about 10 per cent of its expenses, is able to hold street collections twice yearly and receives over DM 100 million yearly from the West German churches. The Hungarian church receives only 1–2 million dollars yearly from Western churches and receives large subventions from the state. The salaries of Baltic church leaders are paid by the state and the rents on church buildings (now state property) place a heavy burden on the church. In terms of the replacement of clergy, again all churches now face chronic shortages of pastors. However, the training of clergy at five state universities and three theological institutes seems to give the GDR church an advantage over Hungary (one theological institute) and the Baltics (one institute and correspondence courses, each with enrolment limited by the state). In addition, the loss of over half the clergy via emigration and deportation during the war left the Baltic churches already in a crisis in the 1940s. Finally, the autonomy in decision-making of the church is greater in the GDR. The regime lobbies the church leaders and elected synod members, but has never exacted loyalty pledges from clergy or prevented the election of church officials. Hungary and the Baltics, on the other hand, saw considerable political interference in the churches in the 1940s and 1950s, which continues to compromise the churches' credibility in the 1980s. The state exacts a loyalty pledge from clergy in Hungary and insists on 'consultation' privileges in selection of church leaders; in the Baltics, state authorities appear to exercise control within the church administration.

The churches appear to differ in their levels of internal church democracy, an extremely important precondition for receptiveness toward non-religious dissent. Hungarian clergy are bound to uphold the 'theology of service' and risk disciplinary action by the church hierarchy if they criticize this, as the case of a dissident who appealed to the LWF in 1984 illustrates. In both the Baltic and Hungarian cases, the bishops have attained considerable clout, overshadowing the elected synod. In the GDR, dissent is facilitated by the extent to which the grass-roots laity in the various regional churches is able to articulate varying viewpoints. Clergy have been disciplined by church administrators, but they are more likely to incur discipline as a result of an unorthodox lifestyle than divergent theological, or even political views. As a result, the synodal element remains strong and church leaderships are under considerable pressure to respond to the often more critical views of the grass roots.

The fourth factor that explains the divergent responses to dissent is the political significance of the church to the respective regime. A regime in which the church is more significant in achieving its goals of foreign policy and domestic stability is more likely to tolerate church-based dissent. The national factor, for example, places the GDR church in a more advantageous position than the other churches. Its implicit role as a manifestation of the German cultural nation redounds to its benefit in the context of Honecker's overtures to the FRG and attempts to anchor the GDR in the historical tradition of Prussia. In the Baltics, on the other hand, the national factor seems to work to the disadvantage of the churches. Notwithstanding the dominant influence of the Germans prior to 1918, the identification of the Estonian and Latvian churches with their respective nations paralyses the churches, since any form of dissent inevitably is seen by regime and dissenter alike as part of a drive for national autonomy. The national factor has little effect in the Hungarian case, since the Lutherans are a minority not identified with a national movement and, moreover, are of less use to the state's foreign policy than the GDR church and of less threat to the state's foreign policy than the Baltic churches.

The international ties of the respective churches are significant to the regime in another sense: greater ties to the West bring greater exposure and increase the costs involved in limiting the churches' role. The close ties of the GDR churches to those of West Germany, to the World Council of Churches, and to the Lutheran World Federation, make it prudent for the state to tolerate greater church dissent than in Hungary and the Baltics, with their relatively more limited contacts with international organizations. Attempts by the LWF to increase contact with the Baltic Lutherans and the so-called Volga German Lutherans have met with mixed success.

Finally, the varying historical experiences with Stalinism in the several countries have had differential impact on the churches' involvement in dissent.[44] The Stalinization process in the Baltics and Hungary was certainly more extreme than in the GDR. The Baltic experience of mass deportations and crushing of opposition and the Hungarian experience of rapid collectiviz-ation, purges and show trials both contrast with the Stalinization process in the GDR, which was characterized by a slower tempo and fewer excesses. Thus the church's role was reduced less dramatically in the GDR than in Hungary and the Baltics. The compromises which the churches in these latter systems were forced to make in order to survive cost them a good deal of their credibility. As a result, societal dissent in them tends to be articulated through secular channels rather than in the church. Because it was not forced to pay this price during the Stalinist period, the GDR church retains more autonomy and credibility with non-religious dissenters today.

My research on the role of the church in dissent leads to the tentative conclusion that, despite the common confessional heritage, the differences between the GDR, Hungarian, and Baltic Lutheran churches considerably outweigh the similarities. The greater role of the GDR Lutheran church as a catalyst and umbrella for various forms of dissent, such as youth alienation, national-cultural dissent, environmental dissent, and dissent on the peace issue, can be explained on the basis of differences of theology, institutional autonomy, internal church democracy, political significance to the regime, and historical experience with Stalinism. Although the GDR church has sought increased contacts with other churches in the Soviet bloc, the GDR 'model' of church–state relations, entailing an activist role *vis-à-vis* non-religious dissent, has not been emulated by Lutheran churches in other East European systems.

NOTES

1. Melvin Croan (1970) 'Is Mexico the Future of Eastern Europe?',

in Samuel P. Huntington and Clement H. Moore (eds) *Authoritarian Politics in Modern Society*, New York: Basic Books.

2. The standard sources in this area remain: Reinhard Henkys (1982) (ed.), *Die Evangelischen Kirchen in der DDR*, Munich: Chr. Kaiser Verlag; Hartmut Zimmermann (1985) (ed.), *DDR-Handbuch*, 720–6 Cologne: Verlag Wissenschaft und Politik; Horst Daehn (1982) *Konfrontation oder Kooperation? Das Verhältnis von Staat und Kirche in der SBZ/DDR 1945–1980*, Opladen: Westdeutscher Verlag. See also Robert F. Goeckel, 'Church and society in the GDR: historical legacies and "mature socialism"', in Marilyn Rueschemeyer (ed.), *The Quality of Life in the German Democratic Republic*, Armonk, N.Y.: M.E. Sharpe (forthcoming).

3. See Bennett Kovrig (1979) *Communism in Hungary: From Kun to Kadar*, Stanford: Hoover Institute Press.

4. *Radio Free Europe Research* (hereafter *RFE*), BR/60, 24 April 1986, 1–6; Rudolf Tökes (1984) 'Hungarian reform imperatives', *Problems of Communism 33*, (5), (Sept.–Oct.), 1–23.

5. *RFE*, SR/5 Hungary, 27 April 1985; *RFE*, SR/3, 25 February 1986, 3–7.

6. For a discussion of the ideas of various opposition groups at a recent round table, see *RFE*, BR/24 Hungary, 13 February 1986, 1–12.

7. Ibid., 2–3.

8. *RFE*, SR/2 Hungary, 6 February 1984, 22–3.

9. *RFE*, BR/24 Hungary, 13 February 1986, 7–11.

10. *RFE*, SR/11 Hungary, 14 October 1985, 23–5; *RFE*, BR/96, 11 July 1986, 1–14.

11. *RFE*, BR/72 Hungary, 30 May 1986. *RFE*, BR/74 Hungary, 27 May 1986.

12. B. Welling Hall (1986) 'The Church and the Independent Peace Movement in Eastern Europe', *Journal of Peace Research 23*, (2), 197–201; Ferenc Koeszegi and Istvan Szent-Ivanyi (1982) 'A struggle around an idea: the peace movement in Hungary', *New Society 21* and *28* (October), 115–8, 163–4.

13. *RFE*, SR/7, Hungary, 1 June 1984, 27.

14. Trevor Beeson (1982) *Discretion and Valour*, 285–6, Philadelphia: Fortress.

15. *RFE*, SR/12, Hungary, 8 November 1985, 9–16.

16. The following discussion of Bishop Kaldy is based on J.V. Eiber (1985) 'Zoltan Kaldy: a new way for the church within Socialism?', *Religion in Communist Lands 13*, (1), (Spring 1985), 33–47, 98–106.

17. *RFE*, SR/9 Hungary, 20 July 1984, 4–7; *RFE*, SR/10, Hungary, 13 September 1984, 18–20. Opposition to Kaldy developed primarily among West German and American Lutherans, but the East Germans were also less than overwhelming in their support. Opposition to Kaldy among Hungarian Lutherans also was manifested in the wake of the dispute. The debate between the East Germans and the Hungarians over the proper role for the church in socialism is an old one. See leading East German theologian Heino Falcke, 'Place of the two kingdoms doctrine in the life of the evangelical churches in the GDR',

versus Zoltan Kaldy, 'Jesus Christ, Lord and Servant', *Lutheran World 24*, (no. 1, 1977), 23–31, 12–21.

18. *RFE*, SR/3, Hungary, 8 March 1985, 9–15.

19. *RFE*, SR/12, Hungary, 8 November 1985, 17–22 on continuing education; *RFE*, SR/1, Hungary, 3 January 1986, 35–9 on trade unions; *RFE*, SR/8, Hungary, 21 June 1985, 1–19 on the new election law; *RFE*, BR/73, 23 May 1986, 1–2, on Chernobyl.

20. State Secretary for Church Affairs Imre Miklos, quoted in *RFE*, SR/2, Hungary, 6 February 1984, 23.

21. Alexander R. Alexiev (1983) *Dissent and Nationalism in the Soviet Baltic*, Santa Monica, CA: Rand; Ronald J. Misiunas and Rein Taagepera (1983) *The Baltic States: Years of Dependence, 1940–1980*, Berkeley: California; Tonu Parming and Elmar Jarvesoo (eds) (1978) *A Case Study of a Soviet Republic: The Estonian SSR*, Boulder, CO: Westview.

22. Alexiev, *op. cit.*, 38–42; V. Stanley Vardys (1983) 'Polish echoes in the Baltic', *Problems of Communism 32* (4), July–August, 21–34. Since 1985 the role of private enterprise in the service and agricultural sectors has been promoted in Estonia. *RFE*, BR/148 Eastern Europe, 23 December 1985, 1–12; *RFE* SR/7, Baltic, 27 October 1986, 7–11. Gorbachev travelled to Latvia and Estonia in February 1987 in order to tout their economic performance. See *RFE*, SR/2, Baltic, 20 March 1987, 3–6, 13–15.

23. *RFE*, SR/1, Baltic, 27 January 1986, 5–15, on the youth problem.

24. Estonia was the first Soviet republic to enact laws to protect the environment in 1957 and the first to establish a national park. *RFE*, SR/6, Baltic, 26 July 1985, 9–23.

25. Rein Taagepera (1986) 'Citizens' Peace Movement in the Soviet Baltic Republics', *Journal of Peace Research 23* (2), 183–92.

26. *RFE*, SR/4, Baltic, 23 April 1985, 13–15.

27. Bishop Matulis, quoted in *RFE*, SR/7 Baltic, 6 September 1985, 10.

28. For recent analyses of dissent in the GDR, see Michael Sodaro (1983) 'Limits to dissent in the GDR: cooptation, fragmentation, and repression,' in Jane Leftwich Curry (ed.), *Dissent in Eastern Europe*, 82–116, N.Y.: Praeger; and Pedro Ramet (1984) 'Disaffection and Dissent in the GDR', *World Politics 37* (1) October, 85–111.

29. For a comprehensive review of the GDR's economic perform-ance and analysis of its economic strategy under Honecker, see Thomas A. Baylis (1986) 'Explaining the GDR's economic strategy', *International Organization 40* (2), Spring, 381–420.

30. Church Province of Saxony Report 1980, as cited in Peter Wensierski (1982) 'Evangelische Jugendarbeit in der DDR', in R. Henkys (ed.) *Die Evangelischen Kirchen in der DDR*, 268.

31. For a review of the controversy, see Matthias Hartmann (1985) 'Als abartig verdammt – zur Ordination berufen?' *Kirche im Sozialis-mus 11* (3) June, 111–6.

32. See Heino Falcke (1985) 'Brief an die Pfarrer . . .', *epd Dokumentation, 41a*, 23 September.

33. 'Wort zum Frieden der evangelischen Kirchen in beiden

deutschen Staaten', *Deutschland Archiv 18*, (6), June 1985, 658–60.

34. Robert F. Goeckel (1984) 'The Luther Anniversary in East Germany' *World Politics 37* (1), October, 112–33.

35. On the church's role in the environmental movement, see Hubertus Knabe (1985) 'Gesellschaftlicher Dissens im Wandel. Ökologische Diskussion und Umweltengagement in der DDR', in *Umweltprobleme und Umweltbewusstsein in der DDR*, 169–99, Cologne: Verlag Wissenschaft und Politik. On Chernobyl, see 'Stellungnahme der Konferenz der Kirchenleitungen betrachtens Tschernobyl-Anfragen', vom 8. July 1986, and 'Appell aus der unabhängigen Friedens-und Ökologiebewegung', *epd Dokumentation* no. 33/86 (28 July 1986), 42–8.

36. 'Aus der Handreichung zur Seelsorge an Wehrpflichtige' (1982) in Wolfgang Büscher and Peter Wensierski, (eds) (1982) *Friedensbewegung in der DDR. Texte 1978–1982*, 54, Hattingen: Scandica Verlag.

37. Various analyses of the churches' high profile in the peace movement exist. See Pedro Ramet (1984) 'Church and peace in the GDR', *Problems of Communism 33* (4) July–August, 44–56; Joyce Marie Mushaben (1984) 'Swords into Plowshares', *Studies in Comparative Communism 17*, (2) Summer, 123–35; Ronald D. Asmus (1983) 'Is there a peace movement in the GDR?', *Orbis 27*, Summer, 301–41. For an excellent post-deployment analysis, see Norman Naimark (1985) 'Militarism, pacifism, and the GDR's peace policy', paper presented at Hamilton College conference, 'A New Germany?', April 26–8 1985.

38. 'Bericht der KKL' and 'Beschlüsse der Synode', *epd Dokumentation* no. 43/85, 7 October 1985, 1–19, 43–4.

39. The Church Province of Saxony maintained in 1985 that the arguments against military service increased following the INF deployments. The Saxony (Dresden) Church indicated that it 'respects' armed service, but continues to see the *Bausoldat* option as the 'clearer signal' of peace service. See *Kirche im Sozialismus 11* (2), April 1985, 41; and *11* (6) December, 1985, 273.

40. Carl Ordnung (CDU), cited in *Kirche im Sozialismus 11* (1), February 1985, 39; *Kirche im Sozialismus 12* (1), February 1986, 30.

41. Detlef Urban (1985) 'Spitzengespräch Staat-Kirche', *Deutschland Archiv 18* (3) March 1985, 231–2.

42. Reinhard Stawinski (1982) 'Theologie in der DDR – DDR-Theologie?', in R. Henkys (ed.) *Die Evangelischen Kirchen in der DDR*, 86–126.

43. Regarding institutional strength, sources on the Baltics include Edward C. Duin (1980) 'Soviet Lutheranism after the Second World War', *Religion in Communist Lands 8* (2), 11–18; Wilhelm Kahle (1979) 'Baltic Protestantism', *Religion in Communist Lands 7* (4), 220–5; Vello Salo (1978) 'The Struggle between the State and the Churches', in T. Parming and E. Jarvesoo (eds), *A Case Study of a Soviet Republic*, 194–201. On Hungary see Beeson, *op. cit.*, 256–87.

44. Zbigniew Brzezinski (1967), *The Soviet Bloc*, Cambridge, MA: Harvard University Press.

Comparisons of consumer market disequilibria in Hungary, Poland, Romania, Yugoslavia and the GDR

Irwin L. Collier, Jr. and Manouchehr Mokhtari

In both socialist and capitalist economies one observes the exchange of money for goods and services. However, the role played by money fundamentally differs in these economic systems. Money is virtually synonymous with the power to acquire goods and services or other assets in a capitalist economy. For private households, money matters less in a socialist economy where consumption choices are influenced by pervasive shortage and where non-market processes of distribution play a much larger role. Household choice in socialist economies is typically limited, both by a household's monetary income and a host of other constraints on the quantities of particular goods and services (e.g. formal rationing or empty shelves). Furthermore, non-monetary benefits associated with a job or political position (e.g. connections or privilege) can constitute a very significant addition to a household's real income.[1]

In this chapter we focus on micro-economic disequilibria resulting from quantity constraints on household choice. Our purpose is to contribute to a better understanding of the nature of money in socialism with an empirical comparison of the pattern of shortages experienced by consumers in the German Democratic Republic with that experienced by consumers in Hungary, Poland, Romania and Yugoslavia. In the first section of the chapter we provide an introduction to the methodology of shortage measurement for non-economists. Next we describe the consumer expenditure and price data we have used to calculate our estimates for disequilibrium. The GDR data for the year 1977 were compiled by the Deutsches Institut für Wirtschaftsforschung (DIW) in West Berlin.[2] For Hungary,

Poland, Romania and Yugoslavia, consumer expenditure and price data are taken from Phase III of the International Comparison Project (ICP) for the year 1975.[3] The substantive contribution of the chapter is found in Section 3 where we present and compare our estimates of the extent and pattern of disequilibria in consumer markets for Hungary, Poland, Romania and Yugoslavia with earlier estimates for the GDR.[4] We conclude the chapter with a brief apologia addressed to non-economists, especially those who distrust the application of formal statistical methods to social processes.

AN ELEMENTARY GUIDE TO THE MEASUREMENT OF SHORTAGE

Since the estimates of micro-economic disequilibrium to be presented below have been explicitly derived from an econometric model of consumer behaviour, some understanding of the economic theory behind the estimates is essential in order to assess their strengths and weaknesses for the task of quantifying shortage. In this section we provide the interested reader with a self-contained introduction to the economic interpretation of the structure of consumption expenditure and consumer prices for households facing significant, non-monetary constraints on the quantities of goods and services which they are able to acquire.

We begin by considering the case of a household which consumes only two goods, beer and housing. Possible combinations of beer and housing[5] can be represented geometrically by points plotted on a graph, see Fig. 7.1a where quantities of beer (litres) are measured along the horizontal axis and quantities of housing (square metres) are measured along the vertical axis. The task of consumer theory is to explain the observed structure of household consumption expenditures (i.e. to predict how the pattern of consumption would change as the constraints limiting household choice change). Consumer theory views household choice as the result of the interplay of subjective preferences (tastes) and objective constraints.

Household preferences

In Fig. 7.1a, consumer tastes are represented using the device

Figure 7.1(a) Indifference curve representation of consumer preferences

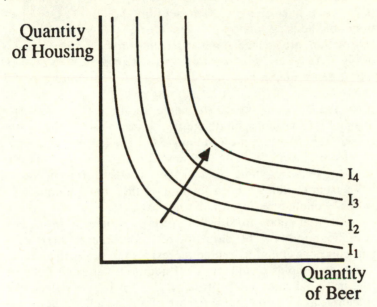

Quantity
of Housing

I_4

I_3

I_2

I_1

Quantity
of Beer

Figure 7.1(b) Budget-constrained choice set of consumers

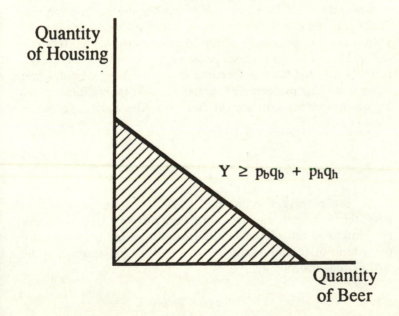

Quantity
of Housing

$Y \geq p_b q_b + p_h q_h$

Quantity
of Beer

of indifference curves which are analogous to the contour lines of a topographic map. The preference map in Fig. 7.1a displays the contour lines of a household's 'utility mountain'. Combinations of housing and beer generating the same level of satisfaction[6] are located along a level line on the preference map of Fig. 7.1a. A household whose tastes are represented by such a preference map is considered to be indifferent among all the combinations of beer and housing which fall along any particular level line, hence the name 'indifference curve'. The assumption that households are utility maximizers means that any household would prefer to move to a higher level of utility, say, from I_2 to I_3. What makes household choice an economic problem is the existence of constraints which prevent households from climbing arbitrarily high on the utility mountain.

The economic reason for the negative slope of indifference curves is that goods are substitutes for each other in producing household utility. The slope of an indifference curve at a particular consumption bundle represents the subjective rate at which households would trade off additional housing for beer (the marginal rate of substitution). The curvature reflects the economic assumption that the more of a good a household has, the more it would be willing to trade in exchange for another good.

Most important for economic analysis is the assumption that tastes (i.e. the contour lines of Fig. 7.1a) are stable. Consumer behaviour can, of course, differ because consumer preferences differ. However, economists generally prefer to leave merely a residual role for taste differences in explanations of consumer behaviour. The preferred candidates for explaining differences in consumer behaviour are differences in the constraints which limit choice.[7]

Budget constraints

In a classic market economy, households are regarded as sovereign economic agents, subject only to a budget constraint (i.e. total consumption expenditures are limited by the wealth or income of the household).[8] The budget constraint may be written algebraically as:

$$Y \geq p_b q_b + p_h q_h,$$

where p_b and p_h are the prices and q_b and q_h are the quantities of beer and housing, respectively. The products of price and quantity – p_bq_b and p_hq_h – are the respective household expenditures for beer and housing. The geometric representation of the budget constraint inequality is found in Fig. 7.1b. The shaded area (plus border) represents the market baskets of beer and housing which are affordable within a budget Y.[9]

The choice set will change as the objective constraints facing the household change. The choice triangle for the household will get larger (greater quantities become affordable) if prices fall and/or if the budget increases. The slope of the top side of the choice triangle represents the (objective) rate in the market for trading housing for a unit of beer.[10]

Unlike a household's preference ordering, the budget constraint (which is determined by the values of Y, p_h and p_b) and the actual consumption bundles (q_h and q_b) are directly observable. These data form the raw material of applied demand analysis.

Household equilibrium (budget constrained)

In Fig. 7.2a, household preferences and the budget constraint have been combined to determine household demands for beer and housing, q_b and q_h. Simple inspection of Fig. 7.2a reveals that household utility will be maximized if the household selects the point where an indifference curve is tangent to its budget constraint.[11] Any other affordable market basket would leave the household on a lower indifference curve. Market demands q_h and q_b are equilibrium choices for the household in the sense that, barring change in the choice set (caused by a change in the total budget or prices) or change in preferences, the household will not change its consumption behaviour from q_h and q_b.

The tangency condition which results from the combination of the utility maximization assumption and the simplicity of the budget constraint provides the crucial link between observed consumer behaviour and unobserved consumer preferences in a market economy. At the equilibrium consumption bundle, the subjective trade-off of housing for beer (the slope of an indifference curve at a point) is equal to the objective trade-off

141

Figure 7.2(a) Consumer's utility maximizing choice for a given budget and prices

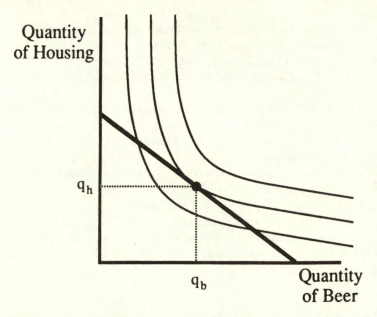

Figure 7.2(b) Observed quantities, budgets and prices. Unobserved indifference curves to be estimated

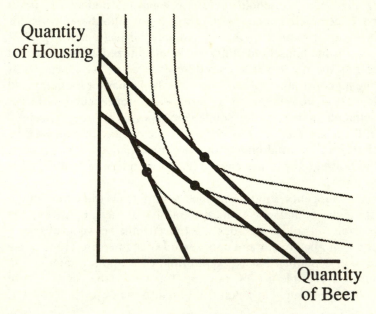

between the two (the slope of the budget constraint which equals the relative price of beer, p_b/p_h).

Applied demand analysis

The basic trick of the applied economist for estimating the contour lines of the unobservable preference ordering in Fig. 7.1a and Fig. 7.2a is to exploit the theoretical insight that the observed budget line will be a linear approximation to the particular indifference curve which passes through an observed consumption bundle. By observing household consumption choices under a variety of price and income situations and employing statistical methods to join the linear 'pieces', in a manner consistent with further assumptions of economic rationality, the empirical economist is able to construct a model of the 'utility mountain'. The purpose of such a model of the preference ordering is to predict which consumption bundle would be chosen for an arbitrary, not yet observed choice set.

Before proceeding to the complications introduced by shortage, we briefly summarize the combination of assumption, observation and inference involved in conventional demand analysis. The three critical assumptions are: utility maximization (i.e. tangency of indifference curve and budget line at the market basket chosen by the household); preferences are stable[12]; and there are no 'unobserved' constraints which affect the choice set (i.e. the choice set looks like Fig. 7.1b). Applied demand analysis can be described as a two-step process: in the first step, one uses observed budget lines (determined by both prices and nominal budgets) and the corresponding consumption bundles chosen by consumers to estimate the unknown indifference map; in the second step, the estimated indifference map is combined with a new budget line to predict the consumption bundle which would be chosen on that budget line (Fig. 7.2a).

Quantity constraints and notional demands

Much of the simplicity of applied demand analysis is lost when quantity constraints become co-determinants of the choice set of households.[13] Consumer sovereignty is diminished. In this case, households are unable to obtain the quantities of certain goods they wish to buy at existing prices. However, they remain sovereign in the limited sense of being free to choose between saving the money which they cannot spend due to shortages or spending more money on those goods which are available.

For the simple two-good example above, let us suppose there is a shortage of housing. In Fig. 7.3a, this is represented by a maximum quantity of housing (H*) which households can obtain. Instead of the entire triangle below the budget line (Fig. 7.1b), the choice set has been reduced to the shaded trapezoid of Fig. 7.3a. What makes H* a binding quantity constraint is that the consumption bundle labelled 'notional demand' lies above the housing constraint H*.[14] Now the highest indifference curve such a household could climb to would be at the corner of the budget and quantity constraints (i.e. where the household is consuming the maximum available housing H* and spending the rest of its budget on beer). The budget and quantity constrained equilibrium is at the consumption bundle in Fig. 7.3a labelled 'actual'.

Unlike the simpler, solely budget-constrained case, there is no tangency between the budget line and the indifference curve at the observed consumption bundle in the quantity-constrained case. The consequence of this lack of tangency for the analysis of the pattern of consumption expenditures is that it is no longer possible to use observations on incomes, prices, and quantities to estimate the unobserved preferences for those economies where quantity constraints are known to be significant.[15] Thus it would appear that the measurement of disequilibrium by comparing notional demands with actual consumption is an impossible task, since the existence of disequilibrium precludes the use of actual consumption expenditures for estimating the indifference curves needed for determining notional demands.

A simple solution to this problem is to seek information on consumer preferences in market economies where quantity constraints may be presumed to be relatively unimportant. In a pioneering paper, the Polish economist Leon Podkaminer 'imported' estimates of the parameters of utility functions for Ireland and Italy to examine disequilibrium in Polish consumer markets.[16] Similarly, one of the authors of this chapter has estimated a demand system for West German households in order to estimate notional demands for quantity-constrained

Figure 7.3(a) Quantity constraint for housing. Actual consumption differs from notional demands

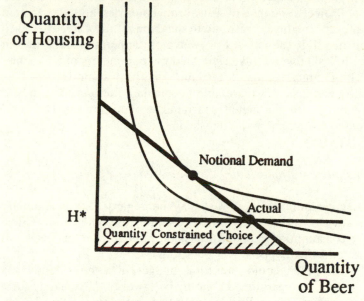

Figure 7.3(b) Effective purchasing power as difference between actual expenditure and minimum expenditure required to remain at same level of utility without quantity constraints

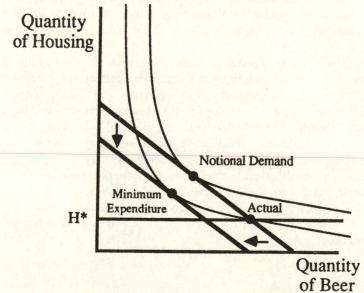

households in the GDR.[17] For this chapter we have reaggregated consumption expenditure data from the International Comparison Project's sample of European countries and the United States to roughly correspond to the expenditure categories used for the GDR estimates. For twelve of the market economies of the ICP sample we have estimated the parameters of a Flexible-Cobb-Douglas demand system.[18] With this model of 'US–European tastes', we are able to calculate notional demands to compare with the actual consumer expenditures in Hungary, Poland, Romania and Yugoslavia.

Quantity constraints and effective purchasing power

Effective purchasing power may be regarded as a summary measure of the extent of microeconomic disequilibrium. Effective consumption expenditure is determined from the answer to the following hypothetical questions:

> How much could the total budget of a household in a quantity-constrained economy be lowered in exchange for a complete elimination of quantity constraints for that household without lowering its utility?

Equivalently,

> What is the most an average East German, Hungarian, Polish, Romanian or Yugoslavian household would pay for the 'bourgeois' right of attaining its notional demands at existing prices?

The lower budget needed to attain the original level of utility in the absence of quantity constraints is defined as effective consumption expenditure. The effective purchasing power (EPP) gap is a summary measure of the extent of microeconomic disequilibrium in consumer markets, defined by Collier as the per cent deviation of effective from nominal consumption expenditure.[19] In Fig. 7.3b this gap can be seen as the difference between the observed budget and a hypothetical budget, which would be the minimum expenditure at existing prices (for a solely budget-constrained household!) required to attain the level of utility associated with the actual quantity-constrained bundle.

THE DATA

International Comparison Project (ICP)

Without a doubt, the most comprehensive collection of consistent price and expenditure data for a large number of countries has been the result of the collaboration between Irving Kravis, Alan Heston, and Robert Summers (University of Pennsylvania) and their associates of the International Comparison Project. From its initial comparison of six countries for Phase I (1967), the ICP has expanded to thirty-four countries in Phase III (1975). Of particular interest for this chapter is the inclusion of Hungary,

Table 7.1. Estimated intermarket spillovers* for Hungary, Poland, Romania and Yugoslavia, 1975

Expenditure category	Hungary	Poland	Romania	Yugoslavia	Sample root mean square percentage error
Food	−6.3	−6.6	−17.0	−22.6	15.6
Beverages and tobacco	47.5	48.2	12.3	16.6	31.7
Clothing	24.1	40.3	50.5	13.7	16.6
Footwear	20.7	14.7	35.2	16.3	24.9
Furniture	38.4	48.5	61.0	62.5	17.7
Appliances	14.8	33.2	32.8	59.2	17.0
Other household expenditures	37.6	31.7	50.8	34.8	30.3
Transportation: equipment	−10.1	−23.2	−45.1	9.5	14.7
Transportation: operation	−90.2	−185.4	−296.3	15.2	10.8
Gross rent	−78.2	−14.6	−5.4	−36.0	20.5
Power and fuel	−5.5	−71.1	−1.3	23.7	20.8
Transportation: purchased	28.3	28.8	56.5	29.7	41.8
Communications	−52.7	−7.5	24.3	−33.7	35.4
All other	−13.0	−27.8	−22.4	−6.3	10.5

* Difference between actual expenditure and estimated desired (notional) expenditure expressed as a percentage of actual expenditure.
Source: Authors' calculations from ICP data in Irving B. Kravis, Alan Heston, and Robert Summers (1982) *World Product and Income: International Comparisons of Real Gross Product*, Baltimore, MD: The John Hopkins University Press.

Poland, Romania and Yugoslavia in the Phase III sample. The ICP was financially supported by the Statistical Office of the United Nations and the World Bank. National statistical authorities and international agencies such as the Statistical Office of the European Communities co-operated with the ICP in the collection, collation, and transmission of the enormous volume of data required for this project.

Per capita gross domestic product for each country of the ICP was broken down into 151 standard categories of expenditure. Consumption expenditures account for 107 of those categories. In order to compare the ICP data with those few available for the GDR we have collapsed the ICP data into the fourteen categories seen in Table 7.1.

The number of individual price comparisons which were used by the ICP research team in Phase III to generate the purchasing power parities (PPP)[20] for the 151 standard categories varied across countries in the sample. At the high end of the spectrum were Austria and Hungary, which provided almost 600 price comparisons for consumer goods, and at the low end Denmark and the UK – with just over 350 consumer prices for the ICP.[21] Enormous efforts were made by the ICP to assure that the price comparisons were made for similar quality goods.

The thirty-four countries of Phase III ICP include many countries from Africa, Asia and Latin America. Rather than attempt to justify using statistics on consumer expenditures and prices in Japan, Sir Lanka, Malaysia and so forth to interpret the structure of consumption expenditure in Eastern Europe, we have limited our sample to the US and European countries of the ICP.[22] Specifically, the ICP data we have used for the estimates of Table 7.1 have been taken from the augmented binary comparisons of fifteen ICP countries (eleven market and four socialist) with Austria.[23]

Deutsches Institut für Wirtschaftsforschung (DIW)

In comparison to the ICP, the effort of the DIW has been much narrower in focus and modest in scale. Until 1981 the collection of comparable consumer price data for East and West Germany by the DIW was largely the result of the work of a single researcher, Charlotte Otto-Arnold. The data for purchasing power parities between the Deutsch mark and the GDR-mark, and the structure of GDR expenditures in 1977, were taken from her 1979 monograph.[24]

Since the DIW is unable to rely on data delivered by a co-operative State Central Administration for Statistics of the GDR,[25] the collection of price data from the GDR consists mostly of scavenging statistical yearbooks, catalogues and press reports. Given the importance of these data for inter-German comparisons, we present a translation of the relevant passage from Otto-Arnold which represents the *sole* published account of DIW price collection procedures:

A systematic observation of GDR prices is not possible. [Published] official price statistics when compared to West Germany's are extraordinarily meagre (85 items). For this reason comparable price data were assembled using a variety of methods:

Officially reported prices have been used [whenever available]. In addition catalogues of the 'Consumer Mail-Order House' for different periods were available from which it was found that prices of identical items as a rule have not changed; furthermore the Winter 1975 catalogue provided a rather complete picture of product assortment and range of qualities available. From the sense of GDR prices acquired from this source, efforts to assemble price information from press reports *and other sources* [our italics] were intensified at the beginning of 1977. For comparison West German prices have been taken from official statistics whenever appropriate, though frequently prices have also been taken from the leading mail-order catalogue of the Federal Republic (Quelle).

(Otto-Arnold, C. (1979) Das Kaufkraftverhältnis zwischen D-Mark und Mark (DDR): 27–8.

While these GDR price data are of somewhat uncertain origin, it is the authors' belief that the individual price comparisons used by DIW researchers are very reliable, since a consumer price check in East Germany is usually no more difficult to arrange than a visit to East Berlin. Prices paid for goods and services by the East German population, unlike prices for producer goods, require no privileged access to special price lists. The PPPs for the year 1977 from Otto-Arnold's study were based upon slightly more than 400 individual price comparisons.

Published data on consumer expenditures are not available at anything like the detail of the 107 consumption categories of the ICP. The GDR Statistical Yearbook only publishes household budget statistics for about fifteen categories of expenditures. The DIW expenditure data for the GDR household budgets are broken down into a few additional categories based on individual studies published by the Institute for Market Research in Leipzig. The price and expenditure data used to estimate 'German' preferences are gathered by the Federal Statistical Office of the FRG: family budgets are gathered and published on a continuing basis, as are indexes of consumer prices. Both the price and expenditure data used for this chapter come from the West German Statistical Yearbook.[26]

Differences between ICP and DIW data

Before proceeding to the empirical results of the next section, it is important to list the major differences between the ICP data set for Hungary, Poland, Romania, and Yugoslavia, and the DIW data set for the GDR.

1. Government subsidies to private consumption expenditure are included in the ICP data but the data for the GDR are valued in actual market prices paid by consumers.
2. The expenditure data for the ICP are for aggregate consumption expenditure expressed on a per capita basis whereas the GDR data and the West German demand system are for households of wage and salary employees only.
3. Medical expenditures are included in the ICP and do not appear to be included in the DIW reconstruction of East German budgets.
4. The item 'Gross Rents' in ICP includes imputed rents for owner-occupied housing and there is almost certainly no such adjustment in GDR expenditures for this item.
5. The expenditure data of the US and European countries in the ICP is of excellent quality (with the likely exception of Romania). Some of the GDR expenditure categories of the DIW are estimated and the matching of West German categories to available East German statistics necessarily involves a large element of judgement.
6. The calculated demand system used for Hungary, Poland,

Romania, and Yugoslavia has the interpretation of average US–Western European tastes (Table 7.1). The demand system used for the GDR was estimated on West German household data, hence average 'German' tastes are the reference for estimates of inter-market spillovers in the GDR (Table 7.2).

Table 7.2. Estimated intermarket spillovers* – all wage/salary employee households GDR 1977

Expenditure category	Percent of actual expenditure
Food	1.1
Tobacco and alcohol	46.4
Outer garments	−17.3
Shoes	14.7
Other textiles	39.9
Furniture	39.8
Electric durables	24.0
Other household goods	−166.3
Motor vehicles and parts	−34.3
Gasoline	38.0
Housing	−274.7
Gas/electricity	−99.0
Public transportation	−42.5
Communications	−92.5
Other goods	58.5
Other services	−26.7

* Difference between actual expenditure and estimated desired expenditure expressed as a percent of actual expenditure.
Source: Calculated from Irwin L. Collier, Jr. (1986) Effective purchasing power in a quantity constrained economy: an estimate for the German Democratic Republic, *Review of Economics and Statistics 68*, February, Table 1.

Because of these differences, we have been careful to separate our empirical findings for Hungary, Poland, Romania, and Yugoslavia from the earlier estimates for the GDR. The temptation to compare all five countries is strong. However, the reader is advised to regard the estimates of Tables 7.1 and 7.2, based on the ICP and DIW data respectively, as a form of scholarly parallel play justified by the early developmental stage of the application of demand analysis to centrally planned economies. While the evidence points to a shortage of housing in all the economies (cf. the rows 'Gross rent' and 'Housing' in Tables 7.1 and 7.2, respectively), we would not wish to assert much confidence in our ability to rank the seriousness of the housing shortage in the four socialist countries of the ICP, much less in comparing those countries with the estimate for the GDR.

INTER-MARKET SPILLOVERS AND EFFECTIVE PURCHASING POWER

In Tables 7.1 and 7.2 we present calculations of inter-market spillovers for the four socialist economies included in the International Comparison Project and the GDR, respectively. The difference between actual expenditure and notional expenditure for particular commodity groups is given as a percentage of actual expenditure. A positive percentage indicates a spillover category of expenditure (i.e. consumers cannot buy some other goods in the quantities they desire so they spend more of their money on such goods) and a negative percentage is a clear indication of a quantity constraint.[27]

For Table 7.1, the underlying US–European demand system was estimated for a Flexible-Cobb-Douglas specification of the direct utility function using the twelve market economies listed in Table 7.3. The last column allows us to assess the significance of the estimated inter-market spillovers. The sample root mean square percentage error[28] given in the last column of Table 7.1 gives information on the accuracy of the fitted values of the individual commodity group expenditures for the solely budget-constrained consumers (by hypothesis) of the US and Western Europe. Wherever the estimated spillover exceeds the root mean square percentage error for the market sample, we have highlighted the number in bold-face type.

The figures in Table 7.1 allow the following conclusions:

1. The pattern of the direction of the spillovers and excess demands (i.e. the numeric signs) in the four countries shows overwhelming agreement. Hungary and Poland show an *identical* pattern of excess demands (−) and spillovers (+). With the exception of the communications category, the same pattern of excess demands and spill-

overs is found in Romania.[29] Given the more decentralized nature of the Yugoslavian economy, we are not surprised to find that Yugoslavia displays differences in three categor-

---

Table 7.3. Estimates of effective purchasing power: Hungary, Poland, Romania and Yugoslavia 1975 (per cent of total consumption expenditure)

Market economies, US and Western Europe

Country	Goodness-of-fit of FCD demand system*
US	2.9
France	0.4
Luxembourg	0.8
West Germany	0.4
Belgium	1.0
Denmark	2.1
Austria	1.9
Great Britain	1.7
Netherlands	1.5
Spain	2.6
Italy	1.1
Ireland	1.6
Average for market economies:	1.4
Standard deviation:	0.7

Socialist Economies, ICP Sample

Country	Effective Purchasing Power Gap
Yugoslavia	3.5
Hungary	4.4
Poland	6.2
Romania	7.0

---

* The parameters of the Flexible-Cobb-Douglas demand system were estimated using data for the market economies of the US and Western Europe. Since by hypothesis, quantity constraints for those market economies are considered insignificant, the 'effective purchasing power gap' calculated for them is more properly regarded a measure of the goodness of fit of the demand system. A perfect fit would be zero percent by this measure. The estimated effective purchasing power gaps for the socialist economies of Eastern Europe given in the table are still large compared to the average goodness-of-fit for the market economies. Data for the calculations are taken from the International Comparison Project as published in Kravis, Heston and Summers.

---

ies: transportation equipment, transportation operation, and fuel and power, which appear to be spillover categories in Yugoslavia but categories of excess demand in Hungary, Poland, and Romania.

2. Contrary to Podkaminer, we fail to find evidence of a spillover from undersupplied non-food to food. Since our calculations involve a finer disaggregation than Podkaminer's, the findings are not directly comparable. None the less, only for Romania and Yugoslavia are the differences between actual and notional expenditure for food large when compared to the calculated root mean square percentage errors.

3. Spillover expenditure appears to fall into the categories of furniture, appliances, other household expenditure,[30] clothing (and possibly beverages and tobacco), footwear, and purchased transportation services.

4. Excess demands appear in transportation operation,[31] the residual category 'other expenditure' (which includes medical care, recreation and education, personal care, and miscellaneous services), and possibly housing (gross rent and fuel and power).[32]

5. The size of the root mean square percentage errors of the demand system estimated for US–European market economies calls for caution in interpretation. Our map of US–European tastes is unfortunately crude.

In Table 7.2 we present estimates of inter-market spillovers for households of wage and salary employees in the GDR for the year 1977.[33] Perhaps the most striking figure in Table 7.2 is the very large excess demand for housing in the GDR which we believe reflects both the very low subsidized rents and a fundamental housing shortage in 1977. Similar to the pattern for the ICP socialist countries seen in Table 7.1, a major spillover expenditure in the GDR is found for the category tobacco and alcohol. Household expenditures on tobacco and alcohol accounted for slightly less than 11 per cent of the average East German wage and salary employee household budget in 1977. It appears to be the case that expenditures for home furnishings and appliances also include a component of spillover demand in the GDR as well as the other four socialist economies.[34] The expenditure on motor vehicles and parts in the GDR is seen in Table 7.2 to be quantity constrained as expected. The spillover expenditure for gasoline is somewhat surprising in light of the measured quantity constraints on motor vehicles; on the other hand, the price of gasoline is quite high. Another category which appears different between Tables 7.1 and 7.2 is the expenditure on public (purchased) transportation. For the ICP countries we find that notional demands are below the observed expenditure for that category but for the GDR it appears that there is an excess demand for public transportation – certainly for foreign travel. In light of the many differences between the ICP data used to generate the estimates of Table 7.1 and the East and West German data used for the estimates reported in Table 7.2, the pattern of excess demands and spillovers in Tables 7.1 and 7.2 are remarkably similar.

Table 7.3 provides estimates of the effective purchasing power gap in the consumer markets of Hungary, Poland, Romania, and Yugoslavia. This gap was determined from the answer to the hypothetical question, 'What per cent of total expenditures would one be willing to pay to be free of quantity constraints at existing prices?'. The EPP gap provides a convenient summary measure of the extent of consumer disequilibrium. At the bottom of Table 7.3 one finds that this measure ranges from a low of 3.5 per cent for Yugoslavia to a high for Romania of 7 per cent.

Are these estimated gaps large or small? These numbers are much larger than those we find in identical calculations of the market economies shown in the top half of Table 7.3. As we mentioned earlier in this chapter, with exact knowledge of preferences and the presumption of no quantity constraints, these gaps should be zero for the US and Western European countries of our sample. Hence these non-zero percentages for the market economies reported in Table 7.3 measure the goodness-of-fit of the demand system. We note that the 3.5 per cent for Yugoslavia is a full three standard deviations greater than the average goodness-of-fit for the market economies. Thus, assuming identical preference for the Eastern European countries of the ICP and the twelve market economies of the sample, we have strong evidence for the existence of quantity constraints in Romania, Poland, Hungary, and Yugoslavia, in that order.

There are two senses in which our estimates of effective purchasing power gaps seem small. From a casual survey of economists familiar with these economies but unfamiliar with the calculations of the authors, the response to the hypothetical question about how much consumers would be willing to pay to avoid quantity constraints was invariably higher than the gaps reported here – more on the order of between a quarter and a fifth of total expenditure. This could be due to the high level of aggregation used in demand studies of this kind. A consumer wants black shoes but there are no black shoes so she buys brown shoes. This would be an instance of a genuine spillover of demand but since it occurs entirely within 'footwear', it would remain unobservable at the level of aggregation used here. None the less, the ordering of the countries by size of the measured gaps does correspond to what one expects *a priori*.

The second sense in which these numbers appear low is in comparison to the gap of 13 per cent estimated for the GDR in 1977.[35] It is not clear which of the several differences (listed at the end of the previous section), between the ICP data and the merged data from the DIW/Federal Statistical Office of West Germany, would account for this large difference. This apparent discrepancy underscores the need for expanding the collection of internationally comparable expenditure and price data along the lines of the International Comparison Project. Where we are fortunate to have a historical series of detailed binary comparisons (such as the DIW purchasing power comparisons of the DM and the East German Mark), it should still be possible to make inter-temporal comparisons of the gap between effective and notional purchasing power for a particular quantity constrained economy.[36]

APOLOGIA

Rather than conclude the chapter with a repetition of our findings, we choose to address the non-economist reader for whom the measurement of excess demands, spillover expenditure, and gaps between effective and notional purchasing power must seem a strange, indeed mysterious, art. The techniques of applied-demand analysis may be counted among the most reliable in the practical economist's box of tools. However, these techniques were specifically developed by economists interested in understanding the normal workings of market economies. It is only very recently that economists have had both the opportunity (because of data availability) and the inclination (a question of grafting technical economic training onto country specialists) to adapt the techniques of applied-demand analysis to the socialist economies. One reason that the concepts presented in this chapter are so unfamiliar to the non-economist is that they are still relatively new for professional economists. The elementary guide to the measurement of shortage was included in this chapter to make this new literature – and more particularly the estimates of this chapter – accessible to non-economist researchers interested in the workings of socialist societies.

The strongest argument for the significance of the estimates presented in this chapter is an analogy with the importance of price indexes for interpreting expenditure data from market economies. The observation that the purchasing power of money changed over time led to the development of the methodology of calculating price indexes. It has become second nature to economist and non-economist alike to use price indexes for the purpose of making cost-of-living adjustments. We have argued above that the constraints which bind households in the socialist economies are 'richer' than the simple budget constraint which limits households in market economies. To interpret changes in the level or structure of consumer expenditures in socialist economies (or market economies under the special circumstances of wartime rationing), it is necessary to adjust expenditures for changes in the price level *and* the differential impact of shortage across expenditure categories. Measuring the cost of living or the standard of living in a shortage economy is a more difficult task than it is in a market economy because the constraints on household choice are more complicated in the former. Just as we would use a price index to quantify the purchasing power of money, we use the estimates of this chapter to quantify the extent and pattern of disequilibrium in consumer markets.

We regard the estimates presented in this chapter as initial returns to a long research programme. While we are confident in the reliability of the data and the appropriateness of the methodology used here, our findings may be fairly characterized as tentative. The growth of knowledge in empirical economics is best viewed as a slow, cumulative growth in which patterns are reproduced under a wide variety of model specifications using a range of independent data sources. Engel's law on the inverse relation between a family's income and the share of its consumption expenditure for food has been established as a durable statistical regularity in this sense as compared to the relatively fragile, naïve Phillips' curve, the inverse relationship between wage inflation and the rate of unemployment. The significance of the numbers in this chapter comes from being among the first of their kind rather than as evidence possessing the conclusiveness of a 'smoking gun'.

ACKNOWLEDGEMENTS

Irwin L. Collier's research was supported by funds from a research grant from the National Council for Soviet and Eastern European Research.

NOTES

1. The importance of shortage in socialist economies is the principal theme which runs through the work of János Kornai. See his *Economics of Shortage*, 2 vols. (1980), Amsterdam: North Holland, and *Growth, Shortage and Efficiency – A Macrodynamic Model of the Socialist Economy* (1982), Oxford: Blackwell. The papers in the volume edited by Christopher Davis and Wojciech Charemza (1988) *Modelling of Disequilibrium and Shortage in Centrally Planned Economies*, London: Chapman and Hall, constitute a valuable collection of current work on the economics of shortage. For the relationship between monetary and real income in the Soviet Union, see the survey by Abram Bergson (1984) 'Income inequality under Soviet Socialism', *Journal of Economic Literature 22*, September, esp. 1057–61, 1089–91. Paul R. Gregory and Janet Kohlhase (1988) have written an interesting paper on the relationship between earnings and privilege based upon Soviet emigrant responses to the Soviet Interview Project (SIP) general questionnaire, 'The earnings of Soviet workers: human capital, loyalty, and privilege', *Review of Economics and Statistics 70*, (February), 23–35.
2. Charlotte Otto-Arnold (1979) *Das Kaufkraftverhältnis zwischen D-Mark und Mark (DDR)*, Deutsches Institut für Wirtschaftsforschung, *Sonderheft* 129, Berlin (West): Duncker & Humblot.
3. Irving B. Kravis, Alan Heston, and Robert Summers (1982) *World Product and Income: International Comparisons of Real Gross Product*, Baltimore, MD: The Johns Hopkins University Press.
4. Irwin L. Collier, Jr. (1986) 'Effective Purchasing Power in a Quantity Constrained Economy: An Estimate for the German Democratic Republic', *Review of Economics and Statistics 68* (February), 24–32.

5. Combinations of goods acquired by households are interchangeably referred to as market baskets or consumption bundles.

6. Also referred to as utility, real income or living standard.

7. Cf. Paul A. Samuelson (1974) 'Analytical Notes on International Real-Income Measures', *Economic Journal 84* (September), 595: '. . . a rich fool is merely a poor fool with more real income'.

8. In this chapter we ignore possible spillovers into additional saving caused by shortages. Such spillovers are a potential macroeconomic problem resulting in an imbalance between disposable income and the aggregate supply of consumer goods. The macroeconomic problem of so-called repressed inflation (too much money chasing too few goods with prices stuck) has dominated the empirical disequilibrium literature (see the papers in Davis and Charemza). Macroeconomic disequilibrium is quite distinct from the problem of whether prices and the structure of consumption are in harmony.

9. Why the choice set happens to be the particular triangle of Figure 7.1b can be seen by considering the vertices of the shaded triangle. The horizontal intercept is what would happen if the household budget were entirely spent on beer ($q_b = Y/p_b$ and $q_h = 0$). Analogously, the vertical intercept would mean that the entire budget would be spent on housing ($q_h = Y/p_h$ and $q_b = 0$). Finally, the empty market basket ($q_b = 0$ and $q_h = 0$) is always affordable. The rest of the triangle represents all possible mixtures of those three extreme, affordable cases.

10. The absolute value of the slope of the budget line is equal to the price of beer divided by the price of housing. This can be seen by rewriting the budget constraint as an equality and dividing both sides of (1) by the price of housing and rearranging to obtain:

$$q_h = \left[\frac{Y}{p_h} \right] - \left[\frac{p_b}{p_h} \right] \cdot q_b$$

where $\left[\dfrac{Y}{p_h} \right]$ is the vertical intercept and $-\left[\dfrac{p_b}{p_h} \right]$ is the slope of the budget constraint drawn in Figure 7.1b.

11. The fact that there is only one such tangency point comes from the presumed curvature of indifference curves.

12. Fortunately the same methodology which we employ below to capture the effect of quantity constraints on consumption patterns can be used to check the appropriateness of assuming similar preferences across the countries of the ICP sample. The similarity of preferences in East and West Germany would seem as safe an assumption as one could ever make in statistical demand analysis. For a critical discussion of the assumption of preference invariability, see Martin C. Spechler (1982) 'Taste Variability is Indisputable', *Forum for Social Economics*, Fall/Winter, 15–30.

13. The term 'quantity constraints' is used in this chapter to denote all forms of non-price rationing, e.g., formal rationing with coupons, allocation by waiting lists, queues, elbows, etc.

14. Notional demand is the term economists use for demand in the absence of quantity constraints.

15. While it is posible to observe such effects of shortage as queues, waiting lists and obtain anecdotal sorts of evidence concerning the existence of coloured markets and waiting times for the delivery of automobiles or obtaining an apartment, quantity constraints themselves will have to be measured indirectly (much as preferences cannot be directly observed).

16. Leon Podkaminer (1982) 'Estimates of the Disequilibria in Poland's consumer markets 1965–1978', *Review of Economics and Statistics 64* (August), 423–31.

17. See the reference in note 4.

18. For the motivation and derivation of the Flexible-Cobb-Douglas specification of a direct utility function, see Collier, *op. cit.*, 25–6. The parameter estimates for the Flexible-Cobb-Douglas demand system used for the GDR are reported in Collier, *op. cit.*, Table 2.

19. The reader is encouraged to make a mental note of his or her *a priori* estimate of this percentage gap for any or all the countries discussed in this chapter to compare with our estimates presented below.

20. Purchasing power parity is defined as 'The number of currency units required to buy goods equivalent to what can be bought with one unit of the currency of the base country . . .' Kravis, Heston and Summers, 383. The base country for the ICP data used in this chapter was Austria.

21. Kravis, Heston and Summers, Table 2.2.

22. We believe the reason that Podkaminer *et al.* were led to the surprising conclusion that 'there is no evidence that the world outside the CPEs [authors' note: Podkaminer *et al.* somewhat idiosyncratically include Yugoslavia among the centrally planned economies (CPEs)] is characterized by a fundamentally different demand structure' was that they included too many countries. See Leon Podkaminer, Renate Finke and Henri Theil, (1984) 'Cross-country demand-systems and centrally planned economies', *Economics Letters 16*, 269–71. Although Podkaminer *et al.* omitted Jamaica and the three African countries of Phase III ICP, it strains the assumption of identical tastes to expect that data from, for example, Syria, Iran, Korea, Thailand, Pakistan, and India will shed much light on microeconomic shortages and demand spillovers in Eastern Europe. The authors are currently examining the sensitivity of the methodology used in this chapter to sample (country) selection and to the degree of expenditure disaggregation (e.g. four categories of expenditure vs. eighteen categories).

23. Expenditure and PPP data used in this chapter were taken from Appendix Tables 7.1 and 7.45 through 7.58 in Kravis, Heston and Summers. The twelve market economies used to estimate the parameters of US-European preferences are listed in Table 7.3 in the text.

24. See the reference in note 2.

25. The DIW is not alone. In 1982 the World Bank contacted the national statistical offices of eight centrally planned economies

requesting co-operation with the Bank's research project directed by Paul Marer on methods for computing the levels and growth rates of the GNPs of those economies. Bulgaria, Hungary, Poland and Romania positively responded to the World Bank's request. The GDR did not respond to the request. See Paul Marer (1985) *Dollar GNPs of the USSR and Eastern Europe*, xii, Baltimore, MD: The Johns Hopkins University Press.

26. Statistisches Bundesamt, *Statistisches Jahrbuch für die Bundesrepublik Deutschland*, Stuttgart and Mainz, FRG: W. Kohlhammer GmbH., 1965–1982.

27. It is possible for a category of consumption to have a spillover of demand from other categories and still be subject to a quantity constraint. Think of a household that would limit cheese purchases to cheddar cheese but is faced with a quantity constraint on cheddar cheese. Some of the excess demand for cheddar cheese could spill over into Swiss cheese purchases. It is possible for supplies of Swiss cheese to be limited, too, so that it cannot absorb all of the excess cheddar cheese demand. Hence an outside observer could observe a spillover into Swiss cheese while the consumer feels that there is simultaneously a shortage of both cheddar and Swiss cheese. Apparently vinegar was one item which was always available for spillover demand in Poland even during 1980–81, see Leon Podkaminer (1988) 'Disequilibrium in Poland's consumer markets: further evidence on intermarket spillovers', *Journal of Comparative Economics*, 12 (March), 43–60.

28. Sample root mean square percentage error is calculated according to the formula:

$$100 \cdot \sqrt{\left(\frac{1}{n}\right) \cdot \sum \left(\frac{(X_i - \hat{X}_i)}{X_i}\right)^2}$$

where X_i and $\hat{X}_i$ are the actual and fitted values for a particular expenditure category in market economy i. For Table 7.1, n = 12, the number of market economies in our sample.

29. We note that our estimate of Romanian spillover demand into the communications category is less than the root mean square percentage error for the market economies.

30. ICP line nos. 67–70 which include household utensils and non-durable household goods together with domestic and household services. For further detail in the description of the ICP categories see Appendix to Chapter 2: 'The ICP classification system' in Kravis, Heston and Summers, 60–64.

31. ICP line nos. 80–83. Tyres, tubes, accessories, automobile repairs, gasoline, oil, grease, parking, and tolls.

32. ICP line nos. 71–77, 90–107.

33. The percentages presented in Table 7.2 have been calculated from the first two columns of Table 1 in Collier, *op. cit.*, 27.

34. The large excess demand for other household goods in the GDR

could indicate a problem in matching East and West German expenditure categories.

35. Collier, *op. cit.*, 30.

36. See Michael Keren (1987) 'Consumer prices in the GDR since 1950: the construction of price indices from purchasing power parities', *Soviet Studies 39*, 247–268, for measures of consumer price inflation in the GDR derived from the historical series of PPP estimates made by the DIW.

8

Enterprise and association in Soviet planning: comparisons with the East German experience

Phillip J. Bryson

INTRODUCTION

The relatively low productivity of socialist enterprises is generally attributed to the centralized economic planning system. An enterprise or production association can be evaluated, of course, only in the context of the particular planning environment in which it must function. The purpose of this chapter is to examine the production unit in that environment in both the USSR and the GDR.

The focus of this chapter will be on the first eighteen months or so of the Gorbachev period (in this chapter, the 'early Gorbachev' period) in which it appeared that he wished to pursue East German achievements with some variant of East German economic strategy. Comparisons between the two countries are difficult, for the GDR has brought its economic mechanism through one nearly complete iteration of plan 'perfecting'. In the early Gorbachev period, the Soviet Union was lagging far behind in its own 'plan-perfecting' process. That projected effort appeared to be inspired in part by East German achievements. Since that time, Gorbachev's experience with 'plan perfecting' convinced him that marginal modification would not achieve the desired results. A dizzying flurry of organizational and legislative activities followed through 1987,[1] which demonstrated clear intent to move toward a level of decentralization beyond anything the GDR had attempted to undertake.

Even before Gorbachev's advent, of course, both Soviet and East German leaders had already been searching for ways to modify traditional planning and production activities in order to improve economic performance. In the Soviet Union, progress had been anything but satisfactory. In contrast, GDR economic performance had seemed to improve in recent years, and East German economic organization had been far more innovative than that of the Soviets. This study will attempt to unveil the differences in the two planning systems up to the end of the early Gorbachev period, attempting to induce a few lessons from Soviet/GDR economic experience.

The first section of this chapter reviews the endeavours of the Soviets to establish a planning/management system that motivates workers and managers and functions with acceptable efficiency. The attempts to achieve this objective are briefly retraced through the reform period, the Brezhnev years, and the subsequent transitional period to the present. The second section compares Soviet 'plan perfecting' (*Sovershenstvovaniye*) with the East German version of the same endeavour (*Vervollkommnung*),[2] both of which will be referred to here as 'planning improvement' (PI). PI's significance lies in the fact that, in the period considered, it was the chosen alternative of both the Soviets and the East Germans to economic reform. At that time, economic reality was seen as PI versus economic reform in both countries. The second section also attempts some additional comparisons of the two economies. The implications of this analysis are explored, and an evaluation of Soviet organizational prospects under Gorbachev is undertaken in the third section.

SOVIET ECONOMIC REFORM AND PLANNING IMPROVEMENT ATTEMPTS

In classical Soviet planning, fundamental economic decisions (pertaining *inter alia* to the firm's output level, sales price, mix and volume of productive resources used, and production techniques) are made by the centre. Enterprise management was essentially an engineering task (i.e. combining inputs to produce outputs). The enterprise plan amounted to little more than gross output targets and a set of 'success indicators' used to monitor performance and reward successful managers and workers. There was no single measure of enterprise effectiveness corresponding to the capitalist firm's profit/loss statement.

By the 1960s, the productive performance of the classical Soviet enterprise began to decline very noticeably, and it became apparent that the Soviet planning system required adjustment. The objectives of the economic reform launched in 1965 were manifold, but it sought especially to create greater independence and responsibility for Soviet enterprise managers. This was attempted by making profitability the chief success criterion of the enterprise. A 1967 price reform was to remove some of the system's distortions. Enterprises were permitted to enjoy some profit margin so that a capital charge could be paid by the enterprise to the state budget.[3] The centre instituted new, indirect financial 'levers' to induce appropriate enterprise performance rather than rely on planning imperatives. As is widely known, the same experiment was being carried out in the GDR. In fact, that country's 'New Economic System' had applied the same (Libermanesque) ideas in 1963 in the first Soviet-bloc reform experiment.

In both countries, ministries were instructed to issue indicators to the enterprises (e.g. the value of output sold, payments to the state budget, profits and/or profit rates, centralized investments, and the wages fund), rather than orders. The ministries, however, did little to promote the reforms; they often continued their perennial 'petty tutelage'. Central agents favoured re-centralization almost from the outset of the reform period, smarting from the loss of influence and prerogatives they had traditionally enjoyed.

The reforms never had the powerful impact their advocates had hoped for. The whole Soviet materials allocation system, for example, survived the reform period completely unscathed.[4] This vestige of command planning inhibited the decentralization of decision-making in production. Moreover, the attempt to adopt enterprise profitability (as opposed to gross output) as the principal success criterion was largely frustrated by the failure to overcome sellers' market conditions in the domestic economy.[5] Schroeder's account of the Soviet Union's subsequent 'treadmill of reforms' documents some of the experiments following the demise of the 1965 reform.[6] These reforms were essentially a consistent retreat from decentralization; the term 'reform' not being used in the Soviet Union from the beginning of the 1970s to the April 1985 plenum.[7] The East Germans have likewise never again engaged even in discussion of reforms, and regard the New Economic System as a failure which has been overcome.

The prevailing sentiment during that period was that central planning must simply be rendered more efficient (i.e. that plan 'perfecting' should be pursued through integrated planning techniques, computerized information and control systems, and administrative initiatives). It was common to argue in favour of radical PI, *without mention of reform*.[8] The East Germans willingly embraced the notion of improving rather than reforming the planning system and actively pursued the strategy after 1980.

It sometimes confuses westerners when the Soviets discuss 'decentralization', since that notion is seen as implying the use of some form of the market mechanism. Dyker shows that the Soviets intend no such implication.[9] The alternative envisioned by central planning agents is merely to strengthen the middle rung in the planning hierarchy, to which the centre would delegate some of its powers. The association or combine would also assume some of the decision prerogatives of the enterprise. An important part of more than two decades of Soviet 'reforms' has consisted of the attempt to establish a more effective middle-level tier in the planning hierarchy. In the GDR, a more effective initiative to organize the planning apparatus in this fashion dates back to 1980, at which time the general strengthening of the *Kombinat* system was undertaken.

Apparently, Soviet willingness to discuss increased decision-making powers for enterprises envisions the exercise of such powers over a narrower range of decisions than market-type decentralization would imply. Combines or associations would respect enterprise autonomy except where poor performance mandates intervention. The increased independence would encourage expanded horizontal relationships through a system of inter-enterprise contracts. The intent would be to achieve more efficient materials allocation (traditionally one of the tasks performed by the centre) through decentralized contractual linkages.

Soviet post-reform history has not consisted merely of discussion, of course. Some of the interesting planning innovations undertaken in that period have included: 'counter plans' (*vstrechnye plany*); the Shchekino labour experiment; and the creation of *obyedinyeniye*.

Beginning in 1971, the use of 'counter plans' was intended to overcome supply problems. Enterprises were encouraged to cease understating their production possibilities (striving for soft-plan targets). The centre tried to motivate them to propose

166

plan targets actually greater than those suggested by the official plan. They were to be rewarded even if they only achieved the official plan targets, leaving the counter-plan's more ambitious targets unfulfilled (even more substantial rewards were granted for fulfilling counter-plan targets). This scheme elicited little response from managers, who saw the ratchet principle applied when targets were met.

The initiative undertaken by the Shchekino Chemical Combine in 1967 was to reduce labour hoarding. Enterprises successful in reducing their labour force (or in expanding output without an increase in their payroll) could retain the resultant wage savings for bonuses to be divided among the remaining employees. Alec Nove blames the ministries for the failure of this technique.[10] Their arbitrary rule changes prevented enterprises from reaping the benefits of achieved economies, and the enterprises quickly learned that hoarding labour is still the most prudent practice.

The first experiment following the reforms, announced on April 2 1973, emphasized the immediate formation of *obyedin-yeniye* or economic associations.[11] The primary forms of association were to be (1) multiplant concerns, (2) republic or all-union associations, and (3) combines (vertically integrated multi-plant complexes directly subordinated to ministries).

The reform aspired to achieve greater control over resource and intermediate goods supplies through vertical integration. For this and other reasons, it was decided that power should be increased at the middle (association) level of the planning hierarchy. Unfortunately, the formation of numerous types and sizes of production association failed to generate any noticeably positive effects on Soviet industrial performance, and the movement bogged down after about half of the enterprises had been so organized. The lack of organizational momentum may have reflected a conviction that the effort was not paying off and so need not be vigorously pursued.

The GDR faithfully mirrored each of these Soviet innovations and experienced roughly the same effects, the exception being in the case of industrial reorganization. With greater zeal the GDR pursued and polished the *Kombinat* organizational form, combining it with many new and refurbished industrial regulations.

A CPSU resolution of July 12 1979 announced the next major Soviet planning innovations. Since the economic situation had failed to improve during the 1970s, the Soviets now adopted the following measures:

enterprise passports with detailed production data were to be assembled;

counter plans were re-emphasized;

some 'new' and additional success indicators were introduced;

additional norms were applied;

bonuses were based once again on contract fulfillment;

price surcharges were resurrected for quality products and product quality became a performance indicator;

the bonus system was to be strengthened for labour productivity improvements;

greater inventory 'reserves' were to be accumulated to open bottlenecks and exploit unforeseen international market opportunities;[12]

to achieve greater planning stability, enterprise plan changes introduced during the implementation phase were to be subject to greater sanctions (loss of bonuses);[13]

investment 'self-financing' via enterprise-earned revenues was permitted for production workers;[14]

'brigade' formation was promoted in a more rigorous manner.[15]

In spite of these measures, the system failed to overcome the centralization bias, to reduce the excessive information requirements, or to eliminate inherent incentive incompatibilities. The information overload prohibited the production of consistent micro-level targets and distorted the operation of success indicators. The abject dependence of purchasers on suppliers continued to militate against both quality production and contract fulfillment in Soviet planning.

It would be difficult to argue with the observation of Höhmann (prior to Gorbachev),[16] that little changed in Soviet planning after the 1979 'reform'. After the 1970s, the Soviet economy demonstrated increasing characteristics of crisis, although some scholars debate whether things deteriorated far enough to justify the use of that term.[17] (Gorbachev himself has adopted the expression 'pre-crisis state' to indicate the economy's status at the inception of his reforms.[18]) In any case, plan targets have been too infrequently fulfilled, growth has continued to diminish, consumers have found their level of living stagnant, and producers have found both labour and capital increasingly scarce. There have been some disastrous harvests, the costs of economic development in the east of the USSR have soared, investment policies and programmes have failed to keep the ageing capital stock from continued deterioration, and the labour force has edged toward demoralization and disengagement as effort and creativity have gravitated toward the second economy.

In 1983, Andropov pursued three principle measures of 'reform'.[19] These were: (1) a law on labour collectives; (2) a resolution (July 14) allowing greater enterprise independence and a greater role in planning for *obyedinyeniye*; (3) a resolution promoting accelerated technical progress. Enterprises gained greater investment autonomy, and could accumulate funds for the development of science and technology. Continued formation of brigades was also important to Andropov. An experiment inaugurated on January 1 1984 was effected in only five ministries.[20]

It extended the 1979 decree, still in operation, and also included:

a reduction and reformulation of performance indicators;
greater enterprise participation in plan formulation;
a strengthening of labour discipline;
provision for increased enterprise investments;
greater room for differentiated work achievement rewards;
measures to increase reliability of enterprise contracts.

Much of this was, of course, *déjà vu*.

It is rewarding to review proposals designed to improve the Soviet economy, since they permit one not only to observe the nature of policy deliberations, but also to make inferences about the nature of the economic difficulties that have inspired the proposals for change. Since becoming General Secretary, Gorbachev has frequently argued for a complete restructuring of the economic mechanism. His speeches follow a common format,[21] and (ignoring his *policy* proposals) generally address the following points concerning the *planning* mechanism: a new quality of development is necessary as the economy shifts from extensive to intensive growth; structural policy must be pursued with greater perseverance, and a restructuring of the entire economic mechanism has become necessary to increase the efficiency of centralization in management and planning; an expansion of the rights of the enterprise together with more flexible forms and methods of management must be achieved, and the initiative of the masses must be harnessed.

Gorbachev's PI efforts were not particularly bold. The 1984 economic experiment was to be extended in 1987 to all Soviet industry. Ministries were at that point to focus their attention on long-range planning and large-scale adoptions of innovations, rather than intervene in the detailed, day-to-day affairs of the production units.

Gorbachev intended to reward labour collectives which achieved technical improvements, and enterprises which eliminated obsolete and poor-quality outputs. He hoped to enhance the consumer's influence on the technical level and quality of products. Price formation was henceforth to facilitate the introduction of everything new and advanced. The number of centrally established plan assignments was to be sharply reduced as enterprises were increasingly regulated by economic normatives. 'Everything outmoded' had to be eliminated.

Many of Secretary Gorbachev's recommendations were proposed earlier by Andropov and others; so, in the realm of economic change, the early Gorbachev period merely extended the past. Nevertheless, the current regime drew the parameters for a discussion on approaches to PI,[22] and with their encouragement, planners and academicians initiated such a discussion. It might be worthwhile to mention at the outset of the review of that discussion, that the measures promulgated were then considered a part of the ongoing PI process. Now, after the party has agreed to follow Gorbachev into *perestroika*, those proposals would remain in force as contributions to 'radical reform'.

In the April 1985 plenum of the Central Committee of the CPSU, Ivanchenko[23] expressed the basic objectives of PI as follows: (1) utilization of the achievements of the scientific–technical revolution; (2) intensification of production; (3) a restructuring of management and planning; (4) improvement of structural and investment policy; (5) strengthening economic organization and labour discipline.[23] In Ivanchenko's view, the achievement of these objectives would require the creation of a whole new system of management (*sozdaniya tselostnoi sistemy upravleniya*).

There was consensus in the Soviet literature that PI would require more effective use of economic 'levers', and Bunich and Abalkin provided lists of proposed alterations for normatives and performance indicators.[24] The Soviets remain unable to design incentive-compatible performance indicators, so each round of experimentation elicits a new set of them.

The main issue in the PI discussion was, of course, the question of decentralization. The view that 'democratic centralism' obligated the party to intervene in production processes when necessary remained in force. Since socialist enterprises do not go bankrupt,[25] even when they fail the test of performance, it was agreed that the state must establish the parameters of their activity and reorganize obsolete enterprises. In general, enterprise autonomy was considered a desirable objective. Optimal economic organization was viewed as the assignment of appropriate targets within a system of economic regulators such that actions desirable for society would also be desirable for the enterprise. Kapustin's view was that the failure to achieve greater enterprise independence is the result of an insufficient correspondence of the present economic mechanism to the attained level of development.[26]

At the April 1985 plenum of the Party, Gorbachev indicated that the appropriate function of the upper echelons of the planning hierarchy is to find the most effective manner of combining the functions of science and production.[27] While the ministries are occupied with that problem, production units could respond with greater flexibility to changing market conditions and opportunities,[28] for they would be freed of the necessity of responding to so many directives and norms. Kapustin argued that greater enterprise autonomy must also permit an increased level of self-financed investments,[29] which in turn require a greater availability of funds for this purpose. This had been advocated (perhaps with less fervour) under previous regimes.

Soviet experts were willing to admit that many procedural questions about PI remained unresolved, but some concrete proposals had also been formulated. First, reorganization must affect *all* of industry, including all enterprises in combines or *obyedinyeniye*. W.K. Zentschagev indicated that the important work of creating production associations was going forward;[30] in industry, 22,000 enterprises remain outside associations, which demonstrated to Zentschagev and others the necessity of pushing forward the process of association formation.[31]

Second, reorganization must achieve a two-level hierarchical system, with production units functioning on the basis of full *khozraschet*. Streamlining hierarchical management will require the elimination of unnecessary linkages and information transfers between enterprises and their ministries. Two-level management and the omnipresence in production of the *khozraschet* principle both seem theoretically reasonable,[32] but until some concrete measures are implemented, it may still be considered no more than a matter of discussion.

A standard feature of the discussion on PI was a suggestion to upgrade the entire science/production effort to achieve intensification of production. The goal of the party is to make the productivity of the Soviet worker the highest in the world within a relatively short time. Abalkin believes that this is conceivable, but only if 'deep' reforms in the social organization of production are accomplished.[33] This would include, among a number of other things, flexibly restructuring production by removing the rigidity of plan targets. After all, the current system's planning procedures, norms, and performance indicators have not been successful.

There must be balance in the plans and they must be much less detailed, while enterprises organize themselves more completely on the basis of contracts. Abalkin echoes the aspirations of hosts of socialist economists in proposing a system of greater flexibility and more abundant planning reserves, including reserve production capacities, to enable rapid reaction to technical developments and changing social needs.[34]

Labour and labour collectives are faithfully discussed, both in the speeches of Gorbachev and the writings of the academicians. It is agreed that incentives should be structured so as to command worker loyalty (and that, to this point, they have not done so). The workers should be so organized that discipline and responsibility will be increased.[35] It is hoped that the ongoing process of brigade formation will result in a marked reduction of such phenomena as: (a) absenteeism; (b) on-the-job dipsomania; (c) pilfering of state materials for moonlighting activities; and (d) general socialist shirking. It is thought that the material dependence of collective members on the common results of work will help achieve these goals.[36]

Soviet theoreticians seem to pay less attention to the pricing issue than most of the other issues already mentioned. But it was acknowledged that there is a role for improved pricing in the search for a master plan of PI. Soviet prices are badly distorted and some thought has been given to price reform.

It was both disappointing and unfortunate that the 27th Party Congress revealed no new initiatives for the improvement of planning and management. Nor were there new ideas for increasing the autonomy of enterprises and combines. Gorbachev's address at the congress contained little more than rhetoric and some refurbished ideas from his predecessors.[37] There were no announcements of major change of the PI type, although Gorbachev did review his *policy* strategy.[38]

After the 27th Party Congress, Gorbachev continued to speak in generalities of prospective reforms in the planning system,[39] pointing to the necessity of 'bold experiments and the elimination of bureaucratic and departmental barriers, antiquated, stereotyped ways of thinking, and the underestimation, by some engaged in economic management, of the importance and efficiency of cooperation'.[40] The central feature of the experiments being extended to new Soviet industries, according to Gorbachev, 'is to increase the authority of the central administrative bodies in solving key problems . . . leaving the rest to the grass roots', and to 'draw the broad mass of the people, every work collective, every individual into the process of accelerated development'.[41]

By 1988, not only had Gorbachev's evaluation of the Soviet economy's problems become soberly realistic. His more radical proposals of 1987 were pointing in the right direction. The substantial amount of legislation passed by the beginning of 1988, however, seemed less dramatic in the reading than Gorbachev's rhetoric. As implementation begins in 1988 and beyond, it will become apparent whether the regulations have teeth. Given recent Soviet economic history, some western analysts anticipate that the implementation will diverge as much from the spirit of the new legislation as the laws themselves diverge from the spirit of Gorbachev's speeches. It will become apparent only gradually if the initiatives under consideration will turn out to be bold ones.

RECENT USSR AND GDR EXPERIENCE COMPARED

While the Soviet economy floundered, East Germany was claiming rather unqualified success for its economic performance. Yet the GDR was following the same philosophical approach to central planning as the Soviets. At the 11th party congress, General Secretary Honecker presented an array of statistics on the fulfillment of the 1981–5 plan,[42] highlighting dramatic increases in labour productivity, agricultural production, and incomes. He claimed the GDR had already proceeded 'to full-scale intensification', keeping abreast of revolutionary developments in international science and technology, and even leading in some fields.[43]

It is too early, of course, to establish proof acceptable to Western economists that the East German PI programme of the past five years has been as successful as claimed.[44] The important thing is that the East Germans themselves are convinced that the economic performance of recent years has been highly successful. While Gorbachev and others are bemoaning general and specific inadequacies in the Soviet planning system, the East Germans credit their planning organization with defusing the credit crisis of the early 1980s, with making the GDR viable in hard currency markets, and with helping to 'master' the scientific–technological revolution. Above all, PI has made it possible to achieve full-scale intensification.[45]

Consider now some of the reasons for the apparent success of the East Germans and the increasing difficulties of the Soviets in the realm of economic policy and planning. Systemic *differences* between the GDR and the USSR will be addressed, but it should be remembered that the two countries are remarkably similar in many respects.

The East Germans combine an intrinsic Soviet-type disinclination to rely on market mechanisms with a willingness to pursue orthodox Soviet-style central planning. It has even been averred that the Soviets have occasionally used the GDR as an economic laboratory.[46] From the termination of the 1960 reform era to the 1986 reform legislation, both countries exhibited a strong antipathy to reform. Some western scholars have underestimated this antipathy, and if the reform effort fails (which remained a distinct possibility early in 1988), that could be in part because Gorbachev likewise underestimated it.

In the early Gorbachev period, East Germany's economic ideology remained remarkably close to that of the Soviets.[47] Having observed the similarity of the conceptual approaches to PI, let us now consider some of the more significant differences.

Centralization

The current socialist doctrine of decentralization does *not* embrace the market mechanism, although even during the time of Andropov, Soviet economic authorities advocated greater autonomy and responsibility for the enterprise.[48] Through my discussions with GDR enterprise and combine leaders, and through the literature of both countries, I have the distinct impression that Soviet enterprises have achieved significantly less autonomy than have those of East Germany. From the East German perspective, the enterprise should have authority to make its own decisions, at least the less consequential ones. In those cases where day-by-day operations function effectively, enterprise managers are left with rather independent jurisdiction.

GDR enterprise independence is expressed primarily through the contracts system, which is alleged to link the decisions of central planners and producers.[49] The objective of the system is 'the achievement of the unity of plan, balance, and economic contracts'.[50] GDR planning literature focuses on ways to make the contracts system more effective. Thus, it discourages stocks that are not 'demand justified' (hoarding), while encouraging more punctual deliveries through more effective planning and managing of orders.[51] The system scarcely works flawlessly, but it lightens the centre's computational burdens and provides greater decision manoeuvrability to individual producers.

The Soviet economic experiment of 1984 intended, above all: (1) to strengthen the role of inter-enterprise contracts, making bonus earnings dependent upon the fulfillment of contractual obligations;[52] and (2) to extend the financial independence of enterprises and associations. The current discussion on contracts still has the flavour of futurity. Increased inter-industrial trade will be based on stronger, direct inter-enterprise information flows and contracts.[53]

The intent of proposed contractual relations sometimes seems merely to render centrally-directed production and sales plans more concrete. Lower level management would merely define more specifically the product assortments, quality, and delivery times determined by the centre. The Soviets would like to determine in advance the effectiveness of using such contracts; they would also like to develop contracts between the centre and the production units regulating the input supply function of the centre.[54] It will be necessary for the Soviet Union to gain a good deal more experience in inter-enterprise and agency/enterprise contracts before reaching even the insufficient level of development achieved by East Germany.

Also of significance in GDR decentralization is the role of the ministry. Before the implementation of the Soviet law on enterprises of 1987, the East Germans were further ahead than the Soviets in freeing ministries from day-by-day enterprise operations. The director general of an East German combine is to be both a colleague of enterprise entrepreneurs (being assigned to manage the 'parent enterprise' or *Stammbetrieb*), and at the same time an agent of the ministry (in assuring that industry outcomes correspond with the long-term interests of the economy as a whole). He is independent of the ministry in his production work for the industry, including all functions – from research and development, to production and marketing (domestic and international). Only the minister himself (as opposed to his staff or office) can give an order to a combine director general.

The ministries have been enjoined by Honecker to concentrate their attention on substantive planning issues;[55] for example, the preparation of investment programmes and the development of new norms or planning indicators tailor-made to the relevant industries. Although each combine is nominally free to establish the broad outlines of its own development, ministerial approval must be obtained for such plans.[56] Since the *Kombinat* retains the right of proposal, however, together with the greater knowledge of production costs and possibilities, it can so manage and prioritize its messages from the ministry as to maintain certain advantages in negotiations pertaining to planning issues. These, and other ministry–combine relationships in the GDR,[57] indicate an ongoing search for organizational forms permissive of adequate enterprise independence, production flexibility, and enhanced incentive conditions for the combines.

In the Soviet case one reads much about the continual, ubiquitous interference by Soviet ministries in the daily functioning of industry. Perhaps Gorbachev will be able to gain some greater degree of control over the ministries, but even if that occurs, it will presumably take major organizational change and considerable time before the situation improves markedly.

Combine and Association Formation

Soviet formation of production associations had already begun in the 1960s, but in 1973 the decision was made to base planning and management on that organization form.[58] In spite of the impetus of that year's reform, association formation was never completed. Kapustin, Zentschagev and others advocate completing the process.[59] The same scholars, responding to the principal/agent problem usually also favour the establishment of a two-level system of management (production unit and ministry) to simplify information flows, improve incentives, and eliminate unnecessary linkages.[60]

The GDR was more thorough in its organizational endeavour, completing its combine formation process by 1984. In centrally-directed industry there are 127 combines, and in regionally-directed industry another 94 of smaller size.[61] Whether or not the *Kombinat* is an optimal institution, East German consistency eliminates some of the organizational uncertainty that must exist in stark measure in the Soviet industrial hierarchy. The ostensible benefits of this organization (i.e. *Kombinat*) are also enjoyed in *every* East German industry,[62] so that planning is potentially more simplified, consistent, and effective.[63]

Labour Motivation

The more than formidable challenge of achieving a loyal, motivated, and disciplined labour force did not produce any imaginative Soviet policy initiatives in the early Gorbachev period. The approach consisted basically of the following: (1) an Andropovian call for discipline; (2) an anti-drinking campaign (that has actually affected alcohol production targets); (3) an extension of labour brigade formation (so that workers can help supervise and motivate each other); and (4) a repetition of the old promise that consumer goods would be more abundant in the present (12th) 5-year plan. The programme amounted to a lot of stick and not much carrot, since the promises for consumer improvements were scarcely at the pinnacle of the priority list and the likelihood of achieving the other plan targets was not high.[64] Gorbachev's investment and technology programmes did not leave a lot left over for Soviet consumers in the next decade and beyond. The literature on the second

177

economy makes it apparent that the Soviet planning system provides an incentive to seek the better life in 'coloured' markets rather than in the planned sector.[65]

One might anticipate that the GDR's budgetary situation, without the Soviet's more substantial alliance and geopolitical expenditures, can provide more resources for domestic purposes. The Honecker regime has explicitly recognized the necessity to use such resources to gain and retain labour loyalty. The East Germans are very much aware of the standard of living maintained directly to the west.

The Honecker regime's 'primary task' (*Hauptaufgabe*) has been to provide a better life for the consumer.[66] This has taken the form of (1) a major housing campaign and (2) increased production of consumer goods in general, including the 'thousand little things' that have so often proved unavailable in East Germany.[67] After a credit crisis, reduced oil deliveries from the USSR, and some other difficulties in the early years of this decade, consumer supplies have normalized and improvements are being enjoyed.

Honecker's guiding conception, the 'unity of economic and social policy', has been explained as the 'mutually interdependent relationships among intensification, productivity improvement and higher living standards'.[68] According to a maxim of Marxism–Leninism, the creativity of the workers is the foundation of the socialist economy.[69] To outward appearances the workers have understood and responded to the message. When one compares GDR indices of production, labour performance, and the abundance of the labourer's life with those of the advanced western countries, one may not be impressed with the GDR as a model economy. But when one makes the same comparison between the East Germans and the Soviets, the GDR performance seems distinctly more impressive.

One also finds the East German second economy far less developed than that of the Soviet Union. This may be both cause and consequence of the relatively greater effectiveness of GDR planning. At the level of consumption there is considerable activity, much of which the government sponsors through its *Intershop* hard-currency sales. At the production level, however, one fails to find substantive evidence of whole firms participating as an entity in second economy activity as is done in the Soviet Union.[70]

The Coupling of Production and Science

The Soviets wish to establish closer relations between large production units and research institutes.[71] Yet, to this point, of the Soviet Union's approximately 4,000 production associations, only 200 science-production associations combine the two functions.[72]

In the GDR's combine formation drive after 1980, establishing a more intimate linkage between science and production was a primary objective. The combine's director general is to be responsible personally for the industry's research, as well as for the construction of specialized in-house equipment (*Rationalisierungsmittelbau*) and other investments required for innovations.[73] A recent decree also gives the *Kombinate* direct access through contractual relationships to the institutes of the Academy of Sciences and the universities.[74]

The East Germans have concentrated their technical work on domestic (non-defence) industries: micro-electronics, chemistry, biochemistry, and others. They expect to build viable industrial technologies through the application of computer-aided development and manufacturing, which will also be the means of linking science and production.[75]

SOVIET AND EAST GERMAN ORGANIZATIONAL PROSPECTS

In the early Gorbachev period, the GDR's *Planvervollkommnung* seemed rather durable. East German economists and planners willingly cited positive performance indicators to make the case that combine formation and planning mechanism adjustments had made PI a notable success over a 5-year period. They are not complacent about their achievements, and party and academic statements call for continued improvements in planning and management. At that time only marginal adjustments were anticipated, and these would be confined to the planning style of that period. By the beginning of 1988 things seemed to be on hold, for the additional reason that it was not clear where *perestroika* was going in the USSR and what its implications would be for the GDR. In any case, modest reorganizational adjustments to realign some combines, in an attempt to achieve better intra-industrial communication and co-ordination, could be forthcoming. Further regulatory changes also seem likely to polish the rough edges of the planning process.

From the party's standpoint, the GDR economic system need not function perfectly; it is not even required to perform as well as capitalism directly to the west. Given the natural advantages of socialism (job security, price stability and the absence of poverty), the system is economically viable if it can maintain its productive momentum and current consumer-friendliness. (Political viability is, of course, related to developments in the Soviet Union.) Secretary Honecker would prefer progress to mere viability, however, and he expects the system to reach certain objectives enumerated at the 11th Party Congress.[76]

The ten 'priorities' laid down at that time can be synthesized succinctly. They include the continued ardent pursuit of technological progress and attendant increases in labour productivity. Combined with further reductions in raw materials and fuels utilized per unit of output, this will assure competitiveness of GDR products in international markets. The party's 'primary task' (pursuing improved consumer and labour conditions) continues as a guide for policy,[77] and funds will be made available to improve performance levels through better education programmes. The share of total investments devoted to 'rationalization' purposes will continue to increase. These things, together with the continued, creative efforts of the populace, are expected to bring the economy to the level of 'comprehensive intensification'.

But just how permanent is the Soviet planning system? One wondered in the early Gorbachev period whether PI in the Soviet Union could be made to perform well enough to survive, or whether substantive reform or other significant change was inevitable. Not only were there structural problems of crisis proportions within the economic mechanism, the party's social contract with the workers was also imperilled. Recognizing the significance of proper labour motivation, Soviet functionaries have unfailingly given lip service to improved living and working conditions for the proletariat. Nevertheless, in the early Gorbachev period, neither Gorbachev nor planning spokesmen showed any inclination substantially to increase levels of consumer-goods production. At best, one could find general expressions arguing for 'more favourable conditions for the development of the social activities and the initiatives of labour collectives', and for an enhancement of their 'material interests in increasing output by more complete utilization of the achievements of science and technology'.[78] The 27th Party Congress and the 12th 5-year plan likewise made only modest commitments to consumers.

Soviet prospects seemed less positive for this than for some of the other reasons discussed above: for the next few years of heavy reinvestment, the alienated Soviet workers were unlikely to enjoy significant improvements in their living standards. Rewards in the planned sector were not sufficient to motivate a transfer of their creative efforts out of the second economy and other secondary pursuits.

The adoption of *glasnost* and *perestroika* ultimately led Gorbachev to raise his consumption targets dramatically, particularly with respect to the provision of housing and consumer services. To the extent that the new promises are kept, the necessary support of the workers is more likely to be assured, and the greater the chances of success for *perestroika*.

With regard to the necessity of improving the economic mechanisms in the early Gorbachev period, this observer wondered whether the General Secretary might delude himself into believing that following the East German PI path would assure Soviet planning success. The differences in the two economies, societies, and cultures seem sufficient to make that a high-risk proposition. The early Gorbachev period began to close, however, when the General Secretary became convinced that marginal change would not suffice and that radical reform would be required to end the pre-crisis state of the Soviet economy.

Because one hears so much about the more dramatic Chinese experiment, because Hungarian decentralization retains such appeal for many, and because western systems theoreticians are so preoccupied with Yugoslavian labour management, many Western economists wondered when some kind of reform process would replace the PI effort in the Soviet Union.

To this author's surprise, it did not take long, and it is fortunate that GDR economic successes did not delay the arrival of Soviet change. The Soviets were anxious to share the success the GDR was enjoying, and they had little affinity for the kinds of reforms and decentralization which appeal to 'bourgeois' and some East European economists. China had pre-empted the market decentralization alternative; the Soviets were concerned that their pursuit of the same course would be construed as admission that the Chinese had discovered the 'correct' way. However, after the early period, Gorbachev's perception of the imminence of economic crisis caused all of these considerations to be swept aside in the phoenix-like ascent of *perestroika*.[79]

Venturing a prognosis for the Soviet Union is clearly not recommended for risk averters. Although a good deal of reform legislation is now in place, much remains uncertain and much depends on Soviet experience as they attempt to implement the new laws. Whether or not *perestroika* can rescue the system from imminent economic crisis is not clear even to Gorbachev.

Because no new ideas of substance were announced to promote reform at the 27th Party Congress, the present author was convinced at that juncture that the Soviet Union would merely push ahead with its own 'plan perfecting' for the foreseeable future. I suggested that this course of action would include: (1) an extension of the contracts system to enhance the performance of enterprise and *obyedinyeniye*; (2) an increase in the number of science/production associations to link industry with the kinds of technological processes that have traditionally bypassed the non-military sector; and (3) more direct participation of production units in international transactions. I was wrong in my pessimism about the adoption of reform; at the same time, however, these very strategies (pursued earlier by the GDR) proved to be spiritual pillars of *perestroika*.

Even if the Soviets successfully implement the *perestroika* measures (including price reform) already discussed, proposed, and legislated, important similarities between the GDR and Soviet economies would remain. After all, the East Germans have also promised price reform, the implementation of which would probably be enough to transform East German PI into economic reform similar to *perestroika*.

ACKNOWLEDGEMENTS

For financial support, the author is grateful to the Eller Center for the Study of the Private Market Economy of the University of Arizona. Thanks are also due to the David M. Kennedy Center for International Studies of Brigham Young University for helpful assistance.

NOTES

1. It was in the April 1985 plenum that Gorbachev first talked about a 'restructuring' (*perestroika*) of the economic mechanism. At the 27th Party Congress he first spoke of a structural economic reform, and even used the expression 'radical reform', which became quite common thereafter. By the summer of 1986, his portrayal of the reform was beginning to be colourful, and he emphasized that the changes needed were no less than 'revolutionary'. He began to see the need for new thinking to determine how to proceed with restructuring, and came to believe that such thinking required conditions of greater freedom of expression. In November 1986 the Supreme Soviet legalized private activity for individuals and family firms in twenty-nine consumer-related industries. Significant reforms were drawn up for Soviet foreign economic activity and organization in December 1986 and January 1987. In February 1987, the draft law of the enterprise was published and discussed. In July of the same year, the revised 'Law on the State Enterprise' was published, along with other significant documentation. See *O Korennoi perestroike upravleniva ekonomikoi: Sbornik Dokumentov* (1987) 1, Moscow: Politizdat.

2. In both languages the word 'perfecting' can also be translated simply as 'improving'. But other forms of the more modest verb could also have been chosen. There seems to be an intent (motivated by ideology?) to imply that, although the planning system has worked very well, system designers are engaged in the process of perfecting it. Planning 'amelioration' or, more simply, planning 'improvement' (PI) are adequate for the purposes of this paper.

3. See Alec Nove, 'The soviet industrial enterprise', (1981) in Ian Jeffries (ed.), *The Industrial Enterprise in Eastern Europe*, 29–38, London: Praeger Publishers.

4. See Jeffries, *op. cit.*

5. Given the excess consumer demands omnipresent in central planning, much can be sold that otherwise would not be. If the price attached to an item is randomly high, good profits could be enjoyed for an item which would otherwise languish in inventory.

6. 'The Soviet economy on a treadmill of reform', (1979) in *The Soviet Economy in a Time of Change*, 312–40 Washington: Joint Economic Committee.

7. See Hans-Hermann Höhmann (1983) *Richtung und Grenzen Neuer Wirtschaftsreformen in der UdSSR*, Köln: Bundesinstitut für Ostwissenschaftliche und Internationale Studien.

8. V. Ivanchenko (1984) 'Sovershenstvovania Organizatsii Upravleniya', *Voprosy Ekonomiki 55* (8), 53.

9. David A. Dyker (1981) 'Decentralization and the command principle – some lessons from Soviet experience', *Journal of Comparative Economics 5* (2), June, 121–48.

10. Alec Nove, *op. cit.*, 29–38.

11. Alice C. Gorlin (1977) 'The Soviet economic associations', *Soviet Studies 26* (1), 3–27.

12. Höhmann, *op. cit.*

13. Barbara Dietz, 'Neue Tendenzen im sowjetischen Lenkungssystem?' (1983) *Working Papers: Osteuropa-Institut Muenchen*, (93) October, 6, 7.

14. Morris Bornstein (1985) 'Improving the soviet economic mechanism', *Soviet Studies, 37* (1), 20–21.

15. Irene Gawronski, (1985) 'Les aménagements du système de planification en URSS sous Andropov et Cernenko', *Revue d'Etudes Comparatives Est-Ouest 16*, (1985), 21–42.

16. Höhmann, *op. cit.*, 9.

17. Cf. E. Dirkson and M. Klopper (1986) 'Is there an economic crisis in the USSR?', *Comparative Economic Studies 28* (1), Spring, 66–74.

18. M.S. Gorbachev, (1987) 'Gorbachev defends economic reform', *The Current Digest of the Soviet Press, 39* (26), July 29, 3. This is a translation of a June 26, 1978 article from *Pravda*.

19. Gawronski, *op. cit.*

20. These are the USSR Ministries of Heavy and Transport Machinery, the USSR Ministry of Electrical Equipment, the Ukrainian Ministry of the Food Industry, the Byelorussian Ministry of Light Industry, and the Lithuanian Ministry of Local Industry.

21. Cf. Gorbachev, *op. cit.*, and 'Korennoi vopros ekonomischeskoi politiki partii', *Pravda*, June 12, 1985, 1–2 (cited in *The Current Digest of the Soviet Press 37*, (23), 1–7.

22. Khachaturov, K. (1986), 'Ekonomika na Novom Etape i Zadachi Zhurnala', *Voprosy Ekonomiki*, (5), 3–10.

23. V. Ivanchenko (1986) 'Sovershenstvovania Upravleniya i Metodov Khozyaistvovaniya', *Voprosi Ekonomiki 57* (2), 3–10.

24. See P. Bunich (1985) 'Tsentralizovannoe Upravlenie i Samostoyatelnost Proizvodstvennykh Kollektivov', *Voprosy Economiki* (9), 48–58, and L. Abalkin (1985) Intensifikatsiya i Ekonomichesky Rost, *Planovoe Khozyaistvo* (8), 18–25.

25. Since that time, of course, *one* has.

26. E. Kapustin (1984) 'Sovershenstvovaniye Upravleniya, Narodnym Khozyaistvom', *Voprosy Ekonomiki* (12), 25.

27. M. Gorbachev (1985) 'O sozyve ocherednogo XXVII sezda KPSS i zadachakh s ego podgotovkoi i provedeniem', *Pravda*, April 24, 1–2.

28. Abalkin, *op. cit.*

29. Kapustin, *op. cit.*

30. See E. Kuehn and W. Salecker (1985) 'Zu den Diskussionsbeitraegen auf der 10. Tagung der Geminsamen Kommission der UdSSR und der DDR – Uebersicht', *Wirtschaftswissenschaft 33*, (9), 1312, 1313.

31. See both previously cited works of Kapustin.

32. See R. Hutchings (1984) *The Structural Origins of Soviet Industrial Expansion*, New York: St. Martin's Press; and Boris Rumer (1986) 'Realities of Gorbachev's economic program', *Problems of Communism*, Washington, D.C.: May–June, 20–31. As they show, that idea was first advocated in the Soviet Union in the late 1920s and early 1930s.

33. See Abalkin *op. cit.*, 25, 26.

34. Ibid., 25, 26.

35. V. Ivanchenko (1984) 'Sovershenstvovania Organizatsii Uprav-leniya', *Voprosy Ekonomiki 55* (8), 54.

36. Gawronski, I. *op. cit.* and Bornstein, M. *op. cit.*

37. Rumer (1986) *op. cit.*, p. 22 describes the Gorbachev report disappointedly as 'barely distinguishable from Brezhnev's cliché-ridden rhetoric'.

38. The policy strategy Gorbachev introduced at the congress is not of central importance for our discussion on planning. The strategy is straightforward, the objective being renewed economic growth, primarily through scientific-technical progress. It is to be stimulated by massive new investments addressed to the modernization of the USSR's badly antiquated and dilapidated capital stock, especially in the machine-tool industry (see Ulrich Weissenburger (1986) 'Zur Lage der sowjetischen Wirtschaft am Beginn des 12. Fuenfjahrplans 1986 bis 1990', *DIW Wochenbericht 53* (17), 205), and the rate of retirement of obsolete equipment is to double in this quinquennium (see E.A. Hewett (1985) 'Gorbachev's economic strategy: a preliminary assess-ment', *Soviet Economy 1* (4), 1985, 296). Nor is the consumer forgotten: the planned yearly growth of retail sales is 3.5 per cent to 4 per cent, and that of paid services is 5.5 per cent to 7 per cent, with the promise of 'significant amelioration of product quality and assort-ments' (see the editorial, Peredovitsa (1987) 'Plan Pervogo Goda Dvenadtsatoi Pyatiletki', *Planovoe Khozvaistvo* (1), 6. These modest improvements are designed to encourage greater labour productivity. Labour discipline and anti-alcohol campaigns are invoked to achieve the same objective.

The early Gorbachevian aspirations appeared unrealistic, since there is a limited amount that can be expected from Andropovian discipline campaigns. Productivity and work quality seemed unlikely to increase in view of poor labour motivation, since proposed increases in consumer goods production were still too modest. Given the pervasive, pent-up investment demands in the economy, it seemed unlikely that even the modest, planned consumption improvements could be delivered. Thus, Hewett holds that the major targets in the current 5-year plan 'cannot be attained' (see Hewett, *op. cit.*, 303).

39. Mikhail S. Gorbachev (1986) *Address to the 11th Congress of the SED*, Dresden: Verlag Zeit im Bild.

40. Ibid., 13.

41. Ibid., 10, 11.

42. E. Honecker (1986) *Report of the Central Committee of the Socialist Unity Party of Germany to the 11th Congress of the SED*, Dresden: Verlag Zeit im Bild.

43. Ibid., 31.

44. As presented by the *Statistisches Jahrbuch*, GDR statistics all appear very favourable, but there are two basic problems, even though GDR statistics have apparently not been subjected to wholesale upward manipulation, as Soviet statistics were in the early Gorbachev period. (See E.A. Hewett *et al.*, (1987) 'Panel on the Soviet economic

outlook; perceptions on a confusing set of statistics', *Soviet Economy* 3, (1), 3–39).

First, one would have to run econometric analyses of production data for time series of several years prior and subsequent to the changes introduced after 1980, to determine whether the production function did indeed shift upward at that time. Insufficient time has elapsed since 1980 to permit the empirical work to be done. Second, one would not be sure that the data could be trusted. GDR output increases involve many 'new' products, of which some are genuinely new and others are simply modified in some fashion. Both types justify higher prices. As a result, when one multiplies the new outputs and the new prices one discovers increases in national income.

One remains unsure, however, whether one is seeing spurious increases in output, since (except in cases where exports to the west are involved) 'new' products are not subjected to the market test. To the extent that such products do not represent substantive improvements, increases in national income are merely reflective of socialist inflation. There are, of course, some measures (e.g. of physical outputs) which seem to speak well for East German claims of substantial improvements in economic performance.

45. See Honecker (1986) *op. cit.* 31. Al these accomplishments were acclaimed in a speech lasting more than four hours at the 11th Party Congress in Berlin (East). Visiting dignitary Mikhail Gorbachev also spoke of the 'remarkable results achieved in all the years since your republic came into existence, including the most recent period'. He also observed that 'intensive methods' had 'ensured the sustained growth' of the GDR economy (see Gorbachev, (1986) *op. cit.*, 6).

46. Some have the impression that after a rather protracted public discussion of the Liberman proposals in the early 1960s, the GDR acted at the behest of Moscow in the 1963 implementation of the first Libermanesque reform. See Karl Thalheim (1985) Sozialistische Planwirtschaft in der heutigen Wirtschaft, in Bruno Gleitze *et al.*, *Die DDR nach 25 Jahren*, 124, Berlin (West): Duncker & Humblot.

47. The Joint Commission of Economists of the USSR and the GDR convenes regularly, and their interchange of ideas is extensive. Both countries pursue their own (similar) versions of modification of the historic tenets of central planning. Both have intellectually rejected the cruder notion of 'command' planning, wishing to rely on indirect levers, norms, and other such techniques. The methodologies in vogue in the first period of the Gorbachev era, however, were not of economic reform, but of PI. In both countries, the sense of any proposed (USSR) or endeavoured (GDR) 'decentralization' was not so much a devolution of authority from central to enterprise agents as one from the centre to the director general or manager of an association or combine.

48. Gawronski, *op. cit.*

49. See R. Rytlewski and N. Zornek (1985) 'Wirtschaftsrecht', in H. Zimmerman (ed.), *DDR Handbuch*, 1506–18, Köln: Verlag Wissenschaft und Politik.

50. *Direktive des X. Parteitages der SED zum Funfjahrplan für die*

Entwicklung der Volkswirtschaft der DDR in den Jahren 1981 bis 1985, 89 Dresden: Verlag Zeit im Bild, 1981.

51. H. Feix and A. Schmich (1986) 'Aktuelle Fragen der Einheit von Plan, Bilanz und Vertrag', *Wirtschaftswissenschaft 34*, (5) 1986, 814–26.

52. Weissenburger (1986) *op. cit.*, 206.

53. See Ivanchenko (1986) *op. cit.*, 8.

54. Kapustin (1984) *op. cit.*, 1984, 28, 29.

55. Honecker (1986) *op. cit.*, 1979.

56. P. Boot (1983) 'Continuity and Change in the Planning System of the German Democratic Republic', *Soviet Studies 35* (3), 331–42.

57. P.J. Bryson and M. Melzer (1987) *Planning Refinements and Combine Formation in East German 'Intensification'*, Beck Papers, University of Pittsburgh.

58. See Gorlin (1977) *op. cit.*

59. See note 30.

60. See Ivancheko (1984) *op. cit.*, 52–59.

61. Bryson and Melzer, *op. cit.*

62. Ibid.

63. It is worth observing that the GDR has the advantage of geographic and organizational compactness. Given the limited size of the GDR's industrial/planning hierarchy, it is possible to have an annual meeting of *all* combine directors-general at one time and place. There the leading economic and planning authorities can instruct, encourage, and indoctrinate the entire group in matters of plan conformity with some facility.

64. Hewett *et al.* (1987), *op. cit.*

65. Katsenelinboigen, A. (1977) Colored markets in the Soviet Union, *Soviet Studies 29*, (No. (2), 1977), 62–85.

66. See Bryson, P.J. and Perry, P.J. (1986) *Sozialpolitik*: East German social welfare policies, *Comparative Economic Studies 28* (2), 1–20; and Bryson, P.J. (1987) 'GDR economic planning and social policy in the 1980s', *Comparative Economic Studies 29*, (2), 19–38.

67. Phillip J. Bryson (1984) *The Consumer under Socialist Planning: The East German Case*, Praeger: New York.

68. H. Koziolek (1978) Beduerfnisse des Menschen – Massstab unserer Wirtschaft, *Neues Deutschland*, 4/5 March, 3.

69. H. Schneider (1985) 'Sozialistischer Wettbewerb und umfassende Intensivierung', *Wirtschaftswissenschaft 33*, (12), 1761–71.

70. Gregory Grossman (1981) 'La seconde économie et la planification économique soviétique', *Revue d'Etudes Comparatives Est-Ouest 12* No. (2), 5–24.

71. Gorbachev, (1985) *op. cit.*

72. Kuehn and Salecker (1985) *op. cit.*

73. Cf. Helmut Richter, 'Zu Aspekten der Entswicklung leistungsfaehiger Kombinate in der Industrie der DDR', in E. Sachse (ed.) (1981) *Zu Grundfragen der Betriebswirtschaft in der DDR und in Japan*, Berlin (East): Verlag die Wirtschaft Berlin; and M. Wenzel (1984) 'Leistungsstarker Rationalisierungsmittelbau bringt dem

ENTERPRISE AND ASSOCIATION IN PLANNING

Kombinat hohen Zuwachs an Effektivitaet', *Wirtschaftswissenschaft 32*, (8), 1170–82.

74. *Gesetzblatt der DDR* (1986) 'Beschluss ueber Grundsaetze fuer dir Gestaltung oekonomischer Beziehungen der Kombinate der Industrie mit den Einrichtungen der Akademie der Wissenschaften sowie des Hochschulwesens', Teil I, (2), January 16, 9–12, Berlin (East).

75. W. Heinrichs and K. Steinitz (1986) 'Neuerungen, Produktiv-kraftentwicklung und umfassende Intensivierung', *Wirtschaftswissenschaft 34* (1), 1–20.

76. Honecker (1986) *op. cit.*, 58–65.

77. The literature's concern for the consumer's loyalty to the system has not always been as apparent. Wolfgang Heinrichs asserts that even in the phase of comprehensive intensification, consumer goods production is of paramount importance because it exerts such influence 'on the balanced development' and the 'effective functioning of management, planning, and economic accounting in the entire economy' (see Kuehn and Salecker (1985) *op. cit.*, 1333). Without the commitment of the worker/consumer, a regime's credibility and future are not assured.

78. See the statement of Bellusov, reported in Kuehn and Salecker (1985) *op. cit.*, 1335.

79. The new course of economic reform in the USSR has been dramatic. Perhaps convenience will one day help us to forget the barriers to reform that made its adoption seem unlikely in the early Gorbachev era, and which still leave its implementation very uncertain. We all agree that, in socialism, politics is pre-eminent. While reconsidering the Soviet departure from the PI period, it is apparent that political pre-eminence is a simple fact of life, so long as economic constraints permit it to be.

188

9

The foreign economic policy of the GDR and the USSR: the end of autarky?

Ronald A. Francisco

The Soviet bloc continues to strive to protect its economies from the threatening volatility of market forces in the capitalist world. However, it is increasingly difficult to maintain this insulation in the 1980s. The Soviet Union and its allies have become dependent on western raw materials, western technology, and massive infusions of western credit. Now, paradoxically, the Soviet bloc seeks even greater involvement with the international economic system dominated by the West. The USSR appears ready to accept the substantial risk that greater international involvement will lead to even greater exposure to damaging world forces. In order to compensate for this risk, the Soviet Union has hardened its policy toward Eastern Europe. The USSR has signalled its position to the West and to its allies: it will exert greater control over its own bloc while it increases the bloc's exposure to the uncertainties of the world economy.

This chapter examines the international economic predicament of the Soviet bloc through two of its pivotal members: the Soviet Union and the German Democratic Republic (GDR). The USSR, of course, is the economic bastion of the Council for Mutual Economic Assistance (CMEA). The GDR is the CMEA's stellar performer – it maintains the highest standard of living, the best economic performance, the highest per capita income, and it is an important technology centre. Together, the two countries constitute the core of economic orthodoxy in the CMEA. Now, without substantial changes, each faces challenges beyond the CMEA that it is ill-equipped to master without external support.

THE EVOLUTION OF THE ROLE OF THE SOVIET BLOC
IN THE WORLD ECONOMY

The situation confronting the USSR and GDR today is far from the idealized world envisioned by early post-war Soviet planners. They sought a bloc free from the influence of disruptive external forces – a bloc that could develop a robust socialist system within a shell of autarky. Werner Gumpel traces the evolution of the USSR's economic foreign policy through four phases.[1] The first phase stressed the Soviet bloc's attempt to achieve complete economic autarky within national systems. Of course, only the USSR had the size and resources to pursue autarky as a reasonable goal. Hence, the second phase involved the creation of the CMEA in 1949 and the attempt to establish autarky within the bloc as a whole. Complete isolation from the capitalist world was sought by constructing a rigorous division of labour within the bloc.

During the 1960s the public pursuit of autarky weakened slightly. Many East European states were concerned about their relative decline in technology and economic development. Western nations had clearly surpassed the CMEA. Now East European states began to open their markets to Western technology. Beginning in 1971, the Soviet Union embraced this policy and co-ordinated a plan within the bloc to borrow funds in the West in order to secure needed basic production technology. The final phase of the CMEA's foreign economic relations has seen debt levels rise exponentially while East European states increasingly strengthen their ties to the world economic system. The Soviet Union appears to have abandoned its goal of autarky for at least the short run. It now even seeks for itself more direct interaction with the capitalist Western world.

There is little doubt that the USSR has been frustrated by a series of failures of its own system and the CMEA. It has been unable to keep pace with Western technological development. It could not supply the resource needs of its growing inter-national bloc. And now it confronts a more vexing pair of problems. On the one hand, it needs to borrow in the West in order to buy technology. On the other hand, it needs to sustain its ability to market in the West in order to fund its trade and monetary obligations. Yet the Soviet bloc has long been unable to compete effectively with strong Western industrial states in

Western markets. The 1980s have brought still another challenge. Newly industrializing states in the Third World have crowded many CMEA products out of the world market. Developing nations in Latin America and Asia produce better, cheaper products, and have reduced the CMEA to the role of a basic raw material exporter.[2]

Mikhail Gorbachev, speaking at the 11th Party Congress of the East German SED, called for better CMEA co-operation in order 'to guarantee our invulnerability to the capitalist market'.[3] This, essentially, is the challenge for the Soviet bloc. Whether this goal can ever be met is questionable. In any case, it appears that the Soviet Union and the GDR have little choice but to tie themselves even more closely to the capitalist world before they can ever hope to withdraw to safe isolation.

CHALLENGES TO THE USSR IN THE 1980s

The burdens of the bloc

The Soviet Union has expanded its influence impressively since 1945, much to the frustration of its Western rivals. Yet the costs of the expansion of the Soviet bloc have become burdensome for the USSR. The Rand Corporation attempted to analyse these costs. It found that the annual average growth rate of the ruble costs of the bloc exceeded 16 per cent for the 1970s alone. These costs occur principally in implicit trade subsidies, export credits with doubtful repayment prospects, military aid, economic aid, foreign military activity (e.g. Afghanistan), and covert activities in the Third World. These policies have taxed the Soviet economy heavily. The Rand study estimated that each increase of 1 per cent in the annual bloc-cost share of the Soviet GNP necessitates reductions of 0.6 per cent to 1 per cent in the growth of military production, or about 0.3 per cent in the growth of civil consumption.[4]

The raw material or resource component of the Soviet programme began to falter in the early 1970s. The USSR was unable to produce enough grain to meet the needs both of its own economy and the growing appetites of its East European allies. The East Europeans were told to find the grain elsewhere (i.e. on the world market).

The case of oil developed somewhat differently. The Soviet

Union continued to export enough petroleum to meet almost all of its allies' needs during the 1970s. Until 1982, these deliveries, denominated in soft currency, were made at prices considerably lower than those prevailing on the world market. The USSR chose to supply its own bloc at a substantial cost to its own economy. In 1982, as world oil prices declined, the complex CMEA pricing regime began to turn the terms of trade in the USSR's favour. But the East Europeans rebelled, and in 1984 demanded that the price (still primarily in soft currency) be linked more closely to the world price. The Soviets, however, have consistently held that their pricing regime is subject to change only when much higher quality goods are offered for change by the East Europeans.

During the past decade, the USSR has attempted to wean its allies from total petroleum dependence. Increasingly, it has shifted its sales to the world market in order to bolster its hard-currency earnings. Yet it is cautious even in this policy, since it must be mindful of the effects of economic disruption within the bloc.[5]

Most Western observers predict that the USSR's own economic difficulties will lead it to fewer subsidies, more demand for service on trade-related bilateral debt, and increased insistence on hard currency in intra-bloc transactions. Yet no one really knows how tough the Soviets can be before significant political dangers arise.[6]

Western debt and the Soviet 'umbrella'

The USSR encouraged its allies in 1971 to borrow in the West in order to finance their technology imports and accelerate their growth. In the middle and late 1970s, when oil and raw materials prices rose rapidly, CMEA countries increasingly borrowed in order to finance basic resource imports as well. The result was a massive accumulation of Western debt (Table 9.1). Western lenders were willing to extend this credit because of a widespread belief in the Soviet 'umbrella' – the view that the USSR would rescue any ally encountering repayment difficulties.[7]

When several CMEA countries finally faced the prospect of default, beginning in 1981, there was no Soviet rescue. For the first time, the Soviet Union tacitly acknowledged to the world

Table 9.1. Soviet hard currency debt to the West (in billions of US $)

	1975	1977	1979	1980	1981	1982	1983	1984	1985	1986
Gross debts	14.0	20.8	23.9	20.4	21.4	21.0	22.5	22.8	30.2	38.2
Net debts	10.5	15.8	14.1	11.5	12.2	9.8	10.3	11.2	16.9	23.2

Source: 1975–9 data adapted from Paul-Günther Schmidt, Hard Currency Indebtedness of the CMEA Countries, *Intereconomics 20*: 3 (May/June 1985): table 3, 117; 1980–6 data from Joan F. McIntyre, The USSR's Hard Currency Trade and Payments Position, in U.S., Congress, Joint Economic Committee, *Gorbachev's Economic Plans*, vol. 2 (November 23, 1987), table 5, 482.

that it could maintain neither its ideal policy of autarky nor even insulate the bloc from the world economy. Romania and Hungary found relief in the OECD-dominated International Monetary Fund (IMF). West Germany stepped in to rescue the GDR, and Poland struggled through rugged refinancing austerity until it too was admitted to the IMF in 1986. Only Bulgaria was helped directly by the Soviet Union. In all other cases the USSR stood by and watched the West settle its allies' debt problems – albeit at a cost of greater Western dependence.

During this period the Soviet Union's own Western debt grew substantially, although never to very high levels; on a per capita basis. After reducing the debt in 1984, the USSR borrowed a total of $3.7 billion in 1985 from Western banks.[8] This trend is likely to continue. PlanEcon, a US-based research firm specializing in CMEA economies, estimates that the gross Soviet debt to the West will exceed $50 billion by the end of 1990.[9] While this, too, is a manageable sum for the USSR, it reflects deteriorating trends that affect the Soviet Union and the CMEA as a whole.

Since CMEA nations have been losing ground in the competition for export of manufactured goods to the Western market, they have become increasingly reliant on raw material exports. But commodity prices have been declining in recent years, prompting a deterioration in the CMEA – and the Soviet – trade balance with the West. There is much official optimism in the Soviet bloc, yet one is hard pressed to see how the CMEA will reverse current trends and be able to compete successfully against newly industrializing nations for world markets.

Demands for reform within the CMEA

The Soviets appear to believe that their best prospect for significant improvement lies within the CMEA. The USSR has lamented the lack of true integration in the CMEA for some time. Gorbachev spoke bluntly in the spring of 1986 (at the GDR's party congress) for a substantial increase in the integration of CMEA member activities.[10] These were not welcome words in Eastern Europe. The smaller CMEA states balk at any further erosion of their economic sovereignty.[11] Their reluctance stems in part from their experience with previous Soviet-mandated co-operation efforts. Since 1975, CMEA states have been required to invest in development projects within the Soviet Union. This is quite reasonable from the Soviet perspective, since the USSR shares its resources with the bloc. None the less, East Europeans view these demands as a diversion of needed investment funds from their own national projects. The Soviet Union also demands East European participation in the multilateral International Investment Bank (IIB). The IIB was created in 1970 in order to finance large development projects by pooling convertible funds to buy technology in the West. Some $3 billion were consumed in this way to build the Soviet gas pipeline to Western Europe. Again, the East Europeans pay a proportional sum to IIB in scarce Western currency, and thus many regard it as a real hardship.[12]

The Soviets have also demanded reforms in the bilateral trade sector. Trade in the CMEA is a complex affair. It is part barter, part money-based trade. Often exchanges are made on the basis of equivalent 'hard goods' (e.g. sewing machines for Soviet oil). As a condition for reforming the oil pricing regime in 1984, the USSR demanded more and better goods from Eastern Europe in exchange for its oil.[13] Much of what was sent to Moscow was little more than scrap. Now these goods were supposed to be of 'high quality and reflect world-level technology'. For more than 2 years a high-stakes battle has been waged over this issue at the highest levels of the CMEA. The Soviets insist that the East Europeans are continuing to send substandard goods as barter. The allies plead poverty and insist that they can do no better without more and cheaper oil. Yet the Soviets have not yielded.

In the November 1986 meeting of the CMEA, the USSR did pledge to send more 'fuel' to Eastern Europe during the next 5

years. But little of this increase is likely to be in oil – what the
East Europeans most urgently need. The Soviets have also
increased the investment cost of its energy. It has increased the
price of required participation in joint projects to extract and
transport Soviet energy.[14] These announcements were followed
immediately by an extraordinary summit meeting of national
leaders in Moscow where more wrangling on the economic
burden of energy supplies ensued.[15] It remains to be seen how
far the Soviets can afford to go in their resolve to gain better
terms of trade. What if the East Europeans cannot or will not
co-operate? How far can the Soviets push the allies without
incurring some serious political or economic backlash?

THE GDR

The German Democratic Republic is the most successful
economic performer in the CMEA. It is in many ways a model
ally. Its economic success has been achieved without radical
departures from the Soviet-defined course. Most of the GDR's
domestic reforms have reflected what Paul Marer calls 'ideologically constrained practicality'.[16] In any event, the GDR's
performance has been impressive. It has outpaced any other
CMEA member in growth in the 1980s and even increased its
already sizeable lead over the rest of the bloc in per capital
income.

Mikhail Gorbachev has noted the East German success.
Speaking in Leningrad in 1985, he singled out the GDR as the
only CMEA member determined to make its products competitive in world markets.[17] Together, the GDR and the USSR
constitute the core of the CMEA's drive to achieve competitive
technological status with the West. Yet as both have recognized,
progress must involve greater interaction with the West. For the
GDR, this is at once easier and considerably more awkward
and dangerous.

The GDR's link to the West

As CMEA nations sought to strengthen their Western links
during the past decade, most had to apply for membership in
international organizations or try to nurture bilateral relations.

The GDR, however, is unique. It has a ready partner in the West at all times in the Federal Republic of Germany (FRG). For most of its history, the GDR has attempted to distance itself from the FRG. This neighbour is all too close, all too alluring to the GDR's population, and economically far too strong for the GDR to match.

The East German leadership is justly proud of the economic success of the GDR within the world of the CMEA. For the bulk of the East German population, though, the standard for comparison lies West, not East. As the GDR has widened its margin in living standards over all other East European nations, it has seen the West Germans widen their lead over the GDR. The West Berlin-based Deutsches Institut für Wirtschaftsforschung (German Institute for Economic Research) estimated recently that the net real income (i.e. reflecting differences in purchasing power) of the average GDR household is only about half as high as its counterpart in West Germany.[18] The GDR population is well aware of this difference, and probably exaggerates it, since its most salient source of information is the nightly programming of West German television stations.

The regular reminders, transmitted electronically into most GDR homes, of the political freedom and material affluence of the West are challenges which no other East European state has to face. Thus, a retreat from the policy of high living standards is politically more dangerous in the GDR than in perhaps any other East European state. For the GDR leadership, the situation is grim. As the USSR has curtailed its material support for the regime in recent years, the GDR has opted for the distasteful choice of limited economic dependence on West Germany. Present trends signal no relief from this precarious course. The GDR's technological and financial needs appear to bind it to West Germany for the long term.[19]

The Technological Gap

The GDR has lost some of the esteem it once commanded as the major technological innovator and supplier in the CMEA. The East Germans are now very weak in relation to West Germany and no longer clearly superior to the Soviet Union. In order to arrest this erosion, the GDR has stressed technological progress as its central goal for this decade. The pressure comes from all sides – the Soviet Union, Western and even Third

World competition, as well as the demands of its own population.

None the less, technological improvement implies increased dependence on the West. This must have been abundantly clear to the delegates of the 11th SED Party Congress in 1986, where Günter Mittag, the SED Secretary for Economic Affairs, waxed enthusiastic about the new key to success in the GDR, using its English acronym, 'CAD/CAM' (computer-aided-design/computer-aided-manufacturing).[20] The GDR's successful computer Kombinat (industrial combine) is to produce the machines that will provide the base for CAD/CAM throughout the nation's industrial system.

Yet it is the computer industry itself that is one of the largest areas of GDR dependence on the West. The GDR produces mid-sized mainframe computers for the CMEA under a division of labour introduced by the USSR in 1970. East German computers are among the best available in the CMEA, driven by the GDR's own U-D microprocessors. At present, however, being the best in the CMEA does not amount to much. The vaunted East German computers are basically copies and revisions of IBM's mid-1960s 360 series of mainframe machines, and its microprocessors are much slower than those available in the West. The Soviet Union receives about one-half of the GDR's computer production, but it is reputed to be dissatisfied with the quality and technical standard of the machines, and has even refused to take delivery in some cases.[21] There seems to be little choice, then, but to seek Western technology at its present levels and try to adapt it to production in the GDR.

Technological adaptation and assimilation is difficult in centrally planned systems. The GDR seems to be committed to easing the transition by uniting with established West German firms in co-operative agreements. This is perhaps the most direct route to significant progress in many manufacturing areas. Co-operation agreements are especially sought to restore some of the GDR's traditionally strong sectors (e.g. pharmaceuticals), and to overcome serious environmental problems. The new 5-year plan promises reduction of air and water pollution, but the GDR will need to turn to the Federal Republic for the required technology. Welcome as these contacts are from a technological point of view, they represent political ties that are likely to bind the GDR economy even more closely to Bonn.

Trade and Financial Pressures

The GDR's relative lack of resources and technological progress have generated trade problems which in turn led to severe levels of international debt. The trade problems exist even within the CMEA. The GDR's trade debt to the USSR expanded rapidly during the past decade. During the years of most rapid increases in the price of oil the GDR incurred deficits of increasing magnitude with the USSR. By the end of 1984, its bilateral trade debt to the Soviet Union stood at more than 4 billion rubles.[22] In the past twelve years, the GDR has been able only once to attain a surplus in its trade with the USSR. The credits granted by the Soviet Union to finance these deficits are scheduled to be repaid in the latter half of the 1980s. Much of the GDR's economic fortune will depend on how seriously the Soviets enforce the payment schedule.

The Soviet reduction in oil exports to the GDR led to more trade problems. Like most other CMEA nations, the GDR borrowed money from Third World oil producers in order to finance trade deficits. These debts are denominated in US dollars. They are clear evidence of the cash shortage that afflicted the GDR during the early part of the 1980s.[23]

The most intractable trade problems lie in the GDR's trade with OECD countries. This trade has become increasingly important to the GDR. It now amounts to over 77 per cent of the GDR's total annual trade with the Soviet Union, and this proportion has been growing for the past decade.[24] The terms of the trade, though, have worsened for the GDR. Its own technical and quality problems have resulted in a decline in manufactured exports. It is now dependent largely on raw materials, especially mineral oil, to balance its trade with the West. And while it would like most to obtain needed high technology, it has often been forced to buy basic grains or raw materials from the West.

The GDR's inability to balance its trade has fuelled the nation's serious debt problem. The debt is large and multi-faceted. Its primary components are: (1) convertible currency debt to Western banks; (2) trade debt to oil producing countries; (3) trade debt to the USSR in hard goods or transferable rubles; (4) trade debt to West Germany; and (5) convertible currency obligations incurred through the CMEA's International Investment Bank.

Hoping to bolster its ability to produce competitive goods, the GDR borrowed heavily beginning in the early 1970s (Table 9.2). A decade later, the need for Western currency to service debt obligations and secure important resources led the GDR leadership to desperate action. Normally considered a cautious and defensive government, the GDR was forced to reckless levels of borrowing. By the early 1980s Western banks began to refuse requests for credit.[25] It was rescued in this instance by massive West German loan guarantees. As of mid-1984, the GDR's total Western debt reached a per capita level of $710 (CMEA average, $230). It was forced to allocate 58 per cent of every dollar or mark gained from the West simply to satisfy its debt service obligations.[26] While certainly not in the dire straits of Poland, the GDR's situation is critical. It can neither afford politically to pursue a long-term austerity programme, nor can it afford to purchase even planned technology imports without borrowing further. Given the Soviet Union's present stance, the GDR's only conceivable source for future resources seems to be the West – especially West Germany.

Table 9.2. GDR hard currency debt to the West (in billions of US $)

	1975	1977	1979	1980	1981	1982	1983	1984	1985	1987
Gross debts	5.1	8.3	12.7	14.2	14.8	13.0	12.8	11.8	10.0	n.a.
Net debts	4.1	7.1	10.2	11.4	12.0	10.6	8.9	7.3	6.8	4.4

Source: 1975–9 data adapted from Paul-Günther Schmidt, Hard Currency Indebtedness of the CMEA Countries, *Intereconomics 20*: 3 (May/June 1985): table 3, 117; 1985 data derived from Eastern Europe's Debt, *The Economist*, April 19, 1986, 122; 1987 data from *Süddeutsche Zeitung*, August 27, 1987, 25.

POLICY OPTIONS

In the more than four decades since the end of World War II the Soviet bloc has endured a slow but steady erosion of its ultimate goal of economic autarky. There is widespread recognition within the bloc that this trend must be arrested. The Soviets, under Gorbachev, have publicly underscored the need to reform CMEA practices, while privately pursuing surprisingly bold initiatives in the West. There seems to be no question that we will see substantial effort at reform. For the first time, these efforts are likely to be stronger at the international level than within the national economies of the CMEA nations.

Reform within the CMEA

The Soviets are convinced that considerable improvement could be achieved by still more centralization and rational division of labour within the CMEA. East Europeans are wary of any further demands on their resources, but even Western specialists agree that there is considerable potential for useful reform within the existing institutions of the CMEA.

Intrabloc trading

The CMEA trading system is cumbersome and primitive. There has never been an effective departure from the early post-war system introduced under the policy of national autarky. CMEA trade is still largely barter trade. The Soviets introduced the concept of the 'transferable ruble' in order to handle deficits and clearing functions, but there is no genuinely convertible monetary unit within the bloc. In 1963, the Soviets established the International Bank for Economic Co-operation. It was supposed to ease financing problems in intra-bloc trade, but it has never really been used effectively for its multilateral function.[27] A meaningful convertible monetary unit would solve a number of problems, and recent Soviet policy statements suggest that Moscow is prepared to take this step.[28] The GDR and Romania oppose the policy. Even with their eventual support, no effectively convertible Soviet currency is likely for several years.

Investment Coordination

The USSR has already actively sought to create a system to allocate bloc-wide investment. For the most part, however, this involves the International Investment Bank and pertains principally to East–West arrangements or to the support of Soviet natural resource production. Most East Europeans, concerned by falling rates of real investment, do not welcome still greater demands from the USSR. It is apparent though, that the Soviets have in mind the sort of division of labour they introduced in the computer industry in 1970. This might reduce duplication and increase efficiency while increasing Soviet domination of the CMEA.

Import Curbing

Import curbing is one of the standard practices of any economic unit that seeks autarky. When deficits occur in external transactions, import curbing programmes reduce the inflow until balance can be restored. In practice, however, these policies cause wild swings in trade, disrupt expectations, pressure internal substitution facilities, and create unhappy trading partners. Almost all Western observers feel that the CMEA must abandon this policy as a standard operating procedure.[29] In the short run, of course, this would exacerbate the trade and debt problems of both the USSR and the GDR, and thus it is unlikely to occur without concomitant reforms in other spheres. Some Western economists think that substantial improvement could be attained without wholesale changes in trade policy. The CMEA might simply speed their efforts to reform the present cumbersome interface of East–West trade, with its 'rigid, bureaucratic constraints and its high value on centralism'.[30]

Options in the West

Not even complete implementation of successful reform within the CMEA would obviate greater reliance on the West. Both the USSR and the GDR appear to recognize this. Each is building up its Western bank deposits in preparation for longer-term borrowing throughout the rest of the decade.[31] Both recognize the need to obtain Western machinery and technology. But in a series of startling signals in 1986, the Soviet Union, at least, seems prepared to abandon the goal of autarky for the short run. It seems to be willing to join the world economy, although no one knows yet on what terms this is really feasible.

Trade Reform and GATT

The Soviet bloc has never had much interest in any notion of free trade. It was therefore surprising in the spring of 1986 when the Soviet Union requested observer status at the new round of trade talks under the auspices of the General Agreement on Tariffs and Trade (GATT). The United States vetoed the Soviet application, citing the incompatibility of the USSR's system with the principles of free trade. The Soviet Union, however, intends to pursue its initiative as part of a strategy to gain a larger role in world trade.[32] No one knows at this juncture whether the Soviets would ever accept fully the basic norms of GATT, which would involve much more exposure to world market forces. It is clear, though, that some opening is underway. While the GDR and other East Europeans have established joint venture projects with Western firms, the Soviets have not. Now, under Gorbachev's reform policies, there are clear signals from Moscow that joint ventures are welcome.[33]

The GDR's trade status is unique in the CMEA. Under a series of agreements with West Germany, the GDR is guaranteed tariff-free access to the FRG as well as important financing facilities. The GDR has long been willing to suffer the minor political indignity that these provisions carry (arising from the West German principle that the GDR is not a foreign country). After all, the benefits – tariff-free access to the West German market, plus a cashless facility for inter-German trade – are invaluable and available to no other CMEA member.[34] Some EEC members are unhappy about the legal fiction of the GDR's 'membership' in the EEC. Meanwhile, the GDR is always mindful of the FRG's attempts to exploit these unique provisions with political demands. It is conceivable, then, that the GDR might join the rest of the Soviet bloc and join the world trading community. At present, though, it has no incentive unless the political pressure from Bonn intensifies greatly.

The need for a lender of last resort

The CMEA countries face a serious problem when they seek loans in the West. Western bankers are a security-conscious group, and they are loath to grant funds to economically troubled nations unless there is some credible lender of last resort. During the 1970s, the bankers assumed that the Soviets would play this role for the CMEA as part of their autarky policy. When they did not, a crisis ensued. Three East European nations (Romania, Hungary, and Poland) joined the International Monetary Fund. The IMF is the standard lender of last resort for the Third World, but it does insist upon considerable influence in a nation's economic policies as a condition for assistance. For this reason alone, the USSR's accession to IMF membership for its allies signified a salient retreat from autarky.

The East Germans also experienced a serious cash problem

Table 9.3. Western bank credit ratings of CMEA countries

Nation		1981	1982	1983	1984	1985	1986	1987
GDR	a	115.4	113.3	102.2	112.0	131.0	132.8	146.05
	b	100.0	98.2	90.2	109.6	117.0	101.4	103.05
CMEA	a	95.6	87.8	79.0	88.2	101.2	100.7	107.93
	b	95.2	91.8	103.4	97.1	114.7	98.5	101.10

Note: a = ratios of country rating to global average for a given year (global average = 100)
b = annual changes in relative credit ratings (preceding year = 100)
CMEA in this table includes only the GDR, Bulgaria, Czechoslovakia, Hungary, Poland, and Romania.
Source: Adapted from Bartlomiej Kaminski, East Europe's relationships with the banks: the betrayal of Eastern Europe? Paper delivered at the 1986 Meeting of the American Political Science Association, Washington, D.C., Table 4. Data from *Institutional Investor* (September issues).

in the early 1980s, but they did not join the IMF. Instead, the West Germans stepped in with government-guaranteed loans totalling almost 2 billion marks in 1983 and 1984. The GDR needed the funds badly. Its credit rating had plunged (see Table 9.3) and it was unable to secure loans in the open market. hence, the GDR was willing to accept some political concessions in exchange for the generous West German gesture.[35]

The GDR has become quite dependent upon the FRG's economic system. Much of the East German foreign exchange receipts come in the form of transfer payments from Bonn and West Berlin for services rendered in the GDR. Another considerable sum is brought into the country by visiting West Germans through private gifts and mandatory exchanges. It is difficult to gauge the amount or impact of these inter-German transfers, but Paul Marer has attempted a rough estimate. Marer approximates the net value of the West German payments at about 1.5 per cent of the GDR's total GNP.[36] This is by any measure a considerable sum. Consider, for example, that most European members of NATO spend about 3 per cent of their GNP on national defence. Further, the money comes to the GDR in the form of convertible currency. This is a substantial advantage to the GDR. Its leadership is well aware that no other international source is likely to be nearly as generous. 'It's a devil's bargain', in the view of GDR philosopher Erich Hahn, 'but how can we break away?'[37] At present it seems unlikely, then, that the GDR will follow its allies into the IMF.

Two factors may alter the GDR's view. First, if the West Germans become too demanding on the political front, the GDR might welcome an alternative benefactor. Second, if the Soviets pursue their recent interest in joining the IMF and the World Bank, it would be logical for the GDR to follow suit.

Why would the USSR want to join the IMF? For decades Moscow has excoriated the institution as an instrument of US imperialism. Political power in the IMF and the World Bank is not equally distributed. It is allocated on the basis of each member's contributions. Hence, the OECD nations, with the majority of contributions, control the majority of votes. IMF members are also required to provide a wide array of economic data that the Soviets presently screen from anyone's view.

Two recent developments, though, may account for the USSR's apparent interest. First, it has seen the Romanian and Hungarian experiences with IMF austerity programmes. In both cases, the IMF was remarkably circumspect. Since it seeks primarily to restore a nation's trade capability, the IMF does not demand structural changes. Austerity programmes for CMEA members, then, look very different from the familiar pattern of Third World arrangements.[38] Second, the Soviet Union is likely to need considerable credit in the coming five years.[39] Yet international banks have grown increasingly burdened by debt servicing problems and *de facto* defaults in Poland and in several Latin American countries. They are considerably more cautious about such lending now. The resulting reduction in international liquidity would at least bring higher interest charges for the USSR. The IMF, then, offers a mechanism to finance balance of payments deficits with a lower economic, but higher political cost.

BALANCING POLITICAL COSTS AND ECONOMIC GAINS

The Soviet Union has shown some public ambivalence about the dilemma it faces in choosing political over economic costs. Official Soviet enthusiasm for the idea of IMF membership began to falter some months after the initial suggestion. None the less, progress toward establishing the necessary groundwork seems to be continuing. After a surprisingly public campaign, the politburo ordered a substantial upgrading in the quality of Soviet economic data. This may well be a first step toward compliance with the data requirements of the major international economic organizations.[40]

Internal political wrangling is also a factor in the failure of the Soviet joint-venture plan to generate enthusiasm among Western companies. Most potential investors cannot gain any assurance from Soviet authorities about their range of profit. The Soviets remain wary of the ideological cost of Western surplus value accumulation in the citadel of Marxism–Leninism. They also seem unwilling to make the basic economic compromises that have propelled joint venture projects in Eastern Europe.[41]

Moscow's secrecy and apparent internal political struggles cloud the picture somewhat, but of the most part Soviet behaviour is fully consistent with a strategy that is designed to secure economic benefits while preserving the USSR's hegemony in its own bloc. It is a strategy that seems to have developed during Andropov's tenure as general secretary. Fundamentally, the strategy seeks to improve the USSR's control of the bloc while pursuing policies that bring the CMEA into a closer relationship with the world economy.

What would the ideal world look like in Soviet eyes? In research conducted in 1984, the Rand Corporation noted that the USSR would most like to have a Soviet-dominated system wherein Western Europe would in effect underwrite the costs of the Soviet domination of Eastern Europe.[42] Interestingly, this is virtually the present situation in the USSR–GDR–FRG triad, but it is clear that the West Europeans have no interest in such a system. The most likely outcome, then, is a two-pronged Soviet policy.

First, the USSR seeks to tighten its control over the CMEA. It has been doing this actively during the 1980s. The mechanisms are joint investment projects, joint production allocation systems, and closely co-ordinated policies. Soviet control over bloc energy supplies and other raw materials strengthens the Kremlin's hand. The East Europeans clearly object to this erosion of their economic independence. The USSR will not find it easy to fulfil this goal of tight co-ordination and domination.[43]

Second, the Soviet Union apparently feels freer to integrate the CMEA into the world economy as long as it has established the protection of tighter co-ordination. This bloc approach may well give the USSR better bargaining power and leverage, but at what cost? Will the East Europeans acquiesce? There are sure to be substantial reservations in the United States and Western Europe about any such Soviet plan.

The Soviet bloc's long pursuit of autarky carried it into isolation from the world economy. Yet the bloc failed to keep pace with world economic and technological growth. The Soviet Union and GDR now attempt to redress these failings in a difficult environment. Neither can compete with Taiwan or South Korea in manufacturing exports. Both need substantial Western capital to rebuild their competitiveness. It is doubtful that either country has enough in its political or economic arsenal to carry through these policy goals. Without substantial structural reform, we are likely to see a more contentious, if not more affluent, CMEA.

NOTES

1. Werner Gumpel (1983) *Sozialistische Wirtschaftssysteme*, 85–8 Munich: Günter Olzog Verlag.
2. See Kazimeierz Poznanski (1986) 'Competition between Eastern Europe and developing countries in the Western market for manufactured goods', in US Congress Joint Economic Committee *East European Economies: Slow Growth in the 1980s*, vol. 2, 62–90 Washington, D.C.: Government Printing Office; and Laura D'Andrea Tyson (1986) 'The debt crisis and adjustment responses in Eastern Europe', *International Organization 40* (2), Spring, 239–86.
3. Quoted in Wolfgang Stinglwagner (1986) 'Modell mit Schönheitsfehlrern', *Deutschland Archiv, 19* (6), 1986, 639.
4. Charles Wolf, Jr. (1984) 'Costs of the Empire', *Wall Street Journal*, January 30, 22; for more recent data see Keith Crane (1986) 'The Soviet Economic Dilemma of Eastern Europe', *Rand Research Report*, R-3368-AF (May).
5. See Tyson, *op. cit.*, 242–3; and Paul-Günther Schmidt (1985) 'Hard currency indebtedness of the CMEA countries', *Intereconomics 20*:3 (May/June), 120.
6. See ibid., and Paul Marer, 'Economic policies and systems in Eastern Europe and Yugoslavia', in US Congress Joint Economic Committee, *East European Economies*, vol. 3, 605.
7. Schmidt, *op. cit.*, 115–9.
8. Bank for International Settlements, *Annual Report* (1986), 54, Basle: BIS.
9. S. Karene Witcher (1986) 'Soviets consider joining IMF, World Bank', *Wall Street Journal*, August 15, 14.

10. Quoted in Stinglwagner, *op. cit.* 639.

11. See Albrecht Hinze (1986) 'Der Kremlchef verblüfft den SED-Parteitag', *Süddeutsche Zeitung*, April 22, 5.

12. Heinrich Machowski (1983) 'RGW-integration: fortschreibung oder intensivierung?', in *Die DDR vor den Herausforderungen der achtziger Jahre*, Cologne: Edition Deutschland Archiv, 48–50; and Paul Marer, 'East European economies: achievements, problems, prospects', in T. Rakowska-Harmstone and A. Gyorgy (eds.) *Communism in Eastern Europe*, (269, 1979), Bloomington: Indiana University Press, 269.

13. Michael Schmitz (1985) 'Das Beste für den grossen Bruder', *Die Zeit*, January 25, 12.

14. See Vladimir Sobell (1986) 'Highlights of the 42nd Session of the CMEA', *Radio Free Europe Research*, November 25, 169/3.

15. See Vladimir Sobell (1986) 'The CMEA Leaders Hold a "Working" Meeting', *Radio Free Europe Research*, November 25, 170/1–5.

16. Marer, 'Economic Policies and Systems', 612.

17. See 'A Comecon Exemplar', *The Economist*, July 6, 1985.

18. 'Hoher Einkommensrückstand der DDR-Bürger', *Süddeutsche Zeitung*, May 22, 1986, 24. The data were from 1983. The margin has probably widened since then.

19. See Sarah M. Terry, 'The Implications of Economic Stringency and Political Succession for Stability in Eastern Europe in the Eighties', in US Congress Joint Economic Committee, *East European Economies*, vol. 1, esp. 527–9.

20. Stinglwagner, *op. cit.*

21. Frederick Kempe (1985) 'Silicon satellites', *Wall Street Journal*, September 16, 76C; and Seymour E. Goodman, The partial integration of the CMEA computer industries: an overview', in US Congress Joint Economic Committee, *East European Economies*, vol. 2, 338–52.

22. Schmidt, *op. cit.*, 114.

23. Ibid., 119.

24. Calculated from *Statistisches Jahrbuch der DDR*, 1984, 239.

25. See Roger Pine (1982) 'Uneasy Western banks pulling back on loans', *Wall Street Journal*, July 1, 1 and 10; and Paul Legg (1985) 'West Germany's detente policy boomerangs', *Wall Street Journal*, September 11, 31.

26. Schmidt, *op. cit.*, Table 2, 116.

27. Machowski, *op. cit.*, 43–45.

28. Philip Hanson (1987) 'Converting the inconvertible ruble', *Radio Liberty Research*, July 16.

29. See, for example, Schmidt, *op. cit.*, or Marek Okolski and Jan Winiecki (1984) 'Structural change and adaptation: on reintegrating planned economies into the world economy', *Konjunkturpolitik 30*:1, 148–169.

30. Gumpel, *op. cit.*, 88.

31. Bank for International Settlements, 94–95.

32. Paul Marer (1986) 'Growing Soviet international economic

isolation and severe problems ahead in the foreign trade sector prompt top Soviet economists to advocate membership in the IMF, World Bank, and GATT', *PlanEcon Report* 2:31 (July 31); and Frederick Kempe (1986) 'Moscow easing laws governing foreign trade', *Wall Street Journal*, September 12, 27.

33. Ibid.

34. For a complete account and explanation of these provisions, see John Garland, 'FRG–GDR economic relations', in US Congress Joint Economic Committee, *East European Economies*, vol. 3, 169–206.

35. For an account of this episode, see A. James McAdams (1985) *East Germany and Detente*, 167–200 Cambridge: Cambridge University Press.

36. Marer, 'Economic Policies and Systems', 613.

37. Quoted in David Binder (1988) 'The Shadow Society', *New York Times*, January 6, 7.

38. See Valerie J. Assetto (1988) *The Soviet Bloc in the IMF and the IBRD*, Boulder: Westview Press.

39. 'Soviet trade', *The Economist*, February 14, 1987, 57–58.

40. Mark D'Anastastio (1987) 'Moscow Seeks More Accurate Economic Data', *Wall Street Journal*, April 6, 15.

41. See Thomas Hanke (1976) 'Das Risiko liegt drüben', *Die Zeit*, March 27, 10; and Mark D'Anastastio (1987) 'Capitalists wary of Moscow's hard sell to invest in joint-venture enterprises', *Wall Street Journal*, April 6, 15.

42. John Van Oudenauren (1984) 'The Soviet Union and Eastern Europe', *Rand Research Report* RF-3136-AF (March).

43. Some suggest, e.g. ibid., that the USSR is likely to be more prone to military intervention.

10

The politics of East–South relations: the GDR and Southern Africa

Brigitte H. Schulz

INTRODUCTION

The intensification of the crisis in the southern part of the African continent has focused the attention of much of the world there. Since the mid-1970s, when radical governments in both Angola and Mozambique emerged after protracted wars of liberation against the Portuguese, much of that attention had been devoted to the precise character of the relations between these countries and the Soviet bloc. Increasingly, however, interest has shifted to the deepening struggle inside the Republic of South Africa itself, a country whose racial policy of apartheid has made it the object of growing criticism, albeit of a rather mild sort, by most of the leading Western countries. South Africa is clearly the jewel on the continent, having vast mineral resources, being Africa's most industrialized economy, and strategically located on one of the major global sea lanes – making it of prime geo-political importance. Little wonder, then, that the outcome of events in this part of the world is of intense interest to both East and West.

It is well known that the major Western powers maintain extensive economic and political ties with the white minority government in Pretoria. Eastern Europe and the Soviet Union, on the other hand, support the forces opposing apartheid, principally the African National Congress, which is seen by all of the socialist countries as the legitimate representative of the African majority inside South Africa. This chapter looks at relations between the German Democratic Republic and the Southern African region, arguing that these can be viewed as a model for the East's relations with national liberation movements. We will conclude by examining the extent to which this model applies to overall East–South relations.

The GDR plays a particularly important role in the East's relations with Southern Africa and is generally assumed in the West to be conducting its African policies in close co-ordination with the Soviet Union and its Eastern European allies.[1] Soviet and Eastern European sources, of course, do not deny this overall co-ordination, although as usual there is silence on the specifics. East German scholars, for example, argue that their country's foreign relations can only be understood within the context of being:

> part of a coordinated, agreed upon and in this sense joint foreign policy of the socialist states. This is how it is both conceptualized and executed. This increases its international importance in the struggle with imperialism and simultaneously gives it increasing tasks and responsibilities in overseeing the overall interest of socialism and the support of the interests of each state in the community.[2]

These co-ordinated policies are thus seen to be a vivid expression of a joint commitment to help those countries suffering under the yoke of imperialism.[3] A co-ordinated foreign policy *vis-à-vis* the world of 'national liberation' thus becomes a common expression of 'proletarian internationalism'. It therefore appears reasonable to use the GDR's policies, particularly toward the ANC (the most important South African liberation movement) as being representative of the policies of the East as a bloc. Furthermore, within the co-ordinated division of labour regarding the Third World policies of the East, the GDR has played a leading role in sub-Saharan Africa.

The first part of the chapter gives a brief outline of the ideological underpinnings of the GDR's relations with the South, particularly with regard to national liberation movements. This will be followed by an examination of how the socialist countries view the situation in South Africa. The third part details some concrete ways in which East German 'solidarity' with the ANC is expressed in concrete terms. This leads to the question as to how, in the final analysis, these 'solidarity relations' can be assessed within the overall framework of East–South relations. The question, of course, is of particular relevance for seeking to understand what would happen should the ANC emerge as the new government of a post-apartheid Republic of South Africa.

THE IDEOLOGICAL FRAMEWORK FOR SUPPORT

Like all the countries of 'real existing socialism', the GDR sees itself locked into an epochal clash between capitalism and socialism, taking place as part of an overall global revolutionary process. The main groupings inside this process are:

[the] socialist world system, the communist and labor movements in the developed capitalist countries, and the revolutionary movements in the developing countries, particularly all those social forces which are taking the road of social progress and in the direction of socialist transformation.[4]

There thus exists an *objective* historical alliance between the socialist countries and the other groups involved in this global process toward socialism.

Since, in the East German perspective, different classes as well as different countries occupy differing roles in this world revolutionary struggle, foreign policy is established in accordance with the group toward which it is targeted. It follows that the role of foreign policy is explicitly to serve as a tool for the class struggle carried out at the global level.[5]

In this view, relations with the governments of the advanced capitalist countries are based on the principle of *peaceful coexistence*. Relations with the working classes inside these countries, on the other hand, are based on the notion of *proletarian internationalism*. This principle, although postulated by Lenin, actually has its roots in Marx and Engels, who as early as 1848 in the *Communist Manifesto* called upon the proletarians of the world to unite. Because of many events since the Bolshevik Revolution, however, this 'historical alliance' with the working class in the West exists mainly at the rhetorical level. In fact, few illusions appear to exist in the East with regard to the revolutionary aspirations of workers in the West at the present time.

Thus *proletarian internationalism* is applied as a principle to guide relations with the developing countries (i.e. the world of 'national liberation'). It is this part of the world which has been viewed as the most important ally in the historical struggle against imperialism. Although still optimistic about the working class in the capitalist countries, V.I. Lenin also clearly understood the important nature of this alliance with the South when he wrote:

> We will make every effort to get closer to the Mongols, Persians, Indians, Egyptians, and to effect a fusion with them. We are of the opinion that this is our duty and that it is also in our own interest to do so since socialism in Europe otherwise will not be secured.[6]

When Lenin made this statement much of what is now referred to as the 'Third World' was still under European colonial rule. Unsettled social and economic situations in that part of the world after independence are still seen as representing opportunities for the weakening of imperialism. In addition, the South is of interest because developments there may favour the establishment of socialism along the Soviet model.

The principle of proletarian internationalism was naturally more easily applicable to national liberation as an important constituent of the world revolutionary process as long as colonialism existed formally. Now that most of the world of 'national liberation' has developed into a group of politically sovereign states whose leaders in most cases have opted for a capitalist path in their hopes to develop their countries,[7] the situation has become more complex for policymakers inside the socialist countries. At one level, the Third World as a whole is still seen as being locked into an objective alliance with the East in its struggle for emancipation from foreign capitalist domination. It is at this level that the GDR lends almost automatic approval to any demands made by the developing countries, such as for a New International Economic Order or those raised at various UNCTAD conferences.[8] Like the other countries of the East, however, it only supports these demands provided they are made of the advanced capitalist countries.

Despite the alliance at this macro level, however, developments in the post-colonial era have forced the East into a re-evaluation of its position *vis-à-vis* the 'world of national liberation'. This has led to a differentiation between developing countries embarked on a 'capitalist' versus a more radical, non-capitalist path, now referred to as 'socialist orientation'.[9] Thus, bilateral relations with countries seen to be firmly embarked on a capitalist path (such as the Ivory Coast or Kenya, for example) are based on the principle of 'peaceful coexistence', while 'proletarian internationalism' is applied to those countries 'who pursue a consistent anti-imperialist policy, especially those which have opted for a socialist development path'.[10] Countries in this latter category include Mozambique, Angola, and

Ethiopia on the African continent, as well as the PR Yemen. The late Samora Machel, president of a country with 'socialist orientation', explained the relations between the GDR and Mozambique in the following way:

> We have a solid foundation for our relations: the principles of Marxism/Leninism and of proletarian internationalism which enable us to coordinate our goals and opinions, and the existence of a harmony of interest between us. Our alliance thus has a strategic character. It does not threaten anyone. It promotes the common struggle for peace and socialism, for freedom and independence of people. This alliance contributes toward the progress of the revolutionary world movement.[11]

Irrespective of the type of development path chosen by a Third World country, however, the East applies yet another principle: that of 'mutual advantage'. This means that both partners must benefit from the bilateral relations between them in order to assure their long-term success. What this means in practice is that the GDR seeks relations advantageous to it, both in the political and economic sphere.[12] It is here, then, that *raison d'état* overtakes the principle of 'proletarian internationalism' with the result that, in the post-independence era, revolutionary Third World governments often witness with dismay that the East drives as hard a bargain with them as does the West.[13]

The special circumstances inside the Republic of South Africa, which have added the element of explicitly racist policies to the general colonial theme of economic exploitation, are manifested in another cornerstone of the East's condemnation of the West: the linking of colonialism to racism. The GDR's general party secretary, Erich Honecker, makes this point, which is repeated *ad infinitum* in the East German literature – i.e. that which binds the peoples of the East and the South is:

> the anti-imperialist struggle for peace, freedom, and social progress. It is in this that the fundamental concerns of real socialism and of the national and social liberation struggle intertwine. What binds us is firm solidarity against imperialist tutelage and interference.[14]

In analysing the problems facing the non-European population in South Africa, East German scholars are also quick to point out not only what they consider to be the colonial nature of that country's economic and political structure, but also the complicity of the West in establishing and maintaining it. Alfred Babing, the GDR's leading expert on South Africa, points to the 'economic, political and strategic interests of imperialism in the racist bastion of South Africa'.[15] Thus, while the West blames the stubborn resistance of the Afrikaaner as the main reason for the continuation of legalized racism there, the East emphasizes the long history of complicity between white South Africa and the major Western countries in creating a structure designed to keep Africans in positions of inferiority.[16] This complicity of course was nurtured by solid economic interests: South Africa is one of the major suppliers of minerals to the West, including manganese, chrome, vanadium, platinum, and aluminium, not to mention gold and diamonds.[17] On top of the country's vast mineral deposits, apartheid has proven a bonanza for foreign firms, which have benefited enormously from the conditions imposed by apartheid.[18] These multinational corporations found several beneficial factors in South Africa: near-absolute labour tranquility; a large pool of migrant workers from which to choose; until recently, the absence of a trade union movement for black workers; and wage scales which enabled the extraction of super profits.[19]

Since apartheid, in the view of the East, is not simply the creation of racism made in Pretoria, but that of imperialism using racism as a mechanism of economic control, it follows that the resistance of Africans to apartheid is seen as part of a global struggle against imperialism. The African National Congress, as the main resistance organization to have emanated from South Africa, is thus seen as a legitimate 'national liberation' movement and the East has consistently supported its efforts. Thus, while the main Western countries (such as the United States, the Federal Republic of Germany, and the UK) have sought constitutional ways of resolving the problems facing South Africa within the framework of 'one man – one vote', to the ANC, as well as its friends in Eastern Europe, the abolition of apartheid must include a fundamental shift in property as well as political relations.[20]

This difference has also manifested itself concretely in the policies which East and West have pursued *vis-à-vis* the Republic of South Africa. The major Western powers have, by and large, pursued a policy of 'constructive engagement' with the Pretoria government designed to bring about political reforms while, at least until very recently, leaving economic relations basically untouched.[21] In contrast, the East has supported the ANC materially as well as diplomatically while withholding from the Pretoria regime any type of diplomatic recognition and eschewing any type of official economic relations with the apartheid state.[22] East German as well as Soviet literature also points constantly to the destabilizing role which the Pretoria government, with either the aid or the tacit approval of the major Western powers, plays in the entire Southern African region.[23]

In contrast to the activities of the major Western powers, the German Democratic Republic and the other socialist countries have supported the African National Congress as the only legitimate representative of the south African majority. We will now turn to a brief discussion of how precisely the ANC is supported by the East, by examining relations between that organization and the German Democratic Republic.

EAST GERMAN RELATIONS WITH THE AFRICAN NATIONAL CONGRESS

The German Democratic Republic maintains no diplomatic relations with South Africa, nor does it conduct any formal trade with it. Since the GDR trades very heavily with West German firms, via so-called inter-German trade, it is difficult to say to what extent East German products reach the South African market or vice versa. That some of this trade does take place should be assumed as fact; however, the GDR does not appear to be directly involved in it *per se*.[24]

Since no formal economic or political relations exist with South Africa, ties to the country have been limited to those with the main opposition organization, the African National Congress. Opposition to apartheid had been one of the pronounced positions of the East Berlin government for years and, prior to the GDR's acceptance on the part of the full international community in the early 1970s, was voiced at whatever international forums to which the GDR had access. Since gaining admission to the United Nations on 18 September 1973, the GDR has worked closely with the United Nations' Anti-Apartheid Committee. In 1973, for example, the United Nations called for an International Decade of Action to

Combat Racism and Racial Discrimination. The GDR immediately set up a special committee, headed by leading political figures and co-ordinated by the Solidarity Committee under the chairmanship of Dr Heinrich Toeplitz, President of the GDR's Supreme court, to ensure East German compliance with this call. In May 1974, the GDR hosted a meeting of the UN Anti-Apartheid Committee in Berlin. When the United Nations declared an international anti-apartheid year from 21 March 1978 to 21 March 1979, the GDR set up a government commission headed by Alfred Neumann, member of the Politburo of the SED, in honour of the occasion. In 1981, the Solidarity Committee of the GDR co-sponsored a conference in Berlin with the UN Committee entitled 'International Seminar on Activities and Role of the Mass Media in the International Mobilization against Apartheid'. In the same year, a symposium led by an ANC delegation was held at Karl Marx University in Leipzig in honour of the 70th anniversary of the ANC and was led by an ANC delegation. All of these activities were meant to lend political support to the ANC in its struggle against apartheid in South Africa. Finally, the Solidarity Committee of the GDR is a member of both the presidium and secretariat of the UN's International Committee against Apartheid, Racism, and Colonialism in Southern Africa.

Prior to 1978, ties directly with the ANC were of a close but rather informal nature. Despite numerous visits of ANC representatives to the GDR, more regularized relations did not come about until the late fall of 1978. The establishment of formal diplomatic ties was preceded by a visit from 15 to 22 May 1978 of an ANC delegation under the leadership of its president, Oliver Tambo, on the invitation of the SED Central Committee. The delegation met not only with Erich Honecker but also with Hermann Axen, a member of the SED's Politburo and the man in charge of the GDR's Africa policies.[25] Six months after this visit, on 20 November 1978, the ANC opened an office in East Berlin which is accredited through the Solidarity Committee of the GDR. To show the significance of this event, President Tambo again travelled to the GDR to be present at the ceremonies. Kurt Seibt, the president of the Solidarity Committee of the GDR, assured the ANC ambassador, Anthony le Clerc Mongalo, that 'the GDR, along with the Soviet Union and the other states of the socialist community, as well as all progressive forces in the world, stands firmly on the side of the ANC'.[26] The ANC was accorded diplomatic recognition and its 'ambassador' has since received highest honours through the Solidarity Committee. For example, in March 1986, Mongalo received the highest medal awarded by the Solidarity Committee in the presence of representatives of East Berlin that the ANC co-ordinates its relations with the rest of the socialist countries, including the Soviet Union.[28]

In addition to the international support given to the ANC's efforts as outlined above, the organization also regularly receives direct support from the East Berlin government, both inside the GDR and in various locations in Africa. In line with the overall pattern of East German relations with Third World countries and organizations, various mass organizations inside the GDR are responsible for specific solidarity activities with their respective foreign partner organizations. This means the active involvement of such diverse groups as women (DFD), the trade union movement (FDGB), the journalists' association (VDJ), and the youth organization (FDJ).

The activities of all of these social organizations are co-ordinated by the Solidarity Committee of the GDR.[29] The Committee spends roughly 200 million marks annually on solidarity activities, both inside the GDR and in various parts of the third world. The GDR lends support to the ANC through the Solidarity Committee in various ways, beginning with the accreditation of the ANC in Berlin with full diplomatic recognition. The Committee also provides a variety of material supports. For example, it prints the ANC's monthly English-language journal *Sechaba* and mails it to subscribers world-wide.[30] This enables the ANC, since 1960 an organization in exile, to reach its membership throughout the world. In addition, the Solidarity Committee arranges medical care for wounded ANC fighters in East German hospitals. It also enables thousands of young Africans to come to the GDR to learn particular industrial skills within the framework of 3-year apprenticeship programmes.

On the African continent, the Committee has committed itself in particular to aid the work of the ANC's training camps, especially the 'Solomon Mahlangu Freedom College' located in Tanzania, in which roughly 2,000 young South Africans in exile are being educated. The College over the years has received a steady stream of 'solidarity goods' from the GDR, such as typewriters, food, sports clothing, cement, etc.[31] Other solidarity goods for the ANC, including medicines, have been sent to various African countries in which the ANC has camps, such as Zambia, Angola, and Mozambique. Over the years, the GDR's Solidarity Committee has also sent goods earmarked for the ANC via the OAU's liberation committee, a move certain to be approved by the countries of black Africa who stand united in their condemnation of the white apartheid regime in South Africa.[32]

As mentioned above, other organizations in the GDR also actively participate in solidarity activities with the ANC. East German journalists, for example, have entered into agreements with the ANC to train journalists. These agreements are ratified annually between the GDR journalists' association (VDJ) and the ANC and includes the training of ANC members at the VDJ's international training college 'Werner Lamberz', located in Bernau, near the capital city, which trains journalists from around the globe. The latest agreement between the ANC and the Association of Journalists of the GDR was signed on 31 January 1983 for the period ending on 31 December 1987 and co-ordinates relations between the two organizations.

East German women, through their organization, the DFD, maintain close ties with ANC women. For example, they declared 1984 as the 'Year of Solidarity with the Women of South Africa' and held special educational events throughout the GDR for the occasion. The East German trade union organization, the FDGB, trains ANC cadres at its union college in Berlin-Bermai and also sends solidarity goods to ANC camps in Africa. Workers in the GDR finance these efforts through 'solidarity' contributions taken out of their pay on a regular basis.[33]

The efforts to support the ANC are not limited to adults. Youngsters organized in the country's youth organization, the Freie Deutsche Jugend (FDJ), regularly are in contact with ANC youth. ANC youths are welcomed by these East German youths both for special events and in training courses at the youth college outside of Berlin. FDG members have also shown their support for the struggle in South Africa – for example, by collecting 2.6 million signatures calling for an end to apartheid. Furthermore, young children in 1986 sent 86,000 birthday cards to Nelson Mandela, the ANC's president who has been in South African jails for the past quarter century.[34] In the summer of 1986, East German children sent a shipment of toys to Tanzania for use by children of ANC parents. These toys had been collected through a special effort of the children's magazine *Bummi* and represented donations made by the children of the GDR to the children of South Africa.[35]

Future Relations

As this brief survey of relations between the ANC and the GDR has attempted to show, support for the struggle against apartheid in South Africa takes place at all levels of East German society. There can be no doubt that this assistance is extremely important to the ANC, not only in material terms, but also as moral support in its ongoing struggle. We will now turn to a brief discussion of what the future of relations will be between the GDR and post-apartheid South Africa. This requires (a) some speculation concerning the future role of the ANC as well as its programme for the future of South Africa; (b) an examination of the GDR's policies with already independent Third World countries, particularly those of 'socialist orientation'; and (c) what the likely response of the West will be.

Since the ANC is an organization banned in its own country with a leadership either in jail or exile, the exact level of support for the organization inside the country is nearly impossible to determine.[36] As the rising tide of black trade-union activity inside South Africa has shown, challenges to the system of apartheid increasingly come from within the country itself, with leaders such as Cyril Ramaphosa, general secretary of the National Union of Mineworkers, gaining in stature.[37] Nevertheless, it is clear that the ANC will play an important, if not the leading, part in post-apartheid South Africa. The ANC itself does not appear to have a clear idea of the precise nature of the country after 'independence' from apartheid, however. Oliver Tambo, ANC President, explained his organization's position, as anchored in the 'Freedom Charter', as follows:

South Africa belongs to everyone who lives there, black and white; it will be the home of all citizens irrespective of skin color; its government must have the mandate of the entire people; the country's resources will belong to everyone who produces them; banks and mines will be nationalized. The charter has thus become a political platform and action program for creating a democratic state on our motherland's soil.[38]

In an interview with the *Cape Times* on 4 November, 1985, Oliver Tambo denied that his organization was 'communist-led' or inspired and insisted that travels to Eastern Europe and the Soviet Union count no more than trips to Sweden, Holland, or Italy. What counts, Tambo argued, was that some countries give them assistance and others do not. Since the West has refused to give the ANC any weapons assistance, it is thus forced to take them from those who have been willing to supply them – the countries of 'real socialism'.[39] The ANC has repeatedly made it clear that it wishes to deal with both East and West on the basis of equality in any future relations.[40] Despite these statements, however, it seems reasonably clear that the current leadership of the ANC, as well as most of the black leaders inside the country, will pursue an agenda which is socialist in nature, although it may not now be intended to be one of Soviet-style socialism or even of 'socialist orientation'.

The GDR can thus count on having good relations with the ANC, should that organization indeed make up the new government in post-apartheid South Africa. Since South Africa holds many strategic raw materials and is also situated in a strategically important location, this post-apartheid alliance would have important consequences for both East and West. For the East, it would provide access to natural resources which it currently cannot obtain due to the economic boycott of South African goods. In the zero-sum world of East–West relations, it would undoubtedly also mean an important victory for the socialist countries in geopolitical terms.

After independence, however, the policies of the East *vis-à-vis* this new South African state would shift from 'proletarian internationalism' to those of 'mutual advantage'. What this would mean concretely is that the GDR, just like its socialist 'brother countries', would seek its own advantage in relations with South Africa while claiming that these relations are *a priori* of a superior type to those to be gained from ties with the West. Here, it is instructive briefly to examine relations between the East and Angola and Mozambique, two countries in Southern Africa which opted for a close alliance with the East in the period immediately following their independence. As events over the last decades have shown, relations between the East and the South are neither as unproblematic as the East would like to have us believe, nor as tight as conservative circles in the West would like us to believe, nor as beneficial to these countries as they had hoped at the time of independence.

'Socialist orientation' has proven extremely difficult as a path to overcoming centuries of economic exploitation on the part of colonialism. It is a model which emphasizes changes mainly at the superstructural level, while advocating continued trade and aid relations with the major capitalist countries.[41] Furthermore, the East's capacity to help eliminate economic backwardness and dependence has been minimal. In the past few years, both Mozambique and Angola have been forced into closer relations with the West, including becoming signatories to the Lome III convention with the European Community.

In Mozambique the economic programmes pursued after independence, including the establishment of state farms and the nationalization of industries, are now referred to by the Frelimo government as 'errors'.[42] Great Britain has a military attaché stationed at its Embassy in Maputo[43] and the British army includes Mozambican officers in each military training course it holds in neighbouring Zimbabwe.[44] Mozambique is under increasing siege by right-wing Renamo rebels funded by South Africa who have effectively isolated the countryside through a campaign of terror and murder.[45] According to Unicef, at least 400,000 people are in danger of starvation in Mozambique's northern provinces and the Frelimo government claims that 5.7 million people in their country are affected by food shortages.[46] In early 1984, that Mozambican government signed a special treaty with the hated South African government, the so-called Nkomati Accord, in order to improve the deteriorating economic and military conditions in the country. In this Accord, the Frelimo government promised to cease all support for the ANC inside Mozambique in exchange for South African pledges to end aid to the Renamo rebels. Although the Frelimo government held to its side of the bargain, Pretoria continues to lend material support to the rebels.[47]

The situation in Angola is similarly grim, although not as desperate as in Mozambique. South African and US-backed UNITA rebels have seriously hindered the MPLA government's ability to rule the countryside and to carry out programmes of economic development.[48] According to Western relief workers, over 15,000 people have been killed and an estimated 690,000 displaced by UNITA's activities in the

221

southern provinces, which include mining roads and raiding rural villages. What saves the country from bankruptcy is oil refined by the US-owned Chevron Oil Corporation in Cabinda under the protection of Cuban troops.[49]

Should a post-apartheid ANC government emerge in South Africa with close ties to the East, there is no doubt that the West would also fund anti-government forces. However, it is important to remember that South Africa is unique on the African continent; it has the most industrialized economy and a genuine proletariat, something almost entirely non-existent in the rest of black Africa. This working class has become increasingly militant in its opposition to apartheid as well as to the free enterprise system which it sees not only as having created but also as having maintained apartheid.[50] Thus anti-capitalism is not the pursuit of urban intellectuals or guerrilla fighters only; it appears to dominate the views of much of black South Africa. Preconditions for building Soviet-style social-ism are thus more favourable in South Africa than anywhere else on the African continent. Because it is highly industrial-ized, along with controlling enormous shares of some of the world's most sought-after raw materials, South Africa is clearly the prize on the continent. Because of the East's high level of support for the anti-apartheid struggle, it will enter the post-apartheid era with a great deal of goodwill on the part of south Africans.

CONCLUSION

Support for the African National Congress in many ways is a picturebook situation for the GDR. The ANC is internationally recognized as the legitimate representative of black South Africa, both in the United Nations as well as in the Organization of African Unity (OAU), whose own liberation committee actively supports the ANC's anti-apartheid efforts. Thus the GDR, like its socialist brother countries, can count on being in the majority camp in the world community, therefore giving it a chance to emphasize its practical commitment to 'socialist solidarity'. For the GDR, this fact has an additional element of importance since it sees itself locked into direct competition with the Federal Republic of Germany both globally and in the case of its own population. Support for national liberation movements, therefore, also has an important legitimation function inside the GDR itself. The leadership in East Berlin can point to sharing the views of an international majority, while the Bonn government, along with London and Washington, has been criticized for being among the closest allies of the Pretoria government.[51]

Overall, the GDR's support for liberation movements which often enjoy a high level of sympathy in the Third World, has earned it a very positive image in the global struggle against a post-colonial order considered by many to be fundamentally unjust. As the examples of Angola and Mozambique have shown, however, although the GDR's high level of support for the ANC and other liberation organizations has important internal and external political and ideological functions, it is not typical for the general pattern of its relations with the decolonized South. Nor is the amount of help granted after independence commensurate with the importance of the assistance offered during the era of the anti-colonial struggle. This leads to the following concluding remarks:

1. As the process of decolonization has been almost completed globally, there are fewer and fewer organizations seeking to 'liberate' their region from *colonial* rule.[52] Thus the world of 'national liberation', one of the cornerstones of East German foreign policy, is shrinking rapidly. This will necessarily mean a reduction in the revolutionary rhetoric emanating from Berlin.

2. Even during the era of decolonization, the GDR's policies were *reactive* rather than *initiating*: in other words, Eastern Europe as well as the Soviet Union were successful only if movements in the South chose a close alliance with them. This was mostly due to actions on the part of the West which drove liberation movements into close alliances with the East. Thus the East was never as eager to incite revolutions to the South as the leading analysts in the West, particularly in the United States, maintained. Instead, complex historical interactions between the West and the South culminated in conflicts from which the East was able to benefit ideologically and geopolitically. In other words, the East was able to cash in on the mistakes made by the West.

3. Because of political decisions made by the East in the early 1970s concerning its economic growth, this part of the

world is now firmly embedded in the capitalist world economy. Both East and West thus behave as advanced industrialized countries which seek certain materials from the non-industrialized South. There is no indication that the GDR, or the other socialist countries, is pursuing a Third World policy intent on a radical restructuring of the existing international division of labour. Its trade relations with the developing countries follow the traditional North–South pattern, exporting finished goods for primary commodities. Since the prices are also based on those prevailing on the world market, this aspect of East–South relations does not differ fundamentally from those between West and South, official utterances to the contrary notwithstanding.[53] It is precisely these trading practices that eventually even out the ideological advantages enjoyed by the East in the immediate aftermath of decolonization. In the case of South Africa, it can be assumed that any multiracial South African government would trade with both East and West on the basis of who offers it the best prices for its goods.

4. Even if the East's programmes were aimed at helping Third World countries overcome their level of underdevelopment by radically restricting the types of products exported by them, the *ability* of the East to do so would be severely limited. The GDR, just like the other socialist countries, simply lacks the economic resources to help underdeveloped countries in a sustained development drive independent of the advanced market economies. On top of that, the East itself is more integrated into the world capitalist economy than ever before and thus its own economic well-being now depends on the continuation of the international economic status quo.

5. Cuba, long considered a model for East–South relations, should really be considered a special case. It was fortunate to be located so closely to the United States and thus to be of enormous strategic value to the Soviet Union at the height of the Cold War. It is highly doubtful that any other Third World country would ever become the recipient of such massive aid as Cuba has from the East. Even membership in the CMEA has apparently been closed off to additional developing countries. Only Vietnam and Cuba have been admitted as non-European powers and

thus been able to gain certain benefits which membership in that organization entails. Both Angola's and Mozambique's requests for membership, on the other hand, were denied and they have simple observer status only.[54]

In attempting to reach an overall assessment of East–South relations, the balance sheet is not as clear as propagandists in either East or West would like to have us believe. The East is much more cautious and conservative in its relations with the South than certain circles in the West maintain. The South is not the recipient of massive amounts of assistance from the East, especially in the post-revolutionary phase. While the East's assistance during the period of 'proletarian internationalism' undoubtedly is a great help to national liberation movements, the post-independence state-to-state policy of 'mutual advantage' makes the long-term differences between East and West almost indistinguishable in the end. The support granted to the ANC is thus not representative of East–South relations, although it deserves praise for helping to overthrow a regime which is repugnant to the contemporary conscience.

NOTES

1. American scholarship tends to look upon East German foreign policy very much within the context of its relationship of dependence on the Soviet Union. To Michael Sodaro, for example, East German relations with Africa can be understood only within the context of that country's 'surrogate' role for the Soviet Union. See 'The GDR and the Third World: supplicant and surrogate', in Michael Radu (1981) *Eastern Europe and the Third World*, 106–41, New York: Praeger. In a similar vein, Paul Marer sees East German activities in the Third World as 'proxy interventions' which have 'supported the Soviet Union's global political and military objectives'. See 'Intrabloc economic relations and prospects', in David Holloway and Jane M.O. Sharpe (eds) (1984) *The Warsaw Pact: Alliance in Transition*, 229, Ithaca: Cornell University Press.

2. Autorenkollektiv, *Aussenpolitik der DDR: Sozialistische deutsche Friedenspolitik*, 16, Berlin: Staatsverlag der DDR, 1982. (All translations from German sources were made by the author.)

3. The term 'imperialism' is used here and throughout this paper not as a political slogan, but to refer to a particular type or stage of capitalism on a world scale; i.e., capitalism as it generally exists in the world today.

4. Gemeinsame Kommission der Ökonomen der UdSSR und der DDR, *Sozialistisches Weltsystem und revolutionarer Weltprozess*, Berlin: Dietz Verlag, 1982, 255–6.

5. This is discussed, for example, in Autorenkollektiv, *Aussenpolitik*, 22.

6. V.I. Lenin (1960) *Werke*, Vol. 25, 61, Berlin: Dietz Verlag.

7. Although the numbers fluctuate somewhat, depending on who does the counting, Soviet and Eastern European sources normally cite fourteen developing countries which have opted for the 'non-capitalist' path, out of a total number far exceeding 100. They are Socialist Vietnam, Laos, and Kampuchea in Indochina; the ex-Portuguese colonies of Angola, Mozambique, Ethiopia in Africa; the PR Yemen, Iran, and Afghanistan in West Asia; and Nicaragua in Central America. Grenada, before it was invaded by the United States, once made the total fifteen.

8. For a lengthy discussion of the official GDR position regarding a New International Economic Order, see Helmut Faulwetter (1988) 'The socialist countries and the new international economic order', in Brigitte H. Schulz and William W. Hansen (eds) *The Soviet Bloc and the Third World: The Political Economy of East–South Relations*, Boulder, CO: Westview Press. For a critical comparison of the theory and practice of East–South relations, see Kunibert Raffer's contribution in the same volume.

9. This should not be confused with already being socialist – a label reserved for only a few Third World countries such as Cuba and Vietnam. While socialism in these countries is seen as *irreversible*, 'socialist orientation' is a transitory phenomenon on the way to building socialism under conditions of underdevelopment and is subject to reversals.

10. Autorenkollektiv, *Aussenpolitik*, 15.

11. *Neues Deutschland*, 4 March 1983.

12. Wolfgang Schoeller, for example, has referred to this as 'comparative disadvantage' rather than 'mutual advantage'. See Wolfgang Schoeller (1983), '"Komparativer Nachteil" und "wechselseitiger Nutzen": Zur Kooperation zwischen COMECON and Entwicklungsländern am Beispiel Mosambiks', in *Deutschland-Archiv, 16*, December.

13. For an interesting account of the Sandinista government's relations with the East, see Stephen Kinzer (1987) 'For Nicaragua, Soviet frugality starts to pinch', *The New York Times*, August 20. A more detailed discussion of the situation in both Angola and Mozambique will follow below.

14. Erich Honecker (1981) *Bericht des Zentralkomitees der Sozialistischen Einheitspartei Deutschlands, an den X. Parteitag der SED*, 31, Berlin: Dietz Verlag.

15. Alfred Babing, 'Zur Krise des sudafrikanischen Apartheid-Regimes', in *IPW Berichte*, 1/86, 41.

16. For a Soviet perspective, see S. Pokrovsky (1986) 'The apartheid regime and its imperialist patrons', in *International Affairs*, September, 101–60.

17. For more information on this, see, for example, the official yearbooks of the Republic of South Africa (Pretoria: Department of Foreign Affairs); information circulars published by the South African

Minerals Bureau; Boleslaw Adam Boczek (1986) 'Resource rivalry in the Third World', in Robert W. Clawson (ed.) *East–West Rivalry in the Third World*, Wilmington, Delaware: Scholarly Resources, Inc.; Anthony Sampson (1987) *Black and Gold: Tycoons, Revolutionaries, and Apartheid*, London: Hodder & Stoughton. On specific US investments in South Africa, see Lawrence Litvak, Robert DeGrasse, and Kathleen McTigue (1985) *South Africa: Foreign Investment and Apartheid*, 2nd edn, Washington: Institute for Policy Studies; Elizabeth Schmidt (1985) *Decoding Corporate Camouflage: US Business Support for Apartheid*, 2nd edn, Washington: Institute for Policy Studies. For a review of British interests, see James Barber (1983) *The Uneasy Relationship: Britain and South Africa*, London: Heinemann. For West German relations with South Africa, see, for example, Peter Meyns (1985) 'West Germany's foreign policy in Southern Africa: cooperation without change', paper presented at the Bi-Annual Conference of the African Association of Political Science, Addis Ababa, May 13–15, 1985; Gottfried Wellmer (1983) 'Aufruster der Apartheid; West-deutsche Multis in Südafrika', in *informationsdienst südliches afrika*, 1/2, 1983, 12 ff.; Pressemitteilung Nr. 119/83, 'Grüne fordern keine weitere Unterstützung Südafrikas durch die Bundesrepublik', Bonn, 26 May 1983, outlining the various levels of co-operation between the Federal Republic of Germany and the Republic of South Africa.

18. Babing, *op. cit.*, in *IPW Berichte*, 1/86, 42–43. The sources cited in note 17 above essentially confirm Babing's assessment.

19. The term 'super profits' has a specific technical meaning; i.e. a condition in which capital pays wages which are by themselves insufficient for the reproduction of labour power. Historically this has been a common phenomenon throughout Africa. In South Africa the peasant sector had to be undermined to some degree to create a workforce for the mines and factories. On the other hand, by not allowing its complete dissolution and setting up a system of migrant labour, the state was able to shift some of the burden for the reproduction of labour power to those left behind in the peasant sector. These are usually the elderly, the very young, and the women left behind in the so-called reserves, homelands, and bantustans. The male was then forced into the factories and mines under conditions that allowed wages lower than the cost of reproduction, thus allowing employers to make 'super profits'. For a systematic elaboration of this argument, see Harold Wolpe (1972) 'Capitalism and cheap labor power in South Africa: From Segregation to Apartheid', in *Economy and Society 1* (November).

20. Typically, debates in the West have centred on the type of constitutional arrangement to follow the apartheid structures. While Andrew Young represented the USA in the United Nations, for example, he continuously pointed to the applicability of the American model for South Africa. West German foreign minister Genscher has also emphatically pushed a solution along these lines. Others, such as Chester A. Crocker, US Assistant Secretary for African Affairs, have argued in favour of finding entirely new modes which would guarantee basic rights to all of South Africa's citizens, particularly the whites, of

course, since they are numerically vastly outnumbered by Africans and Asians. For a very useful summary of these Western positions, see Klaus Frhr. von der Ropp (1984) 'Chancen eines Neubeginns im Südlichen Afrika', in *Die internationale Politik, 1981–1982*, Jahrbücher des Forschungsinstituts der Duetschen Gesellschaft für Auswärtige Politik, Munich.

21. West Germany, Great Britain, and the United States have consistently vetoed any efforts on the part of the international community to impose mandatory economic sanctions on South Africa. On February 20, 1987, these three countries again vetoed a UN Security Council resolution, arguing that this would be against the best interests of the South African economy and thus the South African people. *The New York Times*, 21 February 1987.

22. Although there is a deafening silence on this point in all of the East, co-operation appears to be alive and well between Moscow and the South African mining conglomerate Anglo-American in the marketing of gold, diamonds, and platinum. Siberian diamonds apparently are marketed through the DeBeers Company, an Anglo-American affiliate, and its Central Marketing Organization, under the terms of a 1957 top secret agreement between South Africa and the Soviet Union. Since South Africa and the Soviet Union also mine roughly eighty per cent of the world's gold, co-operation in marketing that resource apparently also exists. See Jack Foisie (1986) 'A hole in sanctions: Pretoria–Moscow connection', *The Seattle Times*, 12 August. For a typical Soviet explanation of its interests (or lack thereof) in South Africa, see, for example, V. Midtsev (1986) 'USA–South Africa: a sinister alliance', in *International Affairs*, January, 72–9; Anatoly Gromyko (1982) 'Soviet foreign policy in Africa', in *International Affairs*, February, 30–35.

23. See, for example, Wolfgang Gabelein and Adrej Reder, 'Die Entwicklungsländer in den Kämpfen unserer Zeit', in *Asian, Afrika, Lateinamerika*, 6/86, 949–60; 'International Conference on Apartheid', in *International Affairs*, January 1984, 142–3. South Africa's activities in neighbouring countries have recently also become the subject of some critical reports in the Western press. See, for example, Anthony Lewis (1987) 'Would they call for a deal if the victims were white?', *International Herald Tribune*, 13 October; 'In Angola, a little-noticed war', *International Herald Tribune*, 22 December 1987.

24. This point was brought up by the author when interviewing various authorities while conducting research in the GDR during 1983/84 and the summer of 1985. The answer always was that what the West Germans do with East German products is no longer of concern to the GDR and that this would be stretching things a bit too far. While the author conducted research in the GDR in the summer of 1985 she was told by various East German citizens that Krugerrands now are on sale in local banks. If this is in fact true then this would indeed amount to direct economic involvement with the present South African government. This information could not be verified, however. The GDR apparently also sells some of the fish it catches off the coast of Mozambique to South Africa through a Mozambican middleman.

Again, this information has not been verified by official sources.

25. For further details of this visit, see 'ANC Visits the GDR', in *Sechaba*, third quarter 1978, 38–41.

26. BPA/DDR-Spiegel, 20 November 1978.

27. *Neues Deutschland*, 13 March 1986.

28. Information obtained during personal interview with a highly placed Solidarity Committee representative in March, 1984 in East Berlin.

29. This Committee was founded in 1960, the 'Year of Africa', to conduct 'solidarity' activities with Africa. At that point, of course, formal diplomatic ties with the newly independent countries of Africa were effectively prevented by the West German government through the so-called *Hallstein Doctrine*. The Committee's scope was later expanded to include Asia, and in 1973 it was officially renamed as the 'Solidarity Committee of the GDR'. This coincided with the time that 'normalization' of relations with the West occurred and the GDR was finally admitted into the community of states as an equal member. The work of the Solidarity Committee since then has become somewhat less important in overall foreign policy terms but it still holds the important function of coordinating the GDR's 'solidarity' activities.

30. The editors of the journal actually work out of London but provide the Solidarity Committee with their finished articles for printing and mass mailing. *Neues Deutschland*, 11 February 1987, and interview by the author with an official of the Solidarity Committee, March 1984.

31. As reported by the East German news agency ADN, for example, a shipment made up of these goods was received in Dar es Salaam, Tanzania, on 23 July 1985.

32. For a fuller discussion of how these 'solidarity' activities inside the GDR are both co-ordinated and executed, see Brigitte H. Schulz (1985) *East German Relations with Sub-Saharan Africa: Proletarian Internationalism vs. 'Mutual Advantage'*, Boston University African Studies Center Working Paper No. 100; and 'The road to Socialism in the periphery: East German solidarity in theory and practice', *Journal für Entwicklungspolitik 2* (2), Vienna, Summer 1986.

33. During the author's various research visits to the GDR, workers often proudly showed her their 'solidarity passport' which had monthly 'solidarity stamps' pasted in them. These stamps are purchased through the FDGB and put into the pass. These contributions apparently also are one of the requirements for eligibility for year-end bonuses for workers.

34. *Neues Deutschland*, 14 October 1986.

35. *Neues Deutschland*, 18 July 1986.

36. Inside the country, the ANC is clearly only one of many anti-apartheid organizations, most of which have overlapping followings and/or memberships. However, as an organization, the ANC clearly appears to command the loyalty of a significant majority of black South Africans. In a March 1985 poll conducted by the *City Press* newspaper in Johannesburg, 56 per cent of the respondents favoured the ANC. Other polls conducted inside the country by local as well as foreign

institutions confirm that finding. Other black leaders such as Desmond Tutu and chief Buthelezi, more to the liking of major Western countries as possible choices for a post-apartheid South Africa, have consistently lagged far behind Nelson Mandela of the ANC in these polls. Bishop Tutu, for example, does not consider himself in opposition to the ANC and, thus, one can be both pro-Tutu and pro-ANC. Even Mangosuthu Gatsha Buthelezi, despite tensions with the ANC, is required occasionally to make friendly overtures towards it. For a discussion of the degree of black support of the ANC inside South Africa, see Roger Omond (1986) *The Apartheid Handbook: A guide to South Africa's Everyday Racial Policies*, 217–8, 2nd edn, Harmondsworth: Penguin Press.

37. Ramaphosa was responsible, for example, for organizing the massive strike of more than 300,000 black mine-workers in August 1987.

38. Interview with Oliver Tambo, President of the ANC, with *Pravda*, Moscow, 8 July 1986, 5.

39. *The Cape Times*, interview with Anthony Heard, 4 November 1985.

40. In the *Cape Times* interview of November 1985, Oliver Tambo insisted that South Africa would rejoin the Commonwealth and become a member of the non-aligned group of nations. This, he argued, would also mean trading with any country on earth but also strengthening existing trade ties, presumably to reassure the West that they could continue to count on their supplies of much needed minerals from South Africa.

41. For a full discussion and critique of this development model, see William D. Graf (1988) 'The theory of the non-capitalist road', in B.H. Schulz and W.W. Hansen (eds) *The Soviet Bloc and the Third World: The Political Economy of East–South Relations*, Boulder, CO: Westview Press.

42. Serge Schmemann, 'Mozambique rethinking its dreams', in *The New York Times*, 19 February 1987. How close Mozambique has come to the West can also be seen by the fact that after its President, Joaquim Chissano, visited Washington in October, 1987, Chester Crocker, Under-secretary for African Affairs in the State Department, referred to the country as 'the most cooperative partner we have in Southern Africa', *General-Anzeiger*, 23 November 1987.

43. *General-Anzeiger*, 23 November 1987.

44. *Neue Zürcher Zeitung*, 16 February 1987.

45. In July 1987 for example, Renamo rebels were blamed for the brutal murder of 386 villagers in Inhambane, including women and children as well as patients in the local hospital, *The New York Times*, 25 July 1987. In October 1987, Renamo killed more than 200 civilians in a brutal attack about fifty miles north of Maputo, *International Herald Tribune*, 13 November 1987.

46. *The New York Times*, 19 February 1987.

47. For a fuller discussion of the East's relations with post-independence Mozambique, see Winrich Kühne (1988) 'Nkomati and soviet expansion?', in B.H. Schulz and W.W. Hansen, (eds) *The Soviet*

Bloc and the Third World: The Political Economy of East–South Relations, Boulder, CO: Westview Press.

48. The US provides the rebels with Stinger missiles routed through Zaire and other military aid. In 1986, the Reagan administration gave $15 million to UNITA through CIA funds and apparently is planning to give the same amount of aid in 1987. Jonas Savimbi, the head of UNITA, is also a frequent visitor to South Africa, from which his organization also receives assistance, *The New York Times*, 27 July 1987.

49. *The Seattle Times*, 14 July 1987.

50. The term 'comrade' is commonly used by young militants in the black townships of South Africa, and warm praise is being extended to the Communist Party as the only white group which has lent its unqualified support to black majority rule in South Africa since the 1920s. Support for the ANC is also displayed increasingly openly and militantly, particularly at funerals for anti-apartheid fighters. For example, at the recent funeral of Eric M. Mntonga, an offiical at the Institute for a Democratic Alternative for South Africa which has sought to initiate dialogues between white South Africans and the ANC, exiled leaders of the ANC were hailed, the ANC flag was defiantly displayed, and the South African Communist Party was honoured for its co-operation in trying to end apartheid. The funeral was attended by thousands of people, *The New York Times*, 9 August 1987.

51. The Federal Republic has, in fact, been accused by the ANC and others of particularly close levels of co-operation with the Pretoria regime, including the field of nuclear co-operation. The ANC published details of this co-operation as early as 1975.

52. This distinction is important because movements seeking to overthrow existing neo-colonial governments have not received the open and unambiguous support of the East. Thus it is not surprising that all recently overthrown dictatorships in the Third World, from Marcos in the Philippines to Baby Doc in Haiti, fell without the complicity of the East. Even the Sandinista government came to power without the active assistance of the socialist countries, although it subsequently turned to them in order to defend its revolution from US aggression.

53. This is argued, for example, by Andre Gunder Frank (1988) in B.H. Schulz and W.W. Hansen (eds) *The Soviet Bloc and the Third World: The Political Economy of East–South Relations*. Marie Lavigne, on the other hand, argues that the case is not as simple as that, although in the end she, too, is forced to admit that in economic terms the Eastern bloc's interests are 'linked to those of the developed market economies in an objective collusion', M. Lavigne (1986) 'East–South trade in primary products: a model borrowed from the North–South pattern?', *Journal für Entwicklungspolitick*, Summer 1986.

54. During the author's various research trips to the GDR, she heard over and over that the East simply cannot afford 'more Cubas and Vietnams'. The feeling very clearly was that support for these two countries has already reached the limits of available means.

Index